A commonsense guide
for new
parents

Published in 2004 by Murdoch Books®, a division of Murdoch Magazines Pty Ltd.

Murdoch Books Australia
Pier 8/9
23 Hickson Road
Millers Point NSW 2000
Phone: + 61 (0) 2 4352 7000
Fax: + 61 (0) 2 4352 7026

Murdoch Books UK Ltd
Erico House, 6th Floor North
93–99 Upper Richmond Road
Putney, London SW15 2TG
Phone: + 44 (0) 20 8785 5995
Fax: + 44 (0) 20 8785 5985

Chief Executive: Juliet Rogers
Publisher: Kay Scarlett
Creative Director: Marylouise Brammer
Editorial Director: Diana Hill
Project Manager: Sarah Baker
Designer: Alex Frampton
Photographers: Sue Stubbs (all unless specified otherwise); Joe Filshie (pp. 8R, 97, 98, 216, 229, 255L, 289); and Grant Smith (p. 211)
Child Nutritionist: Sue Thompson
Line Illustrations: Genevieve Huard

ISBN 1 74045 452 9.

Printed by Sun Fung Offset Binding. PRINTED IN CHINA.
Printed 2004.
© Text, design and photography Murdoch Books® 2004.
Murdoch Books® is a trademark of Murdoch Magazines Australia Pty Ltd.

Note: The reader should consult his or her medical, health, or other competent professional before adopting any of the suggestions in this book or drawing inferences from it.

A commonsense guide
for new
parents

Carol Fallows and Shayne Collier

MURDOCH BOOKS

contents

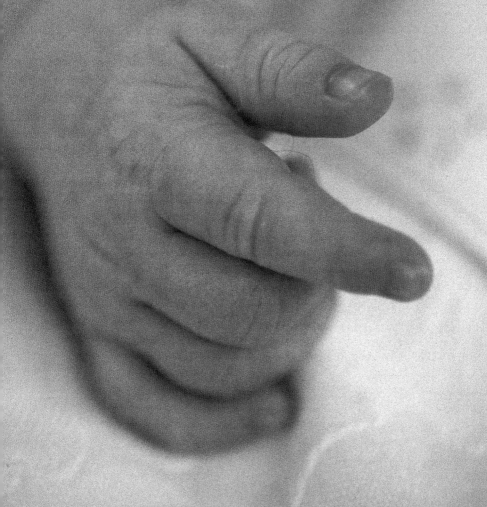

Introduction

Because having a baby is such an all-consuming experience, it can be hard to focus on anything beyond the big day. The truth of the matter is that once your baby is born, your life changes forever. Suddenly, you are responsible for a tiny person who depends on you for absolutely everything. This may sound overwhelming, but it needn't be.

How to use this guide

If you are prepared for parenthood, it can make a big difference to how you cope. And this is where *A Commonsense Guide for New Parents* helps. This book is designed to assist you with the practical aspects of looking after and nurturing your baby and child. In essence, it's a hands-on guide to a range of topics that span birth to three years.

For instance, 'Preparing for your baby' previews the essential items for a nursery and is a handy reference for first-time parents. Similarly, 'Caring' in 'Birth to six months' provides expert tips on perennial issues such as feeding your baby, sleep and immunization, while proving you don't have to be an origami expert to fold a nappy. Even if this is your second or third baby, the advice and product updates keep you informed about the latest trends.

As your baby grows, his* needs change. He becomes more curious and mobile — tiny teeth sprout and he wants to eat what you're eating, the way you're eating it! 'Six months to one year' takes this increased activity into account by addressing safety issues, with practical advice on how to transform your home into a child-friendly haven. An expert in child nutrition

* We will alternate between he/him and she/her on a chapter-by-chapter basis.

has devised the simple recipes. Not only are they tasty, but they also contain natural healthy ingredients — ideal for a baby on the go.

When your child turns one, he is moving, literally, into the mobile world of toddlerhood. However, he may not be walking straight away. In 'One to two years' you'll be reassured by the knowledge that all children are different, and that there is nothing to worry about if your 15-month-old baby decides he's not interested in taking his first step. When it comes to toilet training, the same rule applies — not all children are keen to use the potty at 18 months. So it makes sense to include the often-stressful transition from nappies to potty in 'Two to three years'.

Initially, as a new parent, you're likely to react to every cough, sneeze and slightest rise in your baby's temperature. 'Common illnesses of early childhood' and 'First aid and emergency procedures' are useful resources conveniently located towards the back of the book.

There is no magic formula when it comes to parenting. Some days will be a struggle; others will have you wondering what all the fuss is about! The aims of this commonsense guide are to equip you with the facts, help you feel comfortable in your new role and, importantly, empower you to make informed decisions about what you feel is best for your baby.

Best wishes and happy parenting.

Preparing for your baby

Your baby's birth may be imminent, or it could be that her early arrival has rocked your plans for a leisurely lead-up to the big day. Whatever your situation, now is the time to go shopping! The important thing to remember is to stick to the essentials. There will be plenty of time to add to your baby's nursery after you've stocked up on the basic requirements.

A basic wardrobe for a newborn

Your baby will grow quickly, so don't go overboard buying cute 000-sized outfits. If your baby is born between seasons, buy clothes that will suit the change in temperature. It's a good idea to wash all new items before use.

Here's a list of clothing your baby will need.

6–8 singlets. These should have wide neck openings, which will make it easier for you to dress your young baby. Buy cotton for summer and a thermal fabric (wool/cotton mix) for winter.

4–6 'all-in-one' towelling stretch suits. If it's summer, buy four stretch suits with short sleeves and without long legs, but have two full suits on hand for cool changes and chilly nights. Stretch suits are practical — they don't ride up like singlets or nighties — and can keep your baby warmer in the winter months. The buttoned style is functional because you avoid having to pull the stretch suit over your baby's head. When you're changing a nappy, pop fasteners at the crotch are much easier to handle than buttons. The only real problem with the stretch suit is that a leaking nappy may cause dampness and staining, so you may have to change the stretch suit more often. However, they are easy to wash and dry quickly. Stretch suits made from natural fibres are gentler on your baby's skin.

2–3 nighties. These are an optional purchase, but they are handy for the first few weeks when you're fumbling through a nappy change in the middle of the night. Look for cotton or wool blends, which are kind to your baby's skin and less flammable.

2 jumpers or sweatshirts. You will need these for cool weather.

2 cardigans or hooded jackets. These should be in a stretchy cotton fabric or knitted in soft baby wool.

2 broad-brimmed sunhats for summer and two woollen or 100 per cent stretch cotton fitted hats for winter. In winter the woolly hat will not only keep your baby's head warm but, because

babies lose an enormous amount of heat from their heads, it will also help keep her whole body snug when you're out and about.

3 pairs of socks or booties, two pairs of leggings and two pairs of mittens. Depending on whether your baby is born in summer or winter, or whether you live in a warm or cold climate, you may need more or less of these items. Make sure the socks are not too tight, as a baby's feet are easily damaged. Avoid patterned socks, as there is a risk of tiny toes getting caught in the looped threads inside the socks.

2–3 bibs. Bibs are always useful, especially when your baby begins to enjoy solid foods at around six months. Use them for mopping up excess milk from baby's mouth.

2 good outfits. Your baby will need these for more 'formal' days out.

2–3 bunny rugs or cotton waffle wraps. These are handy for swaddling your baby and can also be used as light blankets.

2 muslin or flannelette wraps. The former are handy in summer, the latter in winter.

2 bath towels and four face washers.

Why natural is better

When you're shopping for baby clothes, always check the labels to ensure the fabric is cotton or wool. These two natural fabrics allow

your baby's skin to breathe and contain good insulating properties, so cotton will keep baby cool in summer while wool will keep her warm in winter. Avoid scratchy synthetic fabrics, as they can be rough on your baby's sensitive skin.

The right size

Babies' rates of growth vary considerably so, rather than using your baby's age as a guide, refer to her weight when selecting clothes. If in doubt, choose an 'all-in-one' stretch suit that is a size too large for your baby so she has room to grow. Later, you could cut the feet out of the suit so she can get more wear out of it.

Now for nappies

It is worthwhile doing some thorough research about nappies before the birth of your baby. There is a huge range of these available — from cloth or terry nappies to the ever-changing variety of disposable ones.

24–36 traditional cloth nappies. Cloth/terry towelling nappies are more economical, but disposable nappies are handy when you're out with your baby. Also available are fitted cloth nappies (see page 63).

36–48 disposable nappies. If you choose disposables, start with three packs of newborn-sized nappies. You could find your baby goes through up to ten disposable nappies per day. See page 64.

4–6 reusable nappy liners. These are placed inside the cloth nappy to provide greater absorbency.

4–6 pairs of pilchers. Pilchers are overpants used with cloth nappies to provide extra protection. See page 63 for further information.

Nappy fasteners or safety pins.

Change mat. Choose one that can be easily wiped clean.

Nappy bag. This will store all your baby necessities when you're out and about.

A change table makes it easy to store everything you need for nappy changes. Have two buckets handy for wet and soiled nappies, but once they're in use, always keep the lids on.

Choosing a pram or stroller

Choose a stroller that is easy to collapse and small enough to fit into the boot of your car.

When you shop for a pram or stroller, look for one that meets your needs. If you'll be hauling it in and out of the boot of your car, ensure it is lightweight and easy to fold and unfold. Learn how to fold and use the pram or stroller before you leave the store and make sure you receive all the instructions. And don't forget to check that it fits into the boot. If you live in a small house or apartment, make sure it's easy to store.

Types of pram or stroller

A pram or stroller should also fit in with your lifestyle. If you enjoy being outdoors and do a lot of walking, you may prefer a jogger stroller. The more traditional pram is suitable for a newborn, but you will need to change to a stroller or convertible pram as your baby grows. Some strollers can lie back at an angle when baby is sleeping, but they are not suitable for a baby who can't hold up her own head (a baby usually achieves this milestone around the age of four to six months).

There are several types to choose from.

Traditional carriage pram. This has a solid body and a collapsible fabric hood.

The convertible pram, a pram or stroller combination. This pram is defined by its backrest, which can be positioned horizontally, like a pram, or vertically, like a stroller. It may also be reversible, so you have the option of lying your baby so she faces you, or when she's older, sitting her up so that she faces either towards you or away from you. The convertible pram can be used for newborns and for toddlers up to around three years. The convertible pram is certainly versatile, but its weight and size make it awkward to lug on and off public transport. If your home is small, it may also be hard to store.

Umbrella stroller. The umbrella stroller gets its name from the narrow shape it forms when folded. This type of stroller is supposed to be easy to fold and unfold, and because of its compactness it should also be easy to store in a small space. Layback and upright umbrella strollers are not recommended for newborns. They are only suitable for a child old enough to support her own head, at around six months.

Jogger stroller. This is a three-wheel stroller made especially for parents who like to jog or go for walks over rough terrain.

What to look for in a pram or stroller

A pram or stroller may look attractive or trendy, but that doesn't necessarily mean that it is safe. You'll get a lot of use from the pram or stroller you do eventually buy — it could last four or five years — so choose carefully. Look for:

Appropriate standard. When you buy a pram or stroller look for one that meets the appropriate safety standard. In some countries the standard is voluntary, so not all strollers will feature the sticker.

Strong components. It should feel rigid but lightweight. If the pram or stroller folds up, make sure that the frame locks are working properly.

One-handed folding operation. You're quite likely to be holding your baby with the other arm while you're dealing with the pram or stroller.

Large wheels and wheel locks. These should work properly. Make sure you can easily activate and release the brake locks with your foot.

Adjustable recline positions and footrests. Ensure these lock securely and adjust smoothly into position.

Easy steering. It can be hard enough to manoeuvre a pram around a crowded shopping centre without having to compensate for poor steering.

Adjustable five-point restraint harness. This should be secured to the stroller frame so that the shoulder straps feed through the backrest at shoulder level.

Stationary handle. This should be at the right height for you.

A jogger stroller is easy to manouevre, but takes up more room than a conventional stroller

Fitted carry basket. Check that it won't destabilize the pram or stroller when it is full, and that it is large enough to accommodate a nappy bag.

Gaps. Check for gaps that could trap small heads, fingers or limbs.

Adjustable hood. This provides protection from rain and sun.

Easy to clean fabric.

Safety tips

- Read the manufacturer's instructions carefully before you use your pram or stroller.
- Check that all frame catches are locked in place and any fabric fastenings are secured before use.
- Always use the five-point restraint harness, so your baby becomes familiar with it.
- A baby should not be left sleeping unsupervised in a pram or stroller because she can slip and get caught on the front of the stroller or on the footplates.
- Avoid placing shopping bags over the handle of a stroller, as their weight can cause the stroller to tip over.
- Remove your baby from the pram or stroller before making adjustments, as small fingers could get caught in the folding mechanism.
- Do not allow more than the intended number of occupants in a pram or stroller — it could easily tip over.

Buy a stroller with a convertible backrest, so your baby can lie down.

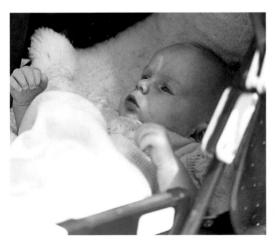

Alternative transport for your baby

Baby carriers are a great choice for hands-free activities, or when a pram is impractical. You can carry your baby in a sling or backpack when you catch public transport, when you go for a walk or when you're shopping. With your baby securely strapped to your body, you are free to move around, performing everyday tasks while your baby feels safe and snug. Soft cloth carriers such as slings are ideal for young babies, while older babies are best carried in more substantial backpacks with aluminium frames.

Slings

Your small baby will love being held close to your body and will be comforted by your warmth, familiar smell, the sound of your heartbeat, and movements similar to those experienced in the womb. Carrying your baby in a sling has many advantages. It helps your baby feel safe and secure, and lets you get on with your daily tasks without interruption. Some slings are two-way; these models are designed to carry the baby facing towards you or facing outwards. Realistically, you can use a sling until your baby is around eight months old or weighs about 8 kg (18 lb).

What to look for in a sling

When shopping for a sling, look for:

Ease of use. You should be able to put on and take off the sling without any trouble. You should be able to easily do up and release clips and buckles.

A comfortable environment. The sling should allow some freedom of movement for the baby's head, arms and legs.

Adequate head support. It should provide support for your newborn baby's head.

Fully adjustable straps. These shouldn't be too long to ensure they don't get caught on anything.

Double lining and double stitching. This is for greater strength and durability.

A sling should be easy to use. Make sure it is well made.

Potential choking hazards. Avoid sharp edges and clips that can trap fingers.

Washability.

Safety tips

- When you put on a sling, make sure it is securely fastened before placing your baby inside it.
- Always put your baby in a safe place before you remove her from a sling.
- When wearing a sling, protect your baby's head with your hands when you bend forward or stretch to one side. A young baby's neck must be supported.
- It is illegal to carry your baby in a sling while you are driving.

- Make sure the sling provides adequate support, and check the fasteners are still intact after washing.

- Be careful of baby overheating. The heat of your body may be too much for your baby on a hot day. In the summer months make sure she is dressed in light clothing.

- Never leave your baby unattended in a sling.

Backpacks

Fixed-frame backpacks, suitable for older babies, are useful in situations where a pram or stroller would be hard to navigate. A backpack is perfect for bushwalking and country rambles, walking on a beach or supermarket shopping. Because it provides minimum support, the backpack should be used only for a baby able to support her own head and neck. A backpack can be hard on the wearer's back, especially since the older baby tends to wiggle around, so be prepared for a little discomfort. However, avoid wearing a backpack if you experience back pain. It is recommended that you try on several packs, with your baby on board, before buying one.

Safety tips

- Remove your baby from the backpack immediately after taking it off, and put her in a safe place where she is out of danger.

- In hot weather, ensure your older baby is protected from the sun when being transported in a backpack. For some brands of backpack, it is possible to purchase a sun shade attachment.

- Never leave your baby unattended in a backpack.

- When you are buying a backpack and have found a type you like, compare it with similar models to make sure the construction is sound.

Choosing a child car restraint

It is dangerous, and also illegal in many countries, to travel with your baby in a car without a child car restraint. It should be used at all times, regardless of the vehicle's speed or the distance to be travelled. When buying or hiring a child car restraint, consider your child's age and weight, and select a restraint that meets the designated standard.

Types of child car restraint

Most child car restraints and harnesses come with fitting instructions. Always follow the manufacturer's instructions and, if you are experiencing any difficulties, contact the manufacturer. A wise and inexpensive option is to have the restraint installed by a specialist fitting service or authorized safety restraint fitting station. Ask at your early childhood health clinic or contact the motoring organization in your area.

You have several options when choosing a child car restraint.

Rear-facing child car restraint

The rear-facing baby child car restraint (baby capsule style) is designed for children up to 9 kg (20 lb) in weight or 70 cm (28 in) in length. The restraint is fitted to the back seat of the car using ordinary seat belts and a top tether. A five-point safety harness, integral to the restraint, is used to keep your child restrained firmly but comfortably.

The advantage of this style is that it is compact and can be lifted from the shell, so you can remove your baby from the car without disturbing her. It's also compatible with most vehicle types, and has been praised by motoring organizations as the safest option for a small baby. It is worth noting that one of these capsules plus baby is heavy to carry.

Convertible child car restraint

The convertible child car restraint can be used as both a baby restraint and for the older child (8 to 18 kg or 18 to 40 lb and approximately six months to four years). Used as a rear-facing child car restraint, most models cater for a baby up to 9 kg (20 lb) or 700 mm (28 in). However, there are some models that can be used in the rear-facing position for babies up to 12 kg (26 lb). This style is handy if your baby weighs over 9 kg (20 lb) but is still unable to support her head in a forward-facing child car restraint.

Booster seat

Once your child doesn't fit into a child car restraint at around four years of age, a booster seat can be used with an adult lap/sash seatbelt. If this is not available, a harness can be used with an adult lap belt until she is about eight years old (14 to 32 kg or 31 to 71 lb). Note that booster cushions without a seat back are not recommended because they fail to provide side-impact protection (so the child's head could hit the car door).

Most child car restraints and harnesses come with fitting instructions. Always follow the manufacturer's instructions and, if you are experiencing any difficulties, contact the manufacturer. Have the restraint installed by a specialist fitting service or authorized safety restraint fitting station. Ask at your early childhood health clinic or contact the motoring organization in your area.

Second-hand or hire?

Because child car restraints are expensive, you might prefer to buy a second-hand product or to hire one from an authorized outlet.

It is advisable to approach the second-hand market with caution, and to check the history of a second-hand child car restraint before you buy. Experts advise against using a child car restraint if it has been involved in an accident, or shows signs of wearing, such as cracks, frayed straps or broken buckles. Contact the consumers' association and motoring organization in your area for information on buying a second-hand child car restraint. It is also advisable to check the features on the latest models to make sure that your second-hand child car restraint is up-to-date and features the latest improvements.

Hiring a child car restraint is the recommended option for a small baby. It is economical and solves the problem of where to store the restraint when it is no longer needed. If your family is growing, you can always hire the latest model as each new family member arrives! Organizations that hire out restraints often provide an installation service and delivery to maternity hospitals. Ask your local maternity hospital or community health service for advice and information.

Setting up your baby's room

Choosing the paint and new furniture for your baby's room can be an enjoyable and satisfying experience. Remember that your baby will grow quickly, so choose a design that will suit your child into toddlerhood.

Sharing a room with baby

You may prefer to have your baby sleeping in the same room as you, and there is nothing wrong with this. In fact, it is reassuring for many parents to have their newborn baby nearby so they can respond to her cries during the night. It is also a bonus in winter because you won't have to leave your room to get your baby, and it's easier to bring her into your warm bed for a feed on a cold night (see 'Sleeping' on page 97).

Sleep essentials

Whether you choose to have your baby with you in your room, or to set aside a room in the house as a nursery, there are many everyday items you will need to help you with the daily routine.

Bassinet or cradle?

You may have to make a decision about the value of buying a bassinet or cradle for your baby, as she'll be ready for a cot at around five months or when she's starting to roll over and pull herself up. The advantage of the bassinet, which may be either woven in traditional willow or cane or made from plastic, is that it's small and portable.

Many bassinets come with a stand, so they can be wheeled around. This is convenient because you can easily move the bassinet from room to room, keeping your sleeping baby by your side around the house. A bassinet basket comes fitted with a foam mattress, with a wheeled stand usually costing extra. The mattress should be firm and a snug fit, and it should not exceed 75 mm (3 in) in thickness. Babies often enjoy the cosiness and smallness of a bassinet.

If you are considering a cradle, which is usually made of wood, experts recommend a

Other essentials for the nursery

Change table. This should have a padded change mat (see 'Now for nappies' on pages 14–15).

Heating/cooling. To avoid overheating, keep the room at a comfortable temperature (23°C or 73.4°F is recommended).

Baby bath.

Manchester checklist

Whether your baby is to sleep in a bassinet, cradle or cot, use this checklist when you go shopping for bedclothes.

Bassinet or cradle

* 1–2 waterproof mattress protectors (used from the waist down)

* 3–4 sets of 100 per cent cotton bassinet or cradle-sized sheets (flat or fitted)

* 1–2 pure cotton bassinet and cradle-sized blankets

* 1 wool blanket for winter

Cot

* 1–2 waterproof sheets/mattress protectors (used from the waist down)

* 4–6 sets of 100 per cent cotton cot-sized sheets (flat or fitted)

* 1–2 cot-sized cellular cotton blankets

* 1 wool blanket for winter

Two nappy buckets. These should have lids, as young toddlers have been known to drown in a nappy bucket. Use one bucket for wet nappies and the other for soiled ones.

Lighting. If possible, install a dimmer switch for night-time feeding and changing, or place a lamp on a low table so baby's eyes will not be hurt by the glare of the overhead light. A night-light also adds a reassuring glow to the room and lets you tiptoe in to check on your baby without disrupting her sleep.

Painting. If you are painting the room, opt for a paint that is non-toxic and lead-free. There is also a wide range of wallpapers and borders with nursery themes available. However, be careful when

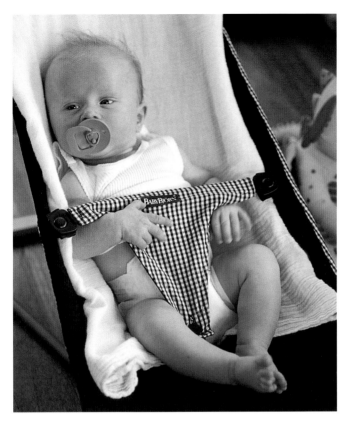

Baby bouncers, suitable for young babies, enable you to move baby from room to room as you attend to various tasks.

choosing because it won't be too long before your baby has outgrown 'Hey Diddle Diddle'. You may prefer to choose more neutral tones and patterns that last through to the school years.

Storage. Storage and shelving are important. Simple open shelving is ideal because you can see where everything is without having to rummage through drawers or heave open cupboard doors when your hands are full. Note that when your baby is mobile, you may want to add doors to prevent mess. A nappy stacker, preferably located near the change table, is also useful. Keep the most frequently used items nearby.

Musical mobile. One of these will soothe baby to sleep and keep her occupied when awake.

Toiletries. It may be useful to start with some basics, such as baby shampoo, wipes, cotton wool and nappy rash cream.

Birth to six months

From the moment of birth your baby begins to learn. In the first year, the senses of sight, taste, hearing, smell and touch, together with the ability to move and control those movements, dominate what your baby learns. At the same time his behaviour is related to whether he is sleeping, crying, waking, feeding, observing or playing.

How your baby grows

Every baby is an individual and will learn new skills at his own rate. A baby learns more in the first 12 months of life than he will in the next 11 years, so he has a great deal of learning to do. If you are worried about your child's development, discuss your concerns with your doctor or an early childhood professional. Also, remember that these developmental milestones are not activities that parents need to teach their child. Your role is to provide a loving environment: talk to, cuddle and be with your baby as much as possible, and watch over your child's safety and development. Children never benefit from being pushed to perform.

Development checklist

Around six weeks

Listens to you and watches you

Smiles at you

Raises his head and holds it up for a couple of minutes

Is excited to see you — he wriggles when he sees you

Around four months

Makes babbling and cooing noises

Turns his head when he hears a loud noise

Can lift his head almost 45 degrees off the floor when lying on his tummy

Turns his head when you shake a rattle or ring a little bell

Loves you to play 'peek-a-boo' games

Watches his fingers, hands and feet as if they belong to someone else — he may even hit himself and get a surprise

If baby is holding something, it will go straight into his mouth (babies use their mouths to explore texture and taste)

Sits quite well when you hold him; his head does not droop

Recognizes the breast or the bottle

Will sleep for six hours without waking up

Will hold a rattle or finger in the palm of his hand

Can roll over from his stomach to his back

Can hold both eyes in a fixed position

Around six months

Will do stand-ups by pushing his feet against your legs when you hold him on your lap facing you

Doesn't like being left alone

Will raise his arms to be picked up

Date you noticed your child doing it

Early arrivals and small babies

Babies who are born early are underweight and, sometimes, babies born on time are also underweight. These babies are known as 'small-for-dates'. Special care is usually necessary for these little ones.

A baby is described as premature, or pre-term, if he arrives before 37 weeks' gestation; prematurity is not defined by birth weight. A baby who is born before reaching full gestation is not mature enough to cope with the world outside the womb.

Small-for-dates babies have not been properly nourished in the last stages of the pregnancy. Some of these babies will need special care because they are having breathing difficulties or suffering from low blood sugar or other medical conditions; others will simply need small frequent feeds and will grow quickly.

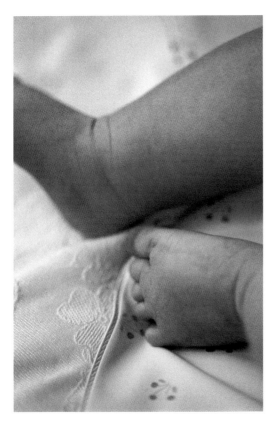

Premature babies

Premature babies need the special attention of an intensive care unit because they cannot move much due to their poor muscle tone; they may also have iron and calcium deficiencies and low blood sugar. Their skin may be red and wrinkly, the bones in their skull will not have hardened, and they are prone to jaundice.

Babies born after 31 weeks' gestation have similar survival rates to babies who are born full-term.

'Micro-prem' is a term given to babies who are born around 24 weeks' gestation and are so immature they need massive medical intervention in order to survive. The treatment needed to keep these babies alive, combined with their extreme immaturity, puts them at risk of a number of disabilities. As well as the problems described above, a micro-prem's eyes will be sealed.

Only about 5 per cent of babies are born prematurely, and in most cases, the cause is unknown. Known causes of prematurity include the following.

- Lack of antenatal care
- Poor nutrition
- Substance abuse
- Teenage pregnancy (less than 18 years)
- A history of a previous premature baby
- Disease or infection (such as urinary tract infection or infection of the amniotic membranes)
- Abnormalities of the uterus, or cervical incompetence
- Premature rupture of the membranes
- Smoking
- Pre-eclampsia or placental problems

Multiple pregnancies nearly always end prematurely.

Feeding premature babies

Premature babies are not strong enough to suck from a nipple or a teat, and their intestines may not be mature enough to absorb food. There are three ways these babies can be fed. The baby's maturity and strength determines which method is used.

Intravenous feeding. A tube is inserted into a vein.

Naso-gastric feeding. A tube is inserted into the stomach via the nose.

A combination of breast or bottle and tube feeding.

Premature babies have tiny stomachs and need to be fed more frequently than full-term babies.

Breathing difficulties

Because their lungs are not mature, premature babies have difficulty breathing and may stop breathing altogether for short periods. This is known as apnoea, and apnoea mats are placed in babies' cribs in intensive care units to detect this problem. Gentle stimulation, such as a light finger stroke, will usually re-start breathing.

Other problems

A premature baby faces a number of problems.

- He is at greater risk of infections, such as pneumonia, than a full-term baby.

- His body is not efficient at regulating his temperature and so he can easily get too hot or too cold. The special care nursery is usually kept warm, and the baby may be in an incubator. It is important to keep the baby warm, as he will grow faster; otherwise, he will lose energy trying to stay warm.

- Low blood sugar (hypoglycaemia) may be a problem. This can cause breathing difficulties and make a baby jittery or limp. A hypoglycaemic baby will need an intravenous drip of glucose.

- Jaundice also creates complications for a premature baby. The yellow skin of neonatal jaundice is caused by an excess amount of bilirubin that has to be excreted by baby's liver; sometimes it can't cope. Sunlight and frequent feeding is usually the treatment, unless it is a more severe form of the condition.

Caring for a premature baby

Parents of premature babies are encouraged to be involved in the care and feeding of their babies. These babies need the touch and comfort of their parents just as much as full-term babies do, and parents will be shown by nursing staff how to stroke their babies and talk to them. Close contact with outsiders is discouraged because of the risk of infection. Parents are required to wash their hands before handling baby and to wear a mask if they have a cough or an infection.

Each mother is encouraged to provide breastmilk for her premature baby, which helps to keep up her milk supply so she can breastfeed her baby when he is ready. Premature babies probably need the precious, unique nutrients that breastmilk provides more than full-term babies do. Not only does breastmilk provide the perfect nourishment, but it also protects against illness and infections, allergies, and problems such as anaemia. Breastmilk also reduces the risk of convulsions and unexplained sudden infant death syndrome (SIDS). When a premature baby's sucking reflex is mature enough, staff will help a mother who is keen to breastfeed her baby to get started.

'Kangaroo care' is used in some hospitals to help stabilize the baby's weight and to keep up the mother's milk supply. The mother (or father) 'wears' her baby against her skin. The baby is dressed in only a nappy and a hat, but is covered by the parent's clothing. This helps the baby's body temperature to stabilize and also reduces crying, which helps to conserve baby's energy. Mothers who use 'kangaroo care' have been found to produce more milk than mothers who do not.

Premature babies are usually allowed to go home when they are gaining weight steadily and have reached their estimated birth date. The staff will provide parents with help and advice on how to care for their baby at home as well as contact numbers for support staff, but nonetheless it can be even more daunting than taking a full-term baby home. Parents are also advised to organize some support for themselves, either from family or other parents who have experienced caring for a premature baby. All this helps to smooth the way.

Preventing premature birth

There are some obvious ways to avoid giving birth prematurely. These include:

* eating a sensible, balanced diet throughout the pregnancy and not putting on too much, or too little, weight; and

* attending regular antenatal checkups to be sure that you are healthy, and that the baby is developing normally.

Sometimes, when a woman goes into labour before she has reached full term, it is possible to delay the birth with appropriate drugs and hospital care until the baby is more mature.

Facts about your newborn baby

Most first-time parents find their newborn baby fascinating. You could probably spend hours gazing at your wondrous creation, although your baby may not be as picture-perfect as you had envisaged.

■ Your newborn's head is disproportionately larger than the rest of his body — about 25 per cent of his entire length.

■ At birth your baby's shoulders and spine may be covered in a fine downy hair. This is called lanugo and it will rub off naturally in the weeks after birth.

■ Many babies are born with a white, cream-like substance, known as vernix, covering their skin. Vernix is a protective coating, produced by the skin cells as they drop off in the amniotic fluid. It is not necessary to wash it off, except perhaps from the face for cosmetic reasons, as it is gradually absorbed by the baby's skin.

■ Some babies develop jaundice. This is a condition where the skin and the whites of the eyes turn yellow. Many healthy babies develop physiological, or newborn, jaundice around the third day of life. It is caused by the baby's blood having a high percentage of red cells that are broken down after birth, releasing a yellow pigment called bilirubin. The jaundice should disappear after a week or so, once the baby's liver is mature enough to process the excess bilirubin.

■ Fontanelles are the soft spots found in the spaces where the skull bones haven't yet joined in the top of the baby's head. Their role is to protect the brain: unfused bones can easily accommodate rapid changes of pressure inside baby's head. They will finally close, or fuse, by the time your baby is 18 months to two years old. If you notice a bulge or a concave area on your baby's head, contact your doctor immediately.

■ Most babies urinate several hours after they are born. Because your baby has no control over his bladder he will continue to 'wee' up to about 20 times in a 24-hour period. This is normal.

■ Your baby will pass meconium within 24 hours of being born. This sticky, dark greenish black substance, which lines baby's

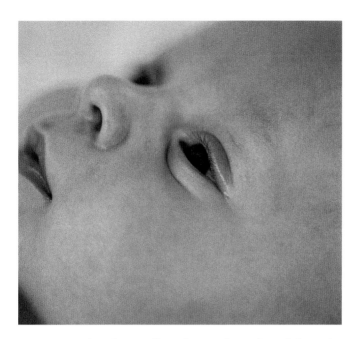

intestine when he is still in the womb, is derived from the amniotic fluid he swallows *in utero*. Your baby's stools will become paler and firmer after he starts feeding. After the fourth day he may pass four or five motions per day.

■ Occasionally, your newborn baby may look cross-eyed. This is because the muscles controlling his eye movements are weak at birth and take over a month to strengthen. By six weeks his eyes should begin to focus.

■ About 1 in 1200 babies is born with teeth. They are early primary teeth, known as natal teeth. Sometimes small grey bumps that resemble teeth appear on a baby's gums, but these subside and disappear a week later.

■ Birthmarks are common in newborn babies. They are usually formed by an abnormal collection of small blood vessels close to the skin's surface. You may find them on any part of your baby and they usually disappear, although some remain and others increase in size.

■ Because it takes several months for a baby's skin to acclimatize after birth, spots and rashes are not uncommon. Milia are small white spots that resemble whiteheads. They appear around the nose and cheeks. You should not attempt to squeeze them, as they are harmless and usually disappear after a few days.

■ If you hold your one-week-old baby gently against your shoulder, he will lift his head in little irregular jerks. By the time he is three weeks old, he can keep his head up for several seconds in this position. By six weeks the neck muscles are getting stronger, so your baby may be able to lift his head from your shoulder for one to two minutes.

■ Enlarged genitals are common in both sexes after birth. The swelling is caused by the presence of the mother's hormones in the baby's bloodstream.

■ If your new baby cries and his navel pops out, he may have an umbilical hernia. After the umbilical cord is cut, stomach muscles grow and encircle the navel from which the umbilical cord once extended, but sometimes not completely. When your

baby cries, pressure is placed on these weak abdominal muscles, causing the intestines to push through to beneath the surface of the navel. The bulge may be small, or as big as a golf ball. Surgery is unnecessary, as the opening usually closes after one or two years.

■ Your baby starts learning language from the moment he is born. He hears sounds in the environment, he is startled or cries at an unexpected noise, and he listens to the voices of other humans who are within his hearing range. Loud noises wake him and he becomes still when he hears a new sound or an unfamiliar voice.

■ Do not panic if your newborn baby has the hiccups. This is a sign that the muscles needed for breathing are growing stronger as your baby reacts to the sudden contraction of his diaphragm.

■ The final colour of your baby's eyes may not become clear until he is 12 months old. This is because there is no melanin, the body's natural pigment, in the eyes or skin at birth.

■ Most babies cry without tears until they are around six weeks old.

■ Stroking your baby's cheek activates the rooting reflex. He reacts by opening his mouth and turning towards the stimulated side.

This reflex can be used to your benefit in the early days of breastfeeding, as you can prepare your baby for 'latching on' in this way (see 'How breastfeeding works' on page 45). It usually disappears around the third or fourth month.

- The sucking reflex works when there is pressure on the upper palate of a baby's mouth. This is why it is important for the whole of the nipple and areola (the area around the nipple) to be inside the baby's mouth, so he is 'latched on' properly and therefore able to feed properly.

- The gagging reflex is important for survival. It is triggered when a baby swallows too much fluid.

- The labyrinthine reflex is named after the organ of balance located in the ear. It is triggered when your baby is placed on his stomach: he automatically raises his head so he can breathe freely. Because he is fighting against gravity, his head will keep dropping down and he will then turn it to one side or the other. (Do not place your baby on his stomach when he is sleeping.)

Amazingly, babies are also born with protective reflexes. For instance, if a hanky or scarf is gently placed over a baby's face, his reaction will be to try to brush it away.

- The stepping reflex is developed in the womb. When a baby is held underneath his arms, with his body upright and his feet touching a hard surface, he will move his legs up and down in a walking or stepping action. The reflex is thought by some to be an exercise in preparation for eventual walking. Another explanation is that when the unborn baby feels resistance on the soles of his feet from, for example, the walls of the uterus, he pushes himself off, ensuring he doesn't get stuck in one position. The reflex usually disappears at around the age of two months.

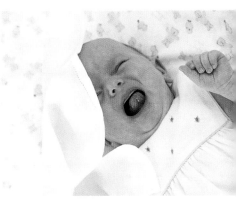

- The crawling reflex is evident when a baby is placed on his stomach. When he kicks out his legs, which are still drawn up, he will look as if he is crawling. Similarly, hard pressure applied to the soles of his feet will cause him to push forward. This reflex will be lost before your baby starts crawling.

- The Babinski reflex is activated when the sole of baby's foot is gently stroked from heel to toe. The toes will turn up and the foot will turn in. This reflex may not disappear until your baby is two years old.

Routine checks

Your doctor, local health nurse or paediatrician will examine your baby from head to toe. He or she will check the head and fontanelles, eyes, ears, mouth and palate (to look for conditions such as cleft palate), heart and lungs, abdomen, umbilical cord, anus, genitalia, testes (to see that they're fully descended), muscle and skeletal formation, skin and reflexes. Also, the legs will be gently manipulated to confirm that baby does not have a congenital hip dislocation. If you regularly visit an early childhood clinic, the nurse will weigh baby and measure his length (from head to toe) and head circumference.

■ The grasp or palmar reflex is triggered when a firm object such as your finger is placed into the palm of a newborn's hand. He will immediately hold on tightly. This reflex disappears around three to four months of age.

■ The Moro, or startle, reflex is used to test muscle tone. The baby is held on his back so his head can drop back. He will react by flinging his arms and legs outwards, before drawing them towards his body. You should not try this at home; leave it to your paediatrician, as it will certainly upset your baby and cause him to cry. However, the reflex might be triggered accidentally when a loud noise or a violent movement startles your baby. The Moro reflex disappears between four and six months.

■ Your paediatrician will test for the galant reflex, a swimming reflex left over from our amphibian ancestors. While holding your baby under the stomach with one hand, the paediatrician will use the other hand to stroke his or her finger along one side of baby's back. The baby will bend his body like a bow and pull his pelvis towards the side stroked. This reflex reveals the development of the spinal nerves and is present until around nine months.

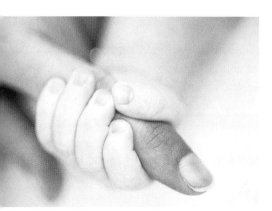

Feeding

After nourishing the baby as he grows in your womb for nine months, your body continues to provide the perfect food for your baby — breastmilk.

Breastfeeding

Breastmilk is designed for human babies. It is a unique and amazing substance. Every mother produces milk which is just perfect for her baby, containing the right amount of nourishment and energy the baby needs at that feed. Beginning in the early days with colostrum, each and every feed will change and adapt to suit your baby's needs. As you and your baby learn about breastfeeding, you come to know your baby's personality, as well as how your baby feeds, so breastfeeding becomes a natural and smooth operation that requires no special equipment.

Benefits for your baby

There are hundreds of properties in breastmilk, and researchers are still discovering new ones. The first milk, colostrum, is an almost clear substance, which bears absolutely no resemblance to the boiled sugary water that was once fed to newborn babies in the mistaken belief that it was better for them. Colostrum is higher in protein and lower in carbohydrates and fat than the later milk produced by the breasts. There are a number of reasons for this.

- Your baby needs only small amounts of breastmilk to get off to a good nutritional start.

- Colostrum acts as a laxative, helping baby's first bowel movement to remove meconium quickly. When this does not happen quickly enough, a baby is more likely to suffer from jaundice.

- Colostrum contains antibodies that protect the newborn baby at a time when your baby is at his most vulnerable.

After a few days the colostrum changes to breastmilk. This milk looks weaker than colostrum and may have a slight bluish tinge. Don't let this concern you. This milk is rich in nutrients and anti-infective properties — everything your baby needs to be able to grow and thrive. As the milk supply settles down, the first milk the breasts produce, called the foremilk, is high in protein, low in kilojoules (calories) and plentiful. As baby's thirst is quenched, the milk changes so that it is higher in kilojoules (calories) but not as plentiful. This is called the hind milk. As this is a gradual process, it is important that the baby feeds until he has had enough and comes off the breast by himself.

We currently know that breastmilk:

- is a complete food and drink for the first six months of a baby's life;

- protects baby against infectious diseases such as diarrhoea;

- safeguards baby against developing allergies;

- nourishes baby's brain (research shows that babies who are breastfed for eight months or more have higher IQs than babies who are not);[1]

- encourages bonding between you and your baby; and

- helps in the development of speech by encouraging the optimum development of the jaw muscles.

Benefits for you

Breastfeeding has long-term benefits for you as well as your baby. It helps your uterus to contract, and in the very early hours after the birth, helps to prevent haemorrhage. The lochia, which is the blood loss from the uterus after giving birth, flows faster and finishes sooner in women who breastfeed. Breastfeeding also helps the uterus return to its prepregnant size more quickly than if you do not breastfeed, and many women also find it helps their figure to regain some of its normal shape. In later life, women who have breastfed their babies seem to be less susceptible to cancers of the breast and reproductive organs.[2]

Breastfeeding does not affect the shape of the breasts, although in the early days it is certainly responsible for the breasts filling with milk as they settle into providing your baby's nourishment. All the major changes to the breasts happen during pregnancy, not while you are breastfeeding. The areola, the dark area around the nipple, will have become darker and the little lumps, known as Montgomery's tubercles, become more obvious. The breasts fill out as the glandular tissue increases in preparation for the breastmilk, and many women find they have the round, full breasts they have always dreamed of. This is also the shape you need to be in order to feed your baby.

How breastfeeding works

The ideal time to first offer your baby the breast is within the first hour of birth. A newborn baby has a strong sucking reflex, and if he is offered the nipple, he will often suck quite vigorously. A healthy newborn baby who is not affected by drugs that have crossed into his system from his mother during labour will eagerly seek his mother's breasts, opening his mouth and turning his head as he does so.

However, if it is not possible for your newborn baby to be put to your breast immediately after the birth, he will still learn to suck from your nipple. You may need help to get started, particularly if you have had a difficult labour and birth.

When your baby first sucks it triggers a flow of two hormones in your system — prolactin and oxytocin. Oxytocin is the hormone that stimulated the uterus to contract while you were in labour. When you and your baby meet each other for the first time, you will probably feel a surge of emotion and happiness. This reaction triggers the release of the hormone which, in turn, triggers the release of the milk. Prolactin is the milk-producing hormone, and it is triggered by the baby feeding at the breasts.

Together, prolactin and oxytocin make milk, and release it from the milk-producing glands in response to baby's sucking. So if the baby does not suck well, and if the breasts are not emptied, then less milk will be made.

Breastfeeding successfully is an amazing experience, but learning to breastfeed is the stage where many people have problems. Breastfeeding combines instinct, reflex, patience and learning. You and your baby both need to learn how to breastfeed, and getting the right advice and support in the early days, from both professionals and family, is a crucial part of success.

The most important thing you need to learn is how to hold your baby so that he can take the nipple into his mouth properly. You need to understand how breastfeeding works for your own benefit as well as your baby's.

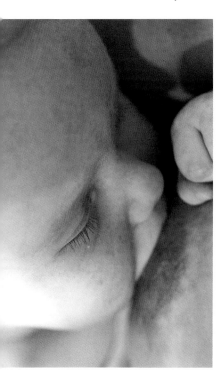

Your family and friends need to know that both you and baby are learning to breastfeed, and they need to understand how breastfeeding works — the most important thing being that supply will equal demand. So a hungry baby needs to feed frequently in order for your supply to build up and meet his needs.

Tips for successful breastfeeding

For your baby to suck properly he needs to take the entire nipple in his mouth. If you look at a diagram of breastfeeding, it looks as if the baby is almost swallowing the nipple and the areola. The areola needs to just about disappear as the baby sucks. You will also notice that your baby's ears will wiggle as he sucks!

To help your baby to 'latch on' properly, you need to hold him so that he can. Either lay him across your lap, or lay him so that his legs are under the arm of the side on which you are feeding. It is vital that baby has his chin to your breast, and if baby is lying across you, his chest should face your chest. To hold baby in either of these positions you will probably need the support of pillows in the beginning, particularly if you have had a caesarean delivery. It is very important that:

- you feel comfortable. If you are straining your back or bending over in an unnatural way, you will not find breastfeeding easy. Your posture can affect the angle of your breasts and the amount of milk your baby can take. The best place to sit when you begin breastfeeding is in a straight-backed chair. A comfy armchair or sitting up in a bed may seem better, but in fact, when you first start, it is more difficult to get comfortable in these places;

- you hold your baby close to you, so he can reach your nipple comfortably. His head, neck and back should all be in a straight line; and

- your baby takes a mouthful of your breast.

As well as being sure your baby is sucking on the nipple efficiently — sometimes breastfeeding advisors call this ' latched on properly' — it is important in the early days to make sure your baby is feeding well.

Once your breasts have made the milk, they need to release it. They do this through a combination of your baby feeding well and the letdown reflex. When you put your baby to the breast and he starts to suck, the milk will 'let down'. Many women feel this as a tingle in their breasts, but the milk can still let down without the 'tingle'. Some women find their milk 'lets down' when they hear their baby cry or even when they just think about breastfeeding.

Babies use their body language to tell their mothers when they are hungry. A baby who is frantically crying has long passed giving out signals and is distressed. However, a baby who is hungry will seek the breast, he will snuggle and nuzzle, impatiently opening his mouth like a hungry little bird, breathing rapidly and possibly waving his arms about. You will soon get to know your baby's signals and know that you need to feed him straight away, or at least very soon.

Breastfeeding is thirsty work, so make sure you have something to drink nearby — water is ideal and you need around eight glasses a day.

Breastfeeding checklist

* Don't lie baby on his back so he has to turn his head.

* Make sure you hold baby high enough up on your chest.

* Don't take the breast to your baby — the correct way is to take baby to the breast, even if you need cushions to do it.

* Don't stop baby latching onto the nipple properly. This can happen when your nipples feel tender, but when a baby is not taking in all the nipple properly it will make the nipple more tender, not less so.

* Don't resist having baby's chin up against your breast. Babies are born chinless so they can take in their mother's nipple without any hindrance.

Things you should know

■ Babies enjoy breastfeeding and many don't want to stop. As well as the nourishment, your baby is enjoying snuggling up against you, and may doze and then suck a little more and doze again — if you let him. Most of us have other things to do, and sometimes it will be necessary to slip a clean little finger in between your nipple and baby's tongue to break the suction. Then you may find he goes to sleep or is happy lying on the floor watching you, or being carried in a sling.

■ At the end of the day you are likely to have much less milk than you do in the morning or during the night. Your baby may also be fussy because of the time of day, and you may feel you are 'losing' your milk. This is most unlikely if you are feeding according to your baby's needs during the rest of the day.

■ Babies suck in a pattern. Each baby sucks in his own way but all babies suck and pause; some are faster feeders than others.

■ Breastfeeding works best when it is 'baby-led': that means feeding baby when he is hungry, not by the clock or because you have things to do or you think he needs a feed. If you regard breastfeeding as a special time you have with your baby, and accept that this time will only be relatively short, you can put others things aside; let your baby's needs take priority. Use it as a time to relax; put your feet up and have a drink.

■ The easiest and most satisfactory way to feed your baby at night is in your bed. If baby is in your room, this is even easier (see 'Sleeping' on page 97).

Preventing problems

In the modern world there are many obstacles that can make breastfeeding problematical, even unsuccessful, for the mother and baby team. Most of these can be prevented, but if they do happen there are remedies that will help you to continue breastfeeding.

Sore nipples

Most women have tender nipples when they start to breastfeed. When baby is positioned properly on the breast this tenderness will soon go away, but if baby is chewing it will make it worse. Try a different position, and if feeding is making your nipples sore, take baby off and try positioning him again. Feed baby on the sore nipple first and before he is really hungry. Let your nipples get plenty of sunlight and keep them dry. Try leaving a little breastmilk on the sore nipple, or use an ice block on the nipple before baby feeds. Once you have sorted out the positioning, the sore nipple will recover quickly. Soap and creams can also irritate sore nipples. Not feeding on a sore nipple can lead to engorgement, an even worse problem (see below).

Thrush

Small white patches in your baby's mouth that don't go away are thrush, a yeast infection. Both baby's mouth and your nipples will be sore. You need to see a doctor as soon as possible and get a medication that will clear up the infection quickly.

Lumps

Blocked milk ducts usually cause lumpy breasts in women who are breastfeeding. Again, these are a result of poor positioning. They will go away if you adjust your position. In the meantime placing a very warm washer on the lumps may help. Try gently kneading the lumps during and after feeds.

Engorgement

Hard full breasts like melons are normal in the very early days when the milk supply is getting established. Expressing a little milk before baby feeds and using a hot washer on your breasts will soon help baby to latch on. Once you are breastfeeding comfortably and as often as baby needs, the hardness will soon disappear.

Engorged breasts, on the other hand, feel like hot lumps and are extremely painful. Engorgement needs to be treated immediately or it will lead to mastitis. It is caused by not feeding baby when he needs to be fed and by not letting baby empty the breast — hurried feeds are the biggest problem.

If your breasts are full, baby does not want to feed, and you are uncomfortable, express some milk. Giving yourself a gentle massage will also help. A cool, washed cabbage leaf in your bra for two to three hours, with a breast pad to protect the nipple, has been found to relieve engorgement; no one knows why this works.

Mastitis

Mastitis is an inflammation of the breast, and will make you feel as if you have the flu. Your breast may also be lumpy. If you act quickly, you may be able to avoid taking antibiotics. Poor positioning and not feeding baby as and when he needs also cause it. Take your baby to bed with you and do not wear a bra. Have plenty of fluids by the bed. Feed your baby often — this may be every 15 to 20 minutes — and for as long as he wants, and try different positions until you are both comfortable. Gently massage your breasts as you feed and be sure to express any leftover milk (in the shower is often the best place).

You can also try:

- placing an ice pack (or a packet of frozen peas) on your breast after feeding to reduce the swelling;

- smearing breastmilk on your nipples and letting it dry;

- using a hot pack to help the milk start flowing; and

- taking paracetamol according to directions.

If the problem has not resolved itself after six to eight hours, you need to see a doctor about antibiotics, but do not stop feeding. It will definitely make the inflammation worse if you do.

Before you give up breastfeeding

Many women are disappointed with breastfeeding. They find it more difficult than they expected, or they just thought they'd give it a go without any planning or understanding of how it works. Some feel it is an imposition on their time, and others are really overwhelmed by motherhood and other responsibilities.

There are plenty of reasons why you should breastfeed, not the least being that breastmilk is the only perfect food for baby. Ideally, your baby needs your milk for the first 12 months of his life. Six months is almost as good, and any is better than none at all.

Here are some of the reasons mothers commonly give for stopping, and also some things to think about before you give up.

Not enough milk. In a society where we are used to measuring quantities and knowing how much we are getting, the way the human body makes breastmilk is a mystery to many, and any unhappiness in the baby is often attributed to 'not enough milk'. If you feed your baby when he needs to be fed, if you have worked out how to get baby to take all the nipple into his mouth, if you are comfortable and if you wait until baby has emptied the breast at each feed, you will be making enough milk. If you are worried that you are not making enough milk, seek reassurance from a lactation consultant or a breastfeeding counsellor.

Sore nipples. These will soon go away if you follow the advice in 'Preventing problems' (see page 48).

Baby is not satisfied. When babies have growth spurts, they need more milk. The way to solve this is to feed more and make sure the breast is emptied every time. If baby does not empty the breast, express what is left and save it in the freezer for a time when you are not around to feed him yourself.

Bottle-feeding is easier. Others can do it, which frees you up. If you are not enjoying breastfeeding, then bottle-feeding will seem attractive. It is expensive and time-consuming, but many people are not concerned about this. It is also easier for women who are not happy feeding their baby in public.

Unsupportive partner. A supportive partner is very important to the success of breastfeeding. Some men are jealous of their baby or of the time their partner is spending with the baby. Some men feel that breasts are sexual objects and should not be used to feed a baby. If your partner feels like this, then you can try to educate him by giving him the information about how important breastmilk is to his baby's development. If he doesn't come around, then you may find it becomes a battleground you would rather not take part in.

Returning to work. If you need to go back to work in the first year of your baby's life, you may feel that keeping up breastfeeds is going to be too difficult. Many women successfully breastfeed and go out to work, but it does need commitment and planning. (See 'Returning to work and breastfeeding' on page 52 for some strategies before you decide.)

Baby not gaining enough weight. Graphs, known as percentile charts, are used to track a baby and child's growth by comparing it against a national average, and doctors and health professionals can become concerned if a baby is not consistently meeting this average. Sometimes a mother who has difficulty getting breastfeeding established feels her baby would be better off on the bottle. If you want to continue breastfeeding, seek the advice of a breastfeeding advisor about building up your supply before you give up breastfeeding.

Not having enough time. You may find it hard to accept that it could take an hour to feed your newborn, especially if you were used to achieving a lot in a busy day before the birth. Try to learn to relax and enjoy this time with your baby.

Expressing your breastmilk

Learning how to express breastmilk will mean that you can have 'time out' from baby. Many new mothers find they need some time to themselves to sleep — or just to do something they were used to doing before they had the 24-hour responsibility of a baby. Hand-expressing is something you will soon learn to do.

To express milk, start at your breastbone and gently stroke down your breast with both hands. As you get to the nipple, gently squeeze it between your thumb and forefinger and collect the milk in a sterile container.

A breast pump will make expressing easier and more efficient, and many have bottle attachments that make it easy to store the expressed milk. Breastmilk keeps in the back of the fridge for up to 48 hours and in the freezer for two to three weeks. Make sure you label it if it is not in a baby's bottle, as you don't want it confused with other milk!

Returning to work and breastfeeding

If you need or want to return to work before you stop breastfeeding, you need to plan and prepare. First, you need to tell your employer that you would like to continue breastfeeding. Also talk to your fellow employees about what you are doing and why.

In order to express milk at work you will need to organize some things.

Time to express. Ideally, express as often as you would feed baby if you were with him.

Time to properly store, seal and label the milk. You will also need a fridge in which to keep it.

A clean, private place. You will need privacy while expressing.

Flexible work options. Obviously if you are going to take up time expressing and possibly taking milk to your baby during the day, this will need to be taken into account. There may be work you can do at home, or perhaps you can work flexitime to keep up with your commitments. Your employer may have a job-share program, allowing you to work part-time.

If there is childcare for your baby nearby or at work, then you may be able to feed baby during the day. This will also make taking your baby to childcare easier and less time-consuming.

Stress can easily interfere with breastfeeding, and going back to work full-time will definitely make your life more stressful. If you are aware of this and can work in with others, ideally with your partner and other family support, then it is less likely to affect your milk supply. If you begin to express before you go back to work, so you have a bit of a backup in breastmilk, and if you take every opportunity to express once you are back at work, you will find it easier.

Bottle-feeding

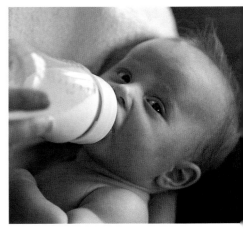

Artificial baby milks, known as formula, were first created at the end of the 19th century. Based on cow's milk, complicated formulae that had to be changed with each feed were given to mothers to ensure that the milk was suitable for their babies — hence the name 'formula'. The strength and quality of this modified milk was altered with lime water, lactose and bicarbonate of soda, in varying amounts. The majority of today's formulae are still based on cow's milk, although there are also soy milk and goat's milk formulae available.

Scientists have created much more sophisticated formulae in the 100 years or so since they were first developed, but these artificial baby milks still lack hundreds of the properties of breastmilk.

Feeding a baby infant formula is an acceptable replacement for human milk when it is made up strictly according to directions, when bottles and other equipment are well sterilized, and when baby is fed according to his needs and not to the instructions on the can or other ideals. Feeding your baby with formula is far less dangerous than feeding him unmodified milks.

If you decide to bottle-feed you need some special equipment.

A can of infant formula. It is best to choose a brand according to price and availability, unless a doctor has instructed you to use a particular brand. All artificial baby milks must meet strict government regulations. They are similar in make-up. There is no benefit to feeding a baby soy or goat's milk-based formula unless you have been given medical advice to this effect. Cow's milk formula is a better choice.

Support

It is easy to feel alone when you are a new mother. Establishing a support network of other mothers with babies the same age — either through a breastfeeding support group or your friends from antenatal class or playgroup — will help you cope with the total change of lifestyle that comes with parenthood and breastfeeding. (See the 'Resources' list on page 349.)

Bottles. Start with four bottles, two small and two large, and choose a couple of different brands. You will soon find one that suits you and your baby.

Teats. Start with four teats, of different types and brands.

A bottlebrush. You'll need one of these for scrubbing bottles and teats.

Sterilizing equipment. You can buy kits for chemical sterilizing or microwave sterilizing, or you can sterilize using the old-fashioned boiling method (see 'Old-fashioned boiling' on page 55).

Making up formula

It is vital that you always make up the formula according to the directions on the can. Making it up too strongly or weakly can cause kidney problems in your baby.

Infant formula must be made up with cooled boiled water and fed to baby from a bottle that has been cleaned and sterilized.

It's best to make up formula as baby needs it; however, if you do make up a bottle in advance, keep it stored in the fridge. When you go out, take formula powder in a separate container and boiled bottle water in the bottle. Mix the two when your baby needs to feed.

Sterilizing

Before you sterilize your bottle-feeding equipment, using the method you have chosen, you need to make sure that all milk residues have been removed from bottles and teats. If baby has a dummy, this can be treated in the same way.

- Rinse everything immediately after a feed.
- Using warm water, detergent and a bottlebrush, scrub bottles and teats.
- Rinse everything thoroughly.
- Rub salt into the inside and outside of teats and rinse them again thoroughly. This will help remove any missed milky bits.
- Put all the equipment into a sterilizing unit and follow the manufacturer's instructions.

Old-fashioned boiling

You can save money by boiling bottles and teats. You need a large pan in which you can submerge everything. Bring the water to the boil and boil for ten minutes. Allow everything to cool in the water, then to dry naturally in the air. Do not use tea towels.

Tips for successful bottle-feeding

Your baby needs to be fed by bottle in the same way as you would feed him by breast during the day and night.

■ Hold your baby in the same position as you would if you were breastfeeding, and let him decide how much he wants and when.

■ At night-time have everything ready for a feed. If you do not have enough time to warm the bottle, don't wait for it while baby gets more and more anxious. An hysterical hungry baby will require much longer to take the bottle and go back to sleep than a baby who has been fed cool or cold milk. At any time, an unhappy baby does not care if the milk is warm or cold. If your baby is hungry and you only have cold milk, both you and he will be happier if you do not wait to warm it up.

■ Be organized with your sterilizing. Two sterilizing units, or boiling as well as using a unit, will make it more efficient. If

Use either a sterilizing unit, like this one, or the old-fashioned boiling method to sterilize baby's bottles.

never

* Never leave made-up bottled formula out of the fridge or carry it around with you.

* Never keep a bottle of milk which baby has not finished. Always discard leftovers. Formula is a great breeding ground for germs.

* Never take warmed made-up formula out with you in an insulated container. This too is an ideal place for bacteria to multiply.

* Never let your baby feed himself with a bottle. He could choke, and you are depriving him of the warmth and closeness that babies need, particularly when they feed.

you have enough bottles and teats, you will only need to do this once a day.

■ Be organized when you go out. Make sure you have sufficient powder in separate containers, and boiled water ready in a sterilized bottle in the fridge.

■ Put the bottle in a jug of hot water to warm the formula. Microwave heating is not recommended as the milk heats unevenly. If you must put it in the microwave, make sure you shake it and test the temperature on your wrist before giving it to baby: babies have been scalded in the mouth by milk which has been heated in a microwave.

Possible problems

Babies who are bottle-fed infant formula do not have the immunity to infections that breastfed babies do. You need to be very careful about sterilizing, and you also need to be aware that your baby is more likely to suffer from colds than a breastfed baby. Babies who come in contact with other children and adults are more vulnerable to infection.

Constipation can also be a problem with bottle-fed babies. Breastfed babies may go for days without passing a bowel motion and not be constipated. If you think your baby is constipated, you need to discuss the treatment with your community nurse or family doctor.

Babies who are bottle-fed can be fussy. It may be that he is still hungry. If he consistently finishes the bottle, then offer him more milk. A hungry baby under the age of six months should not be fed solids. Babies under the age of six months are not ready for other foods, and if they are introduced, these can cause long-term problems, such as allergies and kidney problems. It may be that the teat on the bottle is not large enough. You can enlarge a hole in a teat with a needle that has been sterilized by being held over a gas flame. However, it is better to buy teats with larger holes.

Nonsense about feeding babies

There are plenty of myths about feeding babies, and lots of people ready to tell you how to do it and what you are doing wrong. Here are some of the things you may hear.

Babies need to be fed four-hourly. Since the 18th century men have been telling women that their babies only need to be fed every four hours. Most adults don't go for four hours during the day without food, and their stomachs hold much more than a tiny baby's. In order to grow and develop to their potential, babies need to be fed according to their individual needs.

Giving a baby formula will help him sleep through the night. If a baby has a small stomach, it can only hold so much. A baby fed infant formula may go longer between feeds as formula can take longer to digest than breastmilk, but it won't make a baby who is used to waking every two or three hours for a feed sleep for six or eight hours.

Dummies

Many breastfeeding advocates do not like dummies because they can prevent a baby who needs to be fed from being satisfied. They are also breeding grounds for germs and stop a baby from experimenting with sucking his fingers — an important part of learning about his body. But some babies are 'sucky' and like to have something in their mouth most of the time. You need to decide if you want to give your baby a dummy, and you also need to ensure that you have a good milk supply established. Dummies need to be sterilized in the same way as bottles and teats. There is no truth in the old wives' tale about dummies affecting the development of a baby's teeth.

If you are depressed, you need to stop breastfeeding. Sleep deprivation is one of the contributing factors to much depression. Taking your own sleep needs into account and modifying your lifestyle is a start. A bottle-fed baby still needs to be fed through the night. Admittedly, someone else can bottle-feed your baby for you while you sleep, but the bottle can contain expressed breastmilk rather than formula.

If a baby is chewing on his fingers he is hungry. Babies chew on their fingers because they like the sensation: they are learning about their hands and fingers by sucking on them; it has nothing to do with hunger.

If your mother/sister/cousin couldn't breastfeed, you won't be able to either. Everyone is different and chances are your mother/sister/cousin either wasn't motivated to breastfeed or had inappropriate or inadequate breastfeeding advice and support. You have as much chance as every other woman of breastfeeding, but you need to want to.

My nipples are inverted/too small/too flat to breastfeed. You can still breastfeed: nipples come in all shapes and sizes and baby is very clever at latching on if you have him positioned properly.

Burping

Burping your baby is not something you need to make a ritual of. Babies do not need to be 'burped', but they do need to be held upright after a feed if they are still awake, or gently placed in an upright position over your shoulder if they are asleep, so that any air bubble can be allowed to escape naturally. Some babies are more 'windy' than others, and wind is more likely with bottle-fed babies or babies who are so hungry they gulp their feed. Sometimes your baby will stop in the middle of a feed to burp. Giving your baby the opportunity at the end of a feed to bring up any burps is all you need to do.

Possetting

Possetting is used to describe a small vomit which is quite common in young babies. It is completely harmless, and some babies do it after every feed and between feeds, while others never or rarely do it. If you try to force your baby to burp, he is more likely to bring up milk. If your baby is a 'possetter', he will grow out of it. In the meantime, you need to have a cloth nappy over your shoulder, and perhaps on your lap, at every feed. You also need to wear clothing that can easily be sponged clean or doesn't show marks. The possetting of breastfed babies is less smelly than that of bottle-fed babies.

Worse than possetting is gastro-oesophageal reflux (GOR), which can be distressing for both baby and his parents. You may need to adapt baby's sleeping and feeding patterns. (See 'Gastro-oesophageal reflux' on page 305 for more information.)

Sometimes baby will not burp, but instead will expel wind from his bowel. This is perfectly normal and more common in some babies than in others.

'Colic'

'Colic' is used to describe intense crying — a red-faced baby with knees drawn up to his chest and crying non-stop. It can be worse at the end of the day or at night, and it is very distressing for both parents and baby. Colicky babies are usually healthy and thriving and a lot less irritable than their sleep-deprived parents. Everyone has a theory about colic; some doctors still say that anxious parents cause it, although there is little evidence to support this. Colic is not an illness. It is a distressing pattern of behaviour in babies in their first year. Colic medicines are generally not

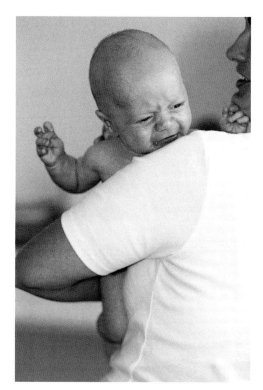

successful, and adopting strategies to help you cope is a far better remedy for a condition that usually disappears round the three to four month mark.

When nothing seems to work, parents are inclined to blame themselves, but this is non-productive. Some strategies will work at some times and not at others.

Making other factors in your life as stress-free as possible will help you to cope with the steep learning curve of early parenting. Taking turns with your partner in trying to comfort your screaming bundle will also help. It can seem like a long haul, but your baby will outgrow colic, and your life will once again return to some kind of normalcy.

If at any time you suspect your baby has a problem other than colic, the wisest course of action is to seek medical advice as soon as possible. It is far better to be sent home with a 'colicky' baby than to ignore your parental instincts.

Caring

Try to establish a routine of caring that suits you and your family. The early days may seem chaotic and overwhelming as you adjust to having a new person in your lives, but gradually, as your baby 'settles', you will choose caring methods and a routine that works for your household.

How to hold a baby

At first your inclination may be to avoid holding your baby; you might be worried about dropping him or holding him incorrectly. This feeling of anxiety is totally natural if you're not used to being around babies. It doesn't help your cause that babies are incredibly intuitive. If you're nervous and fumble, your baby may feel insecure and respond with the Moro, or startle, reflex which is characterized by the arms being flung out wide, an arching back, grimacing and crying. This happens when a baby feels exposed: he is no longer

wrapped in a warm blanket, there is nothing to grab and hold, and nobody is holding him. This reflex has been described as an unconscious attempt by a baby to regain his balance.

So before you even attempt to pick up your baby, relax. You need to be able to approach him in a confident manner: you don't want to squeeze him too tightly, nor should you treat him as if he's wrapped in cotton wool. If you follow these tips, before too long picking up and holding your baby will become second nature. It is recommended that you cradle your newborn baby on your left side, as his head will rest closer to your heart where he will feel reassured by the steady beat so familiar to him while he was in the womb.

Picking up and cradling a baby in your arms

Here are some hints on how to pick up your newborn baby.

1 Lean close to your baby and slide your hand gently under the back of his neck and head.

2 Place the other hand between his legs, so it supports his bottom. Make eye contact and talk soothingly to reassure him that he is in safe hands.

3 Once you are confident he is secure, slowly and gently lift him towards you, still leaning forward. Keep your hands positioned firmly and ensure the back of his neck is cradled.

4 Straighten up as you continue to move him to chest level, then turn his body slightly so it is parallel to yours, keeping his head slightly elevated above the rest of his body.

5 Slide the hand supporting his head under his body so his head rests in the crook of your arm, his body is supported by the length of your arm and his bottom is propped by your hand.

6 Remove your other hand from his bottom and slide it under the supporting arm to provide extra security and comfort for baby. Check that his head and body are still slightly elevated, and allow his legs to remain free. Gently rock your baby if he is unsettled.

Your baby may prefer to be held upright, nestled against your body with his head next to your shoulder. To hold him securely, use one hand to support his bottom and the other to protect his neck and the back of his head.

Holding the older baby

The older baby can sit on your hip with his legs on either side of your waist, while you support his bottom securely with your hand. This leaves your other arm free, or you can use it for extra support. Be careful if you suffer from lower back pain as this hold could make the problem worse.

When holding your baby facing outwards, keep him against you with one arm under his arms and around the front of his body, and the other between the front of the thighs (holding onto his nappy) to hold him steady.

Holding a colicky baby

One method of calming a colicky baby is to position his body so he is resting face down on your forearm, with his head positioned near your hand and his legs either side of your upper arm. Place your other hand firmly on his back. Gently press the heel of your lower hand into his abdomen just below the ribs, while gently bouncing him up and down on your forearm. This may help bring up wind and ease your baby's tummy ache.

Nappies

Keeping baby clean, dry and comfortable may seem like a full-time job in the early months. Your baby has no control over his bladder and bowel functions. The breastfed newborn may have up to 12 bowel movements a day and urinate up to 20 times a day. At times, these bowel movements can be fairly explosive and go everywhere! Fortunately, there's an array of quality products that helps parents achieve their goal of keeping baby feeling fresh as a daisy.

Options

Choosing what's best for your baby will always be foremost in your mind, no matter what the situation. However, many parents may also consider what's best for the environment too.

Traditional cloth nappies

Cloth nappies are significantly cheaper than disposable nappies, and because they are recyclable, can be used for subsequent children. The supporters of cloth nappies point out that they are more environmentally friendly than disposable nappies and don't contribute to landfill. Their detractors, however, point out that they use energy and water-polluting detergents when they are washed. The most absorbent fabric is cotton terry towelling, but this is also the bulkiest.

The traditional cloth nappy requires fasteners or safety pins, liners or pads (optional), and pilchers.

What you will need:

Nappies. Around two or three dozen nappies, usually 100 per cent cotton terry towelling.

Fasteners. A number of fasteners or nappy pins for securing nappies.

Liners. About four to six liners for inside the nappy. These are optional but provide extra absorbency, can draw urine away from the skin and prevent the nappy from becoming too soiled. Disposable and cloth liners or extra absorbent pads are available.

Pilchers. Four to six pairs of pilchers (also called wraps). Pilchers also come in two designs: the fitted design, which fits like a pair of pants, and the open design, which folds out flat and is secured by Velcro or poppers. Avoid plastic pilchers as they trap the moisture inside the nappy; opt for breathable polyester, cotton or wool.

Fitted or shaped cloth nappies

These are like a cloth nappy and pilchers in one (also called baby pants or a nappy system, which may consist of baby pants and same-brand liners and/or pads). Generally, the fitted cloth nappy features around eight layers of cotton flannelette and a waterproof outer layer. Cloth or disposable liners are also required for extra absorbency. The advantages of the fitted cloth nappy are that it:

- is usually a snug fit;
- often has an adjustable waist band or poppers to accommodate a growing baby;
- does not require pins;
- has a waterproof outer layer for maximum protection;
- looks smarter than traditional cloth; and
- is reusable.

Although fitted cloth nappies are initially expensive, over time the cost falls into line with that of the traditional cloth option once you take into account longevity and the cost of pilchers and fasteners.

Disposable nappies

Disposable nappies are praised for their convenience and absorbent qualities. The absorbent padding is made from wood cellulose fibre (also called wood pulp, a fluffy paper-like material) and an apparently 'super absorbent' material called polyacrylate. All the other synthetic materials in the nappy contribute to a snug fit and help stop leaks.

Disposable nappies come in a range of sizes, and the quality can differ markedly from brand to brand. To check for fit and comfort, adjust the waist so you can fit one finger between baby's tummy and the nappy. Also ensure a snug fit around the thighs. Because they can only be used once, disposable nappies end up costing a lot more over time than their traditional and fitted counterparts. They contain large amounts of wood pulp, and their plastic covers take generations to break down. However, they do make travelling with a baby much easier.

If you are concerned about the environment but still looking for the convenience of a disposable nappy, biodegradable disposable nappies are available through the Internet under the entry 'baby pants' and 'fitted cloth nappies'.

Nappy service

A nappy service is a time-saving option that allows you to decide whether you want to continue using cloth nappies. A good service supplies soft, clean, cotton nappies, plastic bags and a large nappy bucket with a lid. The nappies are usually delivered to your door in bags of ten and 20. In the first week 60 nappies are recommended for a girl and 70 for a boy. You place each used nappy in a bucket lined with a plastic bag. At the end of each week you put the full nappy bucket out for collection. The nappy service then washes the nappies according to stringent hospital standard wash processes.

The change area

When you set up your change area, make sure everything you need is no more than an arm's length away so you never have to leave your baby unattended, not even for a few seconds.

A change table is a must if you experience back problems: it stands at around waist height so you don't have to bend over when changing baby. To make sure you're buying a safe product, check that it is sturdy and won't collapse when your baby is on it, that there are no gaps where a baby's head, fingers or limbs could get caught and no sharp edges. A change table that has a shelf underneath stores all changing supplies within easy reach. If there is no storage space, place the change table close to shelves or a table where changing supplies can be kept nearby, but not so close that baby can grab hold of them. A nappy stacker is another useful accessory. It stores towels, linen and nappies, while a small, lined rubbish bin is handy for soiled nappies and used baby wipes.

If there is a safety harness on the change table, it is advisable to use it at all times. If not, gently place one hand on your baby's tummy to hold him in place if you need to reach for fasteners or creams.

Just about all the accidents involving change tables are caused when a baby has been left unattended. If the phone rings or there is an emergency you need to attend to, take your baby with you or remove him to safety, even if he is secured with a safety harness that comes with some change table models.

If space is an issue in your home, a change mat — a foam rectangle covered in vinyl — is a compact and portable option. Simply place it on the surface where you are going to change your baby — a firm bed, table or the floor — and store it away afterwards.

Again, never leave your baby unsupervised on a mat, even for a moment, as he could easily roll. If you've placed the change table near a window, check that there are no choking hazards such as tassels or cords within his reach.

Whether you choose an elaborate change table, a portable mat or a sheepskin protected by a spare nappy, make sure the surface is washable.

To keep your baby occupied while you're changing him, place a colourful mobile, painting or mirror in his line of vision, or simply talk and sing to him. This may help stop the wriggling while you're attempting to fasten a nappy.

How to change a nappy

It is estimated that a baby will have his nappy changed 5000 times. And in the next 12 months you should be prepared to perform this task around ten times a day. If you're using traditional cloth nappies, there are a variety of folds to suit the shape and size of your baby and these include boy and girl folds (see 'Folding cloth nappies' on page 69 for several examples).

Changing a traditional cloth nappy

Fold a clean nappy before you start changing your baby. In fact, you'll save time if you fold nappies as you store them. See 'Folding cloth nappies' on page 69.

What you'll need

- ❏ Clean traditional cloth nappy
- ❏ Baby wipes or clean, damp wash cloth
- ❏ Soft, clean hand towel
- ❏ Cream or lotion (optional)
- ❏ Plastic bag or small rubbish bin for disposal of soiled nappy and wash cloth
- ❏ Nappy liner (preferably reusable cloth liners for nappy rash prevention)
- ❏ Pilchers
- ❏ Fasteners

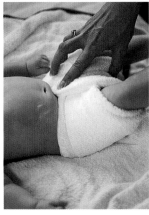

1 Lay your baby on the change mat. If using pins, carefully unfasten them and place them well away from your baby.

2 If your baby has passed a bowel motion, hold his ankles and lift his bottom gently. Use the edge of the nappy to wipe away the poo from front to back.

3 While his bottom is still raised, with your free hand lightly fold the nappy in on itself and slide it out from under your baby before lowering him back onto the mat.

4 Clean your baby's bottom using a non-perfumed baby wipe, a clean, damp wash cloth or dampened cotton wool balls. Dab him dry with the hand towel and, if you like, lightly apply a protective cream or lotion.

5 Holding his ankles again, lift his bottom and place a prefolded nappy and liner underneath him. Pull the absorbent middle pad up between the legs to cover his belly button and then draw the side flaps across so they meet in the middle.

6 Pin or fasten the nappy in the middle, checking that all three layers are secured. If you are using safety pins, always place your hand between the nappy and baby's skin while fastening and unfastening. If the nappy is a little loose, tuck the excess in and under the nappy to form a leak guard around the legs.

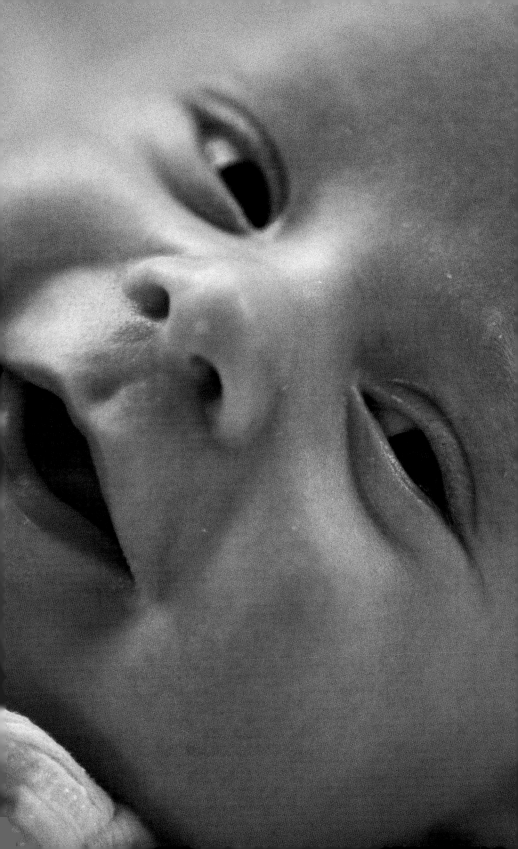

Changing a disposable nappy

You should have a bundle of disposable nappies close to your change table.

What you'll need

- ❑ New nappy
- ❑ Baby wipes or a clean, damp wash cloth
- ❑ Clean hand towel
- ❑ Baby lotion or cream (optional)
- ❑ Plastic bag or lined bin for disposal of soiled nappy

1 Gently lay your baby down on a change mat or other firm flat surface. Unfasten the soiled nappy and grasp your baby's ankles with one hand, gently raising his bottom.

2 Use the front of the nappy to wipe your baby's bottom before sliding the nappy out from under him. Continue to clean his bottom with either baby wipes or a clean, damp wash cloth and finish by dabbing dry with the hand towel.

3 Let go of his ankles and, with one hand on his tummy to keep him secure, apply cream or lotion to his bottom with your free hand.

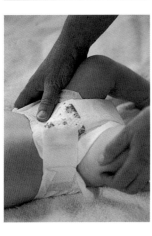

4 Grasp his ankles once more and lift his bottom up gently to slide the new nappy underneath him.

5 Release baby's ankles and bring the front of the nappy up between his legs. Make sure it's on straight for a snug, comfortable fit over the hips. Ensure a boy's penis is positioned downwards, so that he doesn't urinate into the waistband.

6 Peel the backing off one tab at a time and stick it down on either side. Press the overflap down neatly against his tummy so the nappy will hug his waist comfortably.

Nappy changing tips

- When changing a baby girl's nappy, always clean from the front to the back.

- If you are changing a baby boy's nappy, never pull the foreskin back from the penis.

- Never leave your baby unattended on a change table or raised surface while changing a nappy, even for a few seconds.

- When a baby boy's nappy is removed, the sudden feeling of air on his skin may cause him to urinate, so have a spare nappy or cloth to cover his penis, just in case.

- If your baby wears cloth nappies, choose clothes that will accommodate his bulky bottom.

- Do not flush disposable baby wipes or nappies down the toilet. Place nappy and wipes into a plastic bag, tie securely and pop into the rubbish bin.

- You can be fined for placing faecal matter in rubbish collection systems, so before you throw out a nappy, always scrape the bowel motion into the toilet.

Folding cloth nappies

Follow these step-by-step instructions and learn how to do three of the most common nappy folds — the kite, the absorbent and the easy.

Kite fold

This is the most common fold, probably because it's so easy to do. However, it is not as absorbent of some of the other more complicated folds.

1. Place the nappy in front of you. Pull each corner into the middle to produce a kite shape.

2. Fold the top triangle down into the centre.

3. Take the bottom point upwards into the centre. How far you fold it depends on the size of your baby, as it should be aligned with the top of his waist. It's a good fold for small babies. On a small baby each side of this fold may meet in the middle, so only one fastener is needed.

Absorbent fold

This fold suits both boys and girls, and is useful for the larger baby.

1. Fold the nappy in half, taking the top half over the bottom half.

2. Now take the left-hand side across to the right to fold it into quarters.

3. Take the top layer of the bottom right corner and, with your thumb on the remaining three layers to prevent the nappy moving, slide the top layer outwards as far as it will go so it forms a triangle shape.

4. The nappy should now look like a large triangle with a small triangle on top.

5. Turn the nappy over. You now have a square and a triangle shape. Take the left-hand side and fold one-third and then another third so that two-thirds of the square is folded.

6. The nappy should now resemble a triangle with a thick centre pad.

Easy fold

This fold is quick, but loose around the legs.

1. Take the left-hand side of the nappy and fold it in half.

2. Then you can either fold the bottom up one-third for the thickest padding at the front (for a boy), or the bottom down to give the thickest padding at the back (for a girl).

 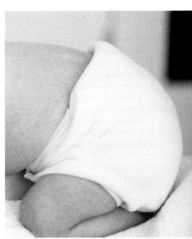

Cleaning cloth nappies

For sterilizing and cleaning nappies you'll need:

- Two sturdy nappy buckets with lids
- Bicarbonate of soda, vinegar or a commercial nappy-sterilizing solution
- Mild and gentle clothes detergent
- Rubber gloves

1 Fill the two nappy buckets with cold water and to each one add 2–3 tablespoons of bicarbonate of soda, vinegar or a commercial sterilizing solution. One bucket is for wet nappies, and the other one is for soiled nappies (although you can get by with one bucket if the soiled nappies are well rinsed). If you are using two buckets, label them clearly to differentiate them. Ensure each bucket holds up to six nappies, has a sturdy handle and a tight-fitting lid. Always wear rubber gloves when cleaning nappies. (*Note:* Nappy buckets pose a drowning risk to mobile babies, toddlers and preschoolers, so always put lids on filled buckets and place them out of the reach of children.)

2 Flush the faecal matter from nappies and cloth liners into the toilet before rinsing them well with cold or warm water.

3 Put the well-rinsed nappies and liners (if fabric) into the appropriate buckets. Secure the lids and soak the items for at least six hours. (It's not advisable to soak pilchers or fitted nappy pants in these solutions. Follow the washing instructions for these.)

4 Rinse the nappies again to remove the sterilizing solution, before placing them in the washing machine, or else program a prewash cycle. Wash the nappies on a 60°C (140°F) cotton or gentle cycle in the washing machine with a mild, fully dissolved detergent. Be careful to measure out the right amount of detergent: too much may irritate your baby's delicate skin, while too little may leave traces of ammonia from baby's urine and bacteria in the nappies, which can cause nappy rash.

5 Hang the nappies on an outdoors clothesline to let the sun bleach out any faint stains. You can use a tumble drier, but it may reduce the nappies' lifespan.

Treating nappy rash

Nappy rash is a skin condition confined to the nappy area and is common in babies. It can affect the genitals, buttocks, groin and thighs, which may look red, spotty and moist. The rash is irritated when the baby passes urine. Usually, it disappears with simple treatment. However, if the nappy rash is severe and prolonged, you should seek medical advice.

What causes nappy rash?

Wetness in the nappy area is the main cause of nappy rash. Urine and faeces contain irritating substances that can cause nappy rash if left in contact with the skin for too long. The longer the nappy is wet, the greater the risk of baby's skin becoming inflamed. If your baby has sensitive skin or your family has a history of psoriasis or seborrhoeic dermatitis, you will need to be vigilant and make regular checks for dampness in the nappy.

Other possible causes of nappy rash may include:

- infection, especially thrush (a yeast-like fungal infection which is bright red and slightly raised, and features spots away from the seriously infected area);
- nappies which, through frequent use, are no longer soft but rough-textured and therefore harsh on your baby's skin;
- detergents and sterilizing solutions that haven't been properly removed from the nappies;
- baby wipes that contain a perfume and remove the natural oil from a baby's skin;
- plastic pants that don't allow baby's skin to breathe and air to circulate around his bottom;

- disposable or cloth nappies that have been left on for too long;
- too much soap, particularly perfumed or medicated, which can dry the skin out;
- talcum powder over the nappy area; and
- very thick ointments, which trap moisture and prevent a baby's skin from breathing.

How to prevent nappy rash

If extra nappy checks help your baby to avoid the discomfort of nappy rash, they're worth it. You can also avoid nappy rash by:

- changing nappies as soon as they become wet or soiled;
- cleaning your baby's bottom with sorbolene diluted with water or warm water with nothing added;
- not using perfumed baby wipes;
- staying clear of plastic pants and using woollen or stretchy synthetic pants;
- using soft cotton liners inside nappies and avoiding disposable liners;
- rinsing cloth nappies thoroughly (see 'Cleaning cloth nappies' on page 71); and
- lightly applying a barrier cream, such as zinc and castor oil or lanolin, to your baby's bottom at every nappy change.

How to treat nappy rash

Despite your vigilance, sometimes your baby will get nappy rash. You should maintain the preventative measures above, and also:

- when changing your baby, wash the affected area gently with cotton wool balls soaked in warm water, then lightly pat dry before applying a cream, such as paw paw ointment. Avoid using too much cream — a thin protective smear is all your baby needs;
- make a nappy-free time for your baby each day so the irritated skin can dry and heal;
- use a soap-free bar at bathtime and don't bath him every day;
- visit your doctor or baby health clinic if the rash is not responding after several days, or if you suspect that it is thrush (which will not respond to nappy rash treatments).

Bathing

For many parents and their babies bathtime is an important part of the daily routine. Most babies love having their bodies immersed in warm water. For these 'water babies' a bath is the blissful end to a busy day.

On the other hand, there are those babies who are startled and respond with a howling scream whenever they are lowered into the water. You can get away with a bath two or three times a week for babies who resist bathtime. However, it is recommended that you 'top' and 'tail' on the other days (see 'Sponge bath for a young baby' on page 78).

The best time to bath your baby is between feeds. If you attempt to bath him after a feed, he may posset (bring up the milk); if you bath him when he is hungry, you'll both end up feeling miserable after he makes it clear he needs food!

Make sure there are no interruptions during bathtime, so before you start, take the phone off the hook, put on some soothing music and hang a 'do not disturb' sign on the front door. The mood should be relaxed and calm, so dedicate as much time as it takes to complete this enjoyable ritual.

Ensure the baby bath is at your waist level, so you don't have to bend and risk hurting your back. If you're using a portable plastic baby bath, place it on a flat, non-slip surface. Check that the room is comfortably warm and also free of draughts.

never

∗ Never take your hands off your baby during a bath or leave him unattended on the change table afterwards, not even for a second.

Bathing your baby

Have everything you need for bathing your baby close by. If you are well organized, bathing your baby should be a fun experience for both of you.

What you'll need

- ❏ Plastic baby bath or spotlessly clean sink
- ❏ One soft, clean, dry towel
- ❏ Two soft face washers (one for the face, the other for the genitals)
- ❏ Sponge (for a younger baby)
- ❏ Mild baby bath lotion or soap
- ❏ Mild baby shampoo (optional for small babies)
- ❏ Sorbolene lotion or nappy rash lotion, if needed
- ❏ Cotton wool pads
- ❏ Cotton buds (only for cleaning around the umbilical cord)
- ❏ Change mat or extra soft towels to lay baby on
- ❏ Plastic apron to keep you dry (optional)
- ❏ Clean nappy, fasteners and pilchers
- ❏ Clean clothes

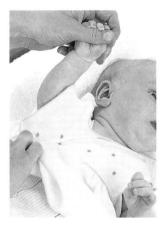

1 If the base of the baby bath isn't non-slip, you could place a small washer on the bottom or a non-slip rubber mat that fits the bath. Launder the washer after every bath, along with the other towels and washers used. And if you're worried about literally losing your grip on baby, avoid using slippery soap products until you're comfortable with the bathing process.

2 Fill the baby bath with warm water to 5 cm (2 in) deep.

3 Before you lower your baby into the water, check that it's comfortably warm. If you're using a thermometer, it should read 30°C (86°F). If a thermometer isn't available, use your elbow or wrist for testing.

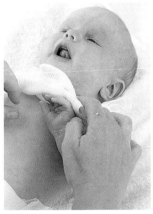

4 To bath your baby, place a towel on your lap and gently undress him completely. If necessary, wrap a towel around him to keep him warm.

5 Before placing a small baby in the bath, clean his eyes and mouth with dampened cotton wool pads (see 'Sponge bath for a young baby' on page 78).

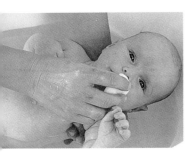

6   Remove the towel and lower your baby into the bath, bottom first, supporting his head and shoulders with one arm and hand, and his bottom with the other hand.

7   Reach around his back and under the opposite arm for a firm grip. The arm around the back supports his head, which has little control in the first month. Chat and sing to your baby as you splash water onto his chest and stomach.

8   Sit him up, with your arm across his chest and your hand under his armpit. Wash his back and the back of his neck, paying close attention to creases.

9   Rinse baby's lower back by turning him around and supporting him across the chest so his face is well above the water.

10   Baby may be a little slippery, so with one hand firmly grasping his arm and the other under his bottom, lift him towards you and out of the bath.

11   To dry your baby, place him in the centre of a clean, soft towel and wrap it around him, but take care not to cover his face. Pat his body dry. Then, unfolding the towel so he is still partially covered, dry first one inner thigh and then the other. Pay attention to the creases around his nappy area, under his arms and around his neck.

Cleaning the umbilical cord

The umbilical cord stump doesn't need any special care, although at bathtime you might like to clean it with a cotton bud and warm water. Afterwards, ensure the area is kept dry and clean to avoid the risk of infection. It is not necessary to wipe the stump with methylated spirits, an old-fashioned and obsolete practice, as it will dry out and fall off without assistance by the time your baby is two months old. Leave the area exposed to fresh air as often as you can to help prevent moisture from damp nappies affecting the stump. If the cord appears red and weepy, seek medical advice.

Washing baby's hair

What you'll need

- ❏ Sponge
- ❏ Warm soft towel
- ❏ Baby shampoo or bath lotion

1 A small baby's head should be washed every few days, using warm water and a sponge. Wrap a young baby in a towel to keep him warm and sit him on your lap. Of course you need to be gentle when washing the fontanelles, but they're fairly tough and can be sponged and then gently patted dry with a towel like the rest of the head.

2 To wash an older baby's hair, hold him tucked under your arm. Support his back with the length of your arm and nurse his head in your hand while moving him towards the baby bath.

3 Use your free hand to gently splash water onto his head. Apply a small amount of baby shampoo and rinse. Some bath lotions double as shampoos so you may not need to add the shampoo directly to his scalp when it's in the water.

Cradle cap

Some babies' skin produces an excess of grease, resulting in yellow, scaly patches. This can irritate the skin, leading to redness, particularly on the scalp. You can soften the scales by massaging olive oil onto the scalp. Leave the oil overnight and the next morning remove the scales using a soft hairbrush.

4 Dry his hair gently with a towel and then brush.

Sponge bath for a young baby

Some parents prefer to ease their baby into a bathing routine by doing a simple 'top and tail' until the umbilical cord falls off and the navel heals. Critical places such as the face, neck creases, hands, feet and bottom require daily attention.

What you'll need

- ❏ A supply of cotton wool pads
- ❏ Lukewarm water for the face, including eyes
- ❏ Slightly warm water with a squirt of baby lotion for the rest of baby's body
- ❏ Cotton buds (only for use on the umbilical cord)
- ❏ Ointment for nappy rash if needed
- ❏ Warm soft towel
- ❏ Clean nappy
- ❏ Comfortable clothing

1   The eyes. Wet a cotton wool pad with some lukewarm water and wipe from the inner to the outer corner of his eye. Repeat for the other eye, using fresh cotton wool pads to prevent infection. If you are unsure about the quality of your local town water supply, you may prefer to boil and cool water until it's lukewarm. Wipe around and behind the ears, but not inside. Don't use soap on his face. Dry his face with a soft towel. Avoid cleaning inside baby's nose or ears as the inner surfaces are lined with mucous membranes that self-clean.

2   Neck, chest and armpits. With new cotton wool pads, wipe around the neck creases to remove any sweat or dirt. Gently lift each arm and wipe in the armpit. Pat dry with a soft towel. Don't use talcum powder and normal bath soap, which tend to dry out sensitive skin.

3   Arms and hands. You will need to extend your baby's arm to get into the creases in the elbows. Use new cotton wool pads to wipe over the hands and to check for dirt under the fingernails. Pat dry with a towel. If your newborn's limbs are curled up against his body, you may need to gently prize them apart.

4   Feet. Wipe the tops and bottoms of the feet and then in between the toes. Pat dry with a towel.

5 **Back.** Place your baby on his tummy with his head to one side and wash the back, including the neck folds. Dry with a towel.

6 **Nappy area.** See 'Cleaning a boy's bottom' or 'Cleaning a girl's bottom' below.

Cleaning a boy's bottom

It's important to clean your baby boy's genitals each time you change his nappy. Baby boys tend to urinate when their genitals are exposed to the air, so be prepared for a spray when you remove your baby's nappy.

1 Check to see if he's dirty, and wipe any excess from his bottom with either the edge of the nappy, disposable wipes or fresh, dampened cotton wool pads.

2 Clean between the leg creases.

3 Wipe his penis clean. If your baby has been circumcised, look out for any signs of infection. If he is not circumcised, never pull back the foreskin, as it is tight and you could easily damage it. Until the skin loosens the area will clean itself, so just attend to the surface creases.

4 Sponge his upper thighs.

5 Clean his bottom by lifting both your baby's legs together with one hand to gently raise his bottom. Using a disposable wipe, clean around the anus.

Cleaning a girl's bottom

When changing a girl's nappy, always wipe from the front to the back to lessen the risk of infection. Use a fresh cotton wool pad for each wipe. Never attempt to clean inside the vulva, as this may spread infection.

1 Remove any excess mess with disposable wipes or fresh, dampened cotton wool pads.

2 Wash the tummy area and navel to remove any urine.

3 Wipe in the leg creases.

4 Clean the vulva. You only need to clean gently around the lips of the vulva.

5 Sponge the bottom. As with a boy, lift baby's legs together with one hand to gently raise the bottom. Remember to wipe from the front down to the anus to avoid the risk of infection.

Baby massage

Baby massage can be an enjoyable and fulfilling experience for both you and your baby. It is also highly recommended for fathers, who can bond with baby through the skin-to-skin contact that mothers often experience when breastfeeding.

Benefits of baby massage

It encourages a deeper connection, as it allows you to communicate your love through the amazing power of touch. And when your baby responds positively, you're bound to feel a sense of satisfaction and contentment as a parent.

For baby

During the massage session your aim is to have your baby feeling comfortable, relaxed, safe and loved. Your baby may also gain from the reported health benefits of this age-old practice. Research suggests that premature babies who receive a regular massage over ten days gain weight 47 per cent faster than those who miss out.[3] This is a result of the nerves from the brain to the gastro-intestinal tract being stimulated, which in turn releases food-absorption hormones such as glucose and insulin. It is also believed that massage:

- helps baby sleep more deeply for longer, and decreases the incidence of apnoea (interrupted breathing);
- increases alertness when baby is awake;
- helps soothe a crying baby;
- improves the immune system;
- helps baby learn to relax and decreases the production of stress hormones;
- aids muscle tone and circulation;
- regulates the respiratory and digestive systems;
- provides relief from the discomfort of wind, colic, teething and congestion;
- teaches baby about communication via your safe touching;
- builds self-esteem and sociability; and
- enhances intellectual development.

For you

If this is your first baby, you may be nervous about handling him, particularly if you haven't had much contact with newborn babies before. By establishing a regular massage routine, you will quickly become confident when handling your baby. And when your baby responds to your gentle rhythmic touch with a beaming smile or satisfied gurgle, you'll fully comprehend what the experts mean when they refer to the significance of bonding with your baby. It is believed that massage:

- helps you become more relaxed;
- makes you more sensitive to your baby's likes and dislikes;
- builds your confidence in your parenting skills and your ability to handle baby; and
- helps develop the parent–child relationship.

Massaging a newborn

Baby massage can start from birth. Even when you lightly stroke your baby's tiny head or cheek you are, in effect, giving him a massage. At this early stage it's best to leave his clothes on during the massage so he doesn't feel exposed and vulnerable. Also, limit the session to five minutes until he becomes more familiar with the routine. Sit on the floor or a chair with your small baby resting on your lap. Start out using butterfly strokes — light fluttery strokes with the tips of the fingers — with both hands in succession over baby's head and face, chest, abdomen, arms, legs and back. As your familiarity with each other grows, expand your repertoire of strokes and increase the time you spend massaging.

Before you start your massage session, make sure you've picked the right time of day for your baby's mood, the room is warm enough and you have everything you need to hand.

Time

Ideally, the best time to give your baby a massage is when he is alert and receptive. If you want to soothe him, try a gentle massage after his bath. It's not recommended that you massage just before or after meals, but about an hour after a feed when your baby is still feeling satisfied. Likewise, avoid massaging your baby if you're feeling at all tense: he will intuitively pick up on your mood and become irritable and uncooperative.

Keep the room warm

If the weather is cool, warm up the room to a comfortable temperature of around 23°C (73.4°F). Then, before you begin, warm up your hands and dim the lights so the atmosphere is calm and soothing. Play some soft, relaxing music if that helps get you both in the mood.

No interruptions

This is your regular, special relaxation time together, so to make sure you can give your baby your full attention, take the phone off the hook to avoid being interrupted. Introduce your young baby to small amounts of massage during the first week with a time limit of five to ten minutes for each session. For older babies extend the session to 20 minutes up to half an hour.

Get comfortable

Before you start, make sure you're both comfortable. You can sit on your haunches (with a pillow tucked between your calf muscles and bottom), with your legs crossed, or with your legs outstretched on either side of your baby. The floor is the safest place, but if this is difficult for you, use an elevated surface. This allows you to stand or sit in a chair while you massage. Whichever position you choose, it is important that you are able to maintain eye contact with your baby at all times: this lets you communicate with him and helps you to interpret his reaction to your touch. The younger baby will probably be happiest lying on his back on a firm surface. If he is a newborn or premature, you may prefer to position him snugly on his back on your lap. In all these situations, make sure your baby is at no risk of falling and that you are feeling totally prepared and at ease.

If your baby is unwell

Avoid massaging your baby if he has a temperature. Check with your doctor before massaging a baby who is unwell.

Different strokes

There are three main types of strokes you can use when massaging your baby.

- Butterfly strokes are most commonly used on newborn babies. Use both hands in succession, making slow, light and rhythmical strokes with the tips of your fingers over your baby's head and face, chest, abdomen, legs, arms and back.

- Effleurage strokes are bigger, firmer strokes you can use when your baby is older and more familiar with massage. Use this stroke on your baby's abdomen, arms, legs and back. Simply stroke with your palms and fingers flat, with one hand always in contact with your baby's skin to maintain a constant rhythm and flow.

- Kneading is a stronger movement than stroking and is done in little circles with thumbs or fingers. It moves the muscles beneath the skin.

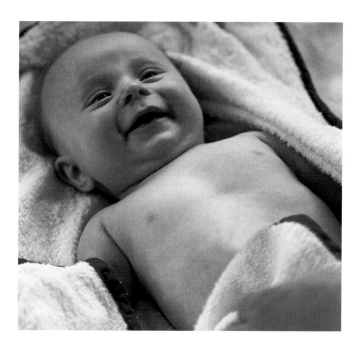

The pressure of the strokes depends on how old your baby is and how familiar he is with massage. When your baby is young, keep the strokes lighter and sprinkle them over his body like a light fall of raindrops. Increase the pressure as he gets older and more familiar with massage sessions. Firm but not too hard strokes are reassuring. Decrease the pressure if his skin appears ruddy or his response is negative. Follow these tips for a massage session that you'll both enjoy.

- When you complete one side of the body, do the same on the other side.
- Keep your stroke light and gentle but not so featherlight that your baby won't feel anything!
- Keep one hand in contact with your baby at all times during the massage.
- Arms, legs, chest, abdomen and back benefit from long, firm effleurage strokes which move outwards from the top of the limbs.
- Hands and feet can handle gentle but firm kneading by your thumbs.
- With an older baby, try gentle circular finger kneading down the back and along the back muscles.

Massaging your baby

This simple step-by-step guide caters for both the younger and the older baby. Many hospitals, baby childcare clinics and privately run organizations offer baby massage classes.

What you'll need

- ❏ Unscented food-based oil (e.g. safflower, canola, olive), warmed in a container of warm water
- ❏ Large soft towel
- ❏ Hand towel
- ❏ Pillow or cushion (optional)

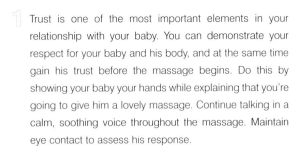

1 Trust is one of the most important elements in your relationship with your baby. You can demonstrate your respect for your baby and his body, and at the same time gain his trust before the massage begins. Do this by showing your baby your hands while explaining that you're going to give him a lovely massage. Continue talking in a calm, soothing voice throughout the massage. Maintain eye contact to assess his response.

2 Pour a small amount of oil onto your palm and rub your hands together. This lets you check the temperature of the oil (if you have warmed it), and you can rub the oil into your palms so your baby gets just the right amount. Start the massage with a 'welcoming' stroke where you lightly brush your fingers from baby's head to his toes. This lets your baby know the massage is about to begin.

3 For the younger baby, massage the chest and abdomen with light 'tinkly' butterfly strokes before gently massaging the tummy in a clockwise direction. For the older baby, massage the chest and abdomen with your palms facing downwards and fingers pointing up the body and close to the shoulders. Using the whole of your left hand, stroke diagonally across the body from baby's right shoulder to the left hip. Then using your right hand, stroke from baby's left shoulder to the right hip. Repeat this sequence twice.

4 Take an arm, and starting at the shoulder, use a 'milking' stroke (as you would gently squeeze a cow's udder) to move from the top of the limb and outwards.

5 Continue moving down the arm until you reach the fingers, which you can gently uncurl, giving each one a little squeeze and rotation. Repeat on the other arm.

6 Go down the leg from thigh to foot using the same 'milking' motion and gently knead the foot, pressing it softly so the toes point downwards like those of a ballet dancer. Repeat on the other leg.

7 To increase the duration of the foot massage, hold your baby's ankle in one hand, with his knee bent and his toes pointing upwards. Place the thumb of your other hand on the sole near the heel. Press lightly, and using a circular motion, take the stroke up the centre of the foot to the base of the big toe and back down again. Do this twice on each foot. Another option is to press in with the thumb all over the base of the foot to stimulate the nerve endings connecting with other parts of the body.

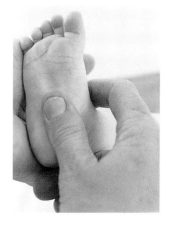

8 Squeeze each toe with your fingertips; then, with your thumb and forefinger, make circles around the ankle.

9 Lay baby on his tummy. For the younger baby, massage his back with broad strokes, moving from the left shoulder to the right hip and then from the right shoulder to the left hip. For the older baby, give his back a massage by pressing your thumbs gently either side of his spine, going up to his shoulders and back down. Finally, give his bottom a soothing circular massage with your thumbs or the heels of your hands.

10 End the session by massaging your baby's head and face. Wipe the excess oil off on a towel, before you start. Form a steeple with your fingers over the top of baby's head. With both hands, simultaneously stroke down his head and over his ears to the jawline.

11 With your hands placed either side of his face, stroke down around the jawline with your fingers until they meet at the chin.

12 Place both your thumbs at the centre of baby's forehead. Simultaneously stroke each thumb in the

opposite direction to the sides of the face. Repeat from the top to the bottom of the forehead.

13. Put your thumbs on either side of baby's head, just above the eyebrows, and make gentle circular strokes on the temples, before gently caressing the eyebrows.

14. Place your thumbs on the cheekbones on either side of the nose and gently rotate your thumbs.

15. Then, with your thumbs, make an outward circle around baby's eyes, going along the eyebrows and back under the eyes.

16. The massage is meant to be a soothing experience. If at any stage your baby appears agitated, stop. Wrap him in a towel and give him a reassuring cuddle. Try again the next day when you are both relaxed. If the response is negative once again, try using different strokes, massage your baby fully clothed or change the environment.

Health and growth check-ups

Many local health services provide support for new parents. This may be in the form of clinics that you can visit in order to have the health and growth of your baby monitored, where you can seek advice from health professionals and meet other parents with children of the same age. Generally these services are free, and you would be wise to take advantage of them.

Some health services also provide a record book, so that both you and health professionals can keep a note of baby's progress as well as immunizations and other health details. Doctors, hospitals and health departments will be able to provide you with details of these health services.

Growth and weight are a matter of concern for most parents and these can be measured during such a checkup. Growth charts are the best means of checking on your baby's progress, but they need to be interpreted carefully.

These charts show the length and weight of babies at a certain age and consist of a series of lines. The lines are known as percentiles. So if a baby's weight is on the 75th percentile, then 75 out of 100 babies would be expected to weigh less. Your baby's weight is dependent on many factors, and there is no ideal place to be on these charts. Babies do not grow or gain weight at the same rate.

You need to know that:

- median birth weights for girls are lower than for boys;
- babies do not gain the same amount of weight every week — it is the overall trend that the health professional will be looking at;
- the weight of a woman's babies usually increases with the number of babies she has, so her third baby is likely to be heavier than her first;
- most growth charts are based on measurements taken mainly from bottle-fed babies. Breastfed babies have been found to be consistently different to the charts. They tend to put on weight sooner, then slow down in weight gain after about three months of age; and

■ babies don't like lying still for long, so if length measurements differ between visits, it could be that baby was wriggling too much for an accurate measurement. Ask to have the measurement taken again.

Immunization

Overwhelmingly, scientific evidence points to the benefits of childhood immunization far outweighing the risks. On a global scale, immunization has led to the eradication of smallpox and many countries are now free from poliomyelitis. The incidence of measles, pertussis, Hib (*Haemophilus influenzae* type b) and other vaccine-preventable diseases has decreased dramatically due to immunization.

Every day you take risks. When you cross the road there is a danger involved and when you have your baby immunized there is a risk involved. However, you may like to consider that there's a far greater chance of being hit by a car than suffering any significant side effects from immunization — that is, the risks of the diseases your child is being immunized against are far greater than the very small risks from immunization.

Child-friendly doctor

It is a good idea to take the time to find a local doctor who relates well to children and with whom you feel you can build up a special patient–doctor bond. It may also be wise to get a recommendation for a good paediatrician because you never know when you will need one.

What is immunization?

When you get an infection, your body reacts by producing substances called antibodies. These antibodies fight the invading virus or bacteria and help you recover. In most instances the antibodies remain in your system to build up your immunity and protect you from contracting the same infection again.

Newborn babies often have immunity to some diseases because they have antibodies from their mothers, but this immunity is only temporary. They are more vulnerable to disease because their immune system cannot easily fight off disease bacteria or viruses. Often, the effects of disease are more serious in infants than in older children. The immune system in young children does not work as well as the immune system in older children and adults because it is still immature. Therefore, more doses of the vaccine are needed.

Immunization is an effective way of keeping children immune from many diseases. Vaccines make the body think it is being infected by a specific disease, and the body reacts by producing antibodies. So if the immunized child is exposed at any time to that disease, he is protected.

What am I protecting my baby against?

Immunization protects young children from various preventable diseases. These diseases are diphtheria, tetanus and pertussis (whooping cough), known collectively as DTP; poliomyelitis (polio); measles, mumps, rubella (MMR); *Haemophilus influenzae* type b (Hib) (which causes meningitis); and hepatitis B (hep B, which can damage the liver).

Diphtheria. Nasal droplets spread diphtheria. The infection causes a sore throat and swollen glands. The toxin from diphtheria can cause nerve paralysis and heart failure. About 1 in 15 of those affected dies.

Hepatitis B. This is a viral infection that causes acute inflammation of the liver. It can be passed from an infected mother to her newborn during childbirth and from one person to another through blood or body fluids, or by intimate contact. About 1 in 4 chronic carriers of hepatitis B develops cirrhosis of the liver (scarring) or liver cancer.

Hib (*Haemophilus influenzae* type b). This is a bacteria spread by mouth as well as by nasal droplets. The infection can cause meningitis and epiglottitis (respiratory obstruction). About 1 in 20 victims dies, while 1 in 4 suffers permanent brain damage.

Measles, mumps, rubella (MMR). The MMR vaccination is given to children at the ages of 12 months and four years, respectively, to provide protection from measles, mumps and rubella.

– Measles is a contagious viral disease that causes fever, rash, runny nose, cough and sore red eyes. It can sometimes lead to complications such as pneumonia (1 in 25 children with measles develops pneumonia). Measles can be caught through the coughs and sneezes of an infected person. About 1 child in 2000 who contracts measles will develop encephalitis (inflammation of the brain; see 'Encephalitis' on page 302). For every 10 children affected by encephalitis, 1 will die and 4 will suffer permanent brain damage. A very rare condition called subacute sclerosing panencephalitis (SSPE) can develop in children several years after a measles infection. SSPE rapidly damages the brain and results in death.

– Mumps causes fever, headache and inflammation of the salivary glands and, in boys, orchitis (inflammation of the testes). Mumps can be caught through the coughs and sneezes of an infected person. Occasionally, it causes encephalitis (brain inflammation) and can also cause permanent deafness and infertility.

– Rubella, although a mild childhood disease, can cause swollen glands, joint pains and a rash on the body that lasts for two to three days. Rubella is most dangerous when a woman contracts it in the first 10 weeks of pregnancy, as it can cause serious abnormalities — including brain damage, blindness, deafness and heart defects — in a newborn baby. Because rubella is highly contagious it is recommended that children be immunized to stop its spread.

Pertussis. Also known as whooping cough, pertussis is caused by contagious bacteria that are spread by coughing and nasal droplets. The infection starts with a runny nose and 'whooping' cough, which may persist for up to three months. Many children develop pneumonia, and the infection can stop a person breathing, particularly in infancy. About 1 in 200 pertussis victims under the age of six months dies from pneumonia or brain damage. In underimmunized populations of the world, 250 000 children die each year from pertussis.

Poliomyelitis. Polio, as it is usually known, is a debilitating disease that had spread to epidemic proportions by the mid-20th century, killing and disabling thousands of babies and children. It is spread by saliva and faeces. Today it appears to have been almost eradicated globally. In Australia, for example, the oral vaccine is given, but in some countries, such as the United States, it is now given as an injection.

Tetanus. This is caused by the toxin of bacteria, which may be present in soil and animal faeces. Those infected by the disease can suffer muscle spasms, convulsions and respiratory failure. About 1 in 10 victims of the disease dies.

It is important to check with your doctor or early childhood nurse for the current version of the immunization schedule in your area.

Possible side effects of vaccinations

Your baby may suffer some soreness, redness, itching and/or swelling or burning at the injection spot for one to two days. Place

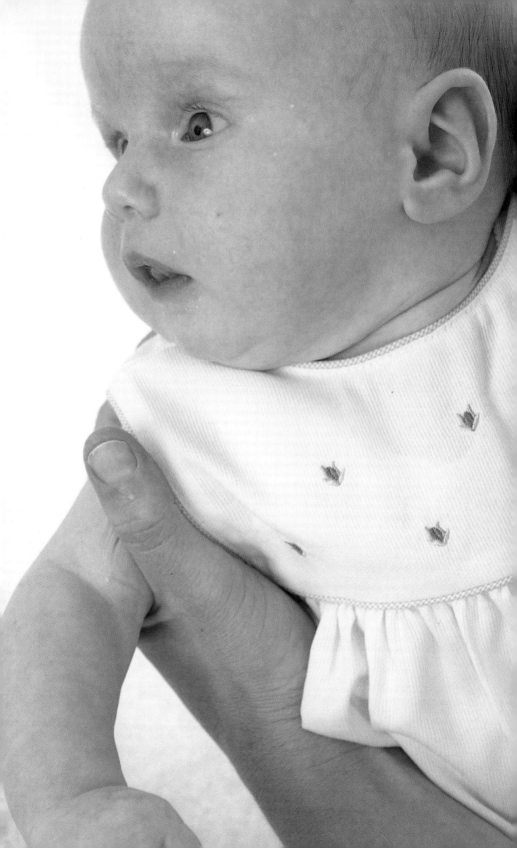

a cold, damp cloth over the affected area to help relieve this. A small hard lump may also persist for some weeks and often longer. This should be no cause for concern, as it will eventually disappear. Do not hesitate to contact your doctor if you are at all concerned about your baby's wellbeing.

The chickenpox vaccination
Chickenpox (varicella) is a highly contagious viral infection. It is usually a mild disease in healthy children. However, it can be more severe in adults, and can cause serious and even fatal illness. The disease can have potentially devastating effects on the foetus of a pregnant woman who contracts the disease: the baby may suffer from skin scarring, severe varicella or congenital malformations.

The average incubation period for chickenpox is 14 to 15 days, followed by the appearance of a spotty, itchy rash. In some countries, such as the US, a vaccine against the chickenpox virus is given to toddlers at 18 months. In the UK, the vaccine is not currently recommended for routine use in children. In Australia, the National Health and Medical Research Council has approved varicella vaccine for children from the age of 12 months. It has been recommended

Possible side effects of vaccinations

	Hib	DTP	Hep B	MMR	Polio
Mild fever on day of immunization	✓	✓	✓		
Unsettled, grizzly behaviour		✓			
Drowsiness		✓			
Soreness, swelling, redness at injection site	✓	✓	✓	✓	
Swelling of facial glands 3 weeks after immunization				✓ (mumps component)	
Head cold, possible runny nose 7–10 days later				✓ (measles component)	
Slight rash, not infectious, 7–10 days later				✓ (measles component)	
Joint pain (less than 1%)					✓
Diarrhoea (less than 1%)					✓
Headache (less than 1%)					✓

that parents who express an interest in the varicella vaccine should be encouraged to have their child vaccinated. Contact your doctor, immunization clinic or baby clinic nurse for more information.

Meningococcal vaccination

Meningococcal disease can affect all ages, with the highest rate being in children under the age of five years and those between the ages of 15 and 24. This rare but serious illness can cause blood infections and bacterial meningitis — an infection of the brain and spinal cord coverings.

It is wise to contact your doctor, immunization clinic or baby clinic nurse for more information and updates on the availability of the meningococcal vaccine.

Treatment of side effects

* Give extra fluids such as breastmilk, or water for the older child. Do not give your child flat lemonade or fruit juice, as this may cause diarrhoea and dehydration.

* Do not overdress your child if he is hot.

* Place a cold, damp washer on the injection site.

* If your child is feeling hot, give him a sponge bath with tepid water.

* If required, give paracetamol every three to four hours to lower baby's temperature. Carefully follow the dosage instructions on the label.

* If the reaction is severe and persists, contact your doctor or local hospital.

Your pre-immunization checklist

Even if your child has a minor illness such as mild fever, cold, mild diarrhoea or is taking antibiotics, vaccinations can be given. The vaccine will still be effective and it will not make your child's illness worse. Receiving all immunizations when they are due is an important way to complete each vaccine series on time and avoid extra visits.

However, before your baby is immunized, tell your doctor or nurse if your child:

- is unwell;
- is suffering from a disease that lowers immunity (such as cancer, HIV/AIDs or leukemia);
- has had an adverse reaction to any specific vaccine or a severe reaction to anything (your doctor should report your child's reaction to the relevant government health authority);
- has had any other immunization in the last month;
- is having treatment that lowers immunity (such as oral steroids like cortisone or prednisone, or radiotherapy or chemotherapy);

- has had an immunoglobulin injection or blood transfusion in the last three months;
- lives with someone who has a disease (such as cancer) or who is having treatment which causes low immunity;
- has a condition of the central nervous system which is still to be determined;
- lives with someone who is not immunized.

If you are pregnant or planning to become pregnant within two months of the immunization, you will also need to discuss immunization options with your doctor.

Vaccination myths

There are many myths circulating about the dangers of vaccination. Here are some important points to consider. If you are still worried about having your child immunized, discuss your fears with your doctor. He or she will be able to reassure you as well as stress the importance of having your child immunized.

Myth: Vaccine-preventable diseases are on the decrease because of better hygiene and sanitation, not because of immunization. Although many infectious diseases have become better controlled as living conditions and hygiene have improved, they still remain serious threats due to occasional outbreaks in vulnerable populations. Dramatic drops in the rates of vaccine-preventable diseases came after the introduction of vaccines. Diseases such as measles and pertussis are highly contagious, regardless of hygiene and living conditions.

Myth: Vaccines weaken the immune system. This is not true. Immunization strengthens the immune system against specific infections. It does not interfere with the body's ability to fight off other infections it is not immunized against.

Myth: It is unwise to give several vaccinations in one day as this overloads the immune system. Scientific data from the United States shows that giving a child several vaccines at the same time has no adverse affect on a normal immune system. Vaccines only affect a small part of the immune system's capacity and do not reduce the body's ability to fight off other infections.

Myth: It is better to let children develop a natural immunity through catching the disease. Vaccine-preventable diseases can be lethal or they can cause permanent disabilities. For example, measles or pertussis may result in permanent brain damage, while polio causes paralysis. Also, some vaccines are more efficient at creating immunity than the natural infection. This is true of tetanus, for example.

Myth: Homeopathic immunizations are an effective means of protecting a child from diseases. Only conventional immunization produces a measurable immune response to diseases. The Faculty of Homeopathy at the Royal London Homeopathy Hospital strongly supports conventional immunization, as long as there are no medical reasons why the immunization should not be given (known as contraindications).

Myth: The measles, mumps, rubella (MMR) vaccination can cause inflammatory bowel disease (IBD) and autism. IBD is a group of chronic inflammatory disorders of the small and large bowel, the most common being ulcerative colitis and Crohn's disease. The cause of IBD is not understood, but a genetic predisposition and an immune mechanism are likely. IBD occasionally occurs in children. Autism is a development disorder that is usually identified around the age of 18 months. Children with autism have difficulty communicating, both verbally and non-verbally, and with socializing and playing with other children. A single cause of autism has not been identified, but research links it to neuro-developmental, genetic and environmental factors. In 1998 the World Health Organisation (WHO) and a group of international experts investigated claims that the measles component of the measles, mumps, rubella (MMR) vaccine is linked to Crohn's disease and autism. They concluded, based on current evidence, that 'there is no link between measles, measles vaccine, and either Crohn's disease or autism'. A conclusive study, recently published, now shows that there is no link between MMR and autism.

Myth: Immunization is associated with sudden infant death syndrome (SIDS). The Australian National Health and Medical Research Council (NHMRC) states that there is no scientific evidence to support this belief, which periodically circulates through the community. The NHMRC says no association with SIDS has been documented. SIDS Australia notes the peak age of SIDS is the same age babies are most often immunized (two to four months), so by chance they can occur around the same time. SIDS Australia also refers to recent studies that found babies who are immunized are at a lower risk of SIDS.

Myth: Children can die from a vaccine. Because most infants are vaccinated during the first year of life, it is likely that a child experiencing medical problems, including those leading to death, will have been immunized. Since vaccination can often occur around the time of these events, parents may pinpoint vaccination as the cause of death. However, there is no evidence at all that vaccines can cause death.

Myth: Some people contract diseases even though they have been vaccinated. Although most vaccines are effective, they do not work in some people. Even when all the doses of a vaccine have been given, not everyone is protected against the disease. Measles, mumps, rubella, tetanus, polio and Hib vaccines protect more than 95 per cent of children who have completed the course. Three doses of whooping cough vaccine protect about 85 per cent of children who have been immunized, and will reduce the severity of the disease in the other 15 per cent of children if they do catch whooping cough. Booster doses are needed because immunity decreases over time. Three doses of hepatitis B vaccine protect 80 to 95 per cent of children.

Sleeping

The first thing you, as a new parent, need to know is that your baby sleeps very differently to the way you do. The description 'sleeping like a baby' is sometimes used about someone who is sleeping peacefully and smiling gently. While newborn babies will sleep like this at times, it is only for a very short time and is not at all how they sleep normally.

What is sleep?

A newborn baby will sleep between 16 and 20 hours in a 24-hour period, but not all at once and often not when the parents would like. Also, your baby's sleep is much more active than the sleep of older children or adults. A baby's face will change expression dozens of times, he will make noises — grunts, snuffles and cooing sounds — and his limbs will move and twitch, sometimes enough to wake him up.

Your baby sleeps in this way because his brain has not matured enough to stop his body being so active. Sleep patterns begin to develop before a baby is born, and this 'active' sleep can be seen at six or seven months' gestation. The other reason that your baby has such active sleep is that he dreams more than an adult; in fact he spends half his sleeping time dreaming. Research suggests that babies dream this much because dreaming helps the brain to develop; it is not simply a replay of the day's events. We continue

to dream throughout our lives — and researchers have yet to determine the value of dreams in old age — but we certainly do not stop, although the amount of time spent on dreaming decreases.

This 'active' sleep is called REM or rapid eye movement sleep. The time spent in more peaceful sleep is known as non-REM sleep. This type of sleep has four stages.

1 Drowsiness. The sleeping person can be easily woken.

2 Light sleep. It is easy to wake someone in this stage.

3 Deeper sleep. It is difficult to wake a person in this stage.

4 All the body's rhythms slow down — very deep sleep.

When humans sleep they drift in and out of these four sleep phases. In babies, non-REM sleep is different: not until a baby is a few months old has he matured enough to fall into the deeper stages of non-REM sleep. All babies mature differently; there is no magic age when your baby will start to sleep more deeply and for longer periods.

Your baby's sleep needs

Your baby is an individual from the day he is born, and therefore each baby has different sleep needs. Although the newborn baby sleeps on average between 16 and 20 hours a day, a few babies will sleep for less and a few for more. One expert has divided this into eight hours during the day and eight and a half at night, broken of course. By four weeks this averages down to six and three-quarter hours during the day and eight and three-quarters at night; by three months the average is five hours during the day and ten hours at night; and by six months it's four hours during the day and ten hours at night.[4]

Most new parents look forward to the night when their baby sleeps through and they too are able to get a 'good night's sleep'. The average time when this happens is three months after the baby's birth. However, once again there will be babies who will 'sleep through' at six weeks and babies who won't sleep through until after the age of six months. And parents also need to know that this first night of 'sleeping through' may not be the beginning of a regular pattern; their baby is just as likely not to sleep through the next night.

Some time between the age of three months and one year, a baby's sleep patterns start to become regular and more like those of his parents. There will be one period in every 24 hours where the baby sleeps for a long stretch of six to eight hours. Even this sleep is likely to be broken and the baby may need comfort from you in order to get back to sleep.

In the first year babies need to sleep during the day, and these naps will generally last from one to two hours.

Babies who do not get enough sleep for one reason or another will not react in the same way as a sleep-deprived adult. They are often jumpy and irritable, and unable to fall asleep because they are overtired. It is essential for baby to get adequate naps during the day, as he will sleep better at night. Inadequate sleep can happen because the baby is being woken to fit in with your schedule, or being kept awake because he is being handled by different people and moved about when he would be better off left quietly to sleep.

Parents' sleep

If you found being pregnant brought the experts out of the woodwork with advice and tales of woe, wait until you ask for advice on getting your baby to sleep. If you are wise you will stop asking because you know that what works for one family may not work for another, and you also know that you need to work out your own strategies based on your baby's temperament and your own attitude.

It is a reality that in their first year new parents can expect to lose between 400 and 750 hours of sleep. Adults average between seven and eight hours sleep a night and most function reasonably well on this amount, but some need more. For most new parents the lost sleep averages two hours a night until their baby is around five months old; after that age it gradually lessens. Also, the sleep parents get is broken and they find they suffer mental as well as physical fatigue. This sleep deprivation has been found to cause some cases of postnatal depression.

By being aware that it is not possible to *force* your baby to sleep, and by aiming to create an environment that *encourages* him to fall asleep and stay asleep, you give yourself the best chance of having better sleep. Many parents desperate to satisfy their own sleep needs have resorted to leaving their babies to cry, and since the early 19th century there have been experts, systems and charts that say this is the only way parents will get their baby to sleep and thus get to sleep themselves. In modern societies sleep problems are growing and sleep clinics are increasing in number too, yet people are not getting more sleep.

Trying to get a baby to sleep by letting him 'cry it out' teaches the baby that he cannot call on his daily carers to look after him; it also desensitizes the carers. Babies are not capable of being manipulative when they cry for attention; it is their only way of communication and when they cry at night it is a call for help. There was a school of thought in the early part of the 20th century that told parents that babies who stopped crying when they were picked up were 'naughty', but this has since been proven to be complete nonsense. There is no evidence to show that 'crying it out', also called 'extinction' or 'controlled crying', is safe or without long-term emotional consequences.

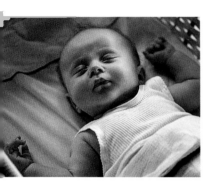

Baby's sleeping place

The baby's nursery is a modern invention and has come about with larger houses, more rooms and fewer children. However, nurseries are not the ideal sleeping place for babies under six months of age. Babies are generally happier sleeping near you, and it can save you a great deal of anguish and broken sleep when your baby is in the same room. This is not fashionable, but it is the natural way for both parents and babies to sleep. Babies sleeping in isolation — that is, alone in a nursery away from you — have been found to be at increased risk of sudden infant death syndrome (SIDS). In most non-Western cultures, babies usually share a bed with their mothers. This has been found to:

- improve the baby's breathing and stabilize the heartbeat;
- lead to fewer episodes of crying;
- help the baby's ability to regulate his body temperature; and
- increase the length and frequency of breastfeeding and consequently the mother's milk production.

The safest place for a newborn baby to sleep is in a cot in your bedroom. Babies over the age of 14 weeks are just as safe, and much happier, sleeping in their parents' bed. This is because of the 'sensory exchanges' that are possible between parents and baby. Baby can hear your presence in the room, and a room with more people in it is warmer and friendlier. You can hear your baby when he whimpers and can comfort him or feed him before his whimpers become cries.

However, many parents find a baby in their bed intrusive. This is particularly so with fathers, and if this is the case in your household, then putting your baby to sleep in a cot in the same room is an ideal alternative. If you are concerned or uncomfortable about having your baby in your bed for any reason, including possibly squashing and suffocating the baby, which has been found to be most unlikely except under certain conditions (see 'When sleeping with baby is risky' below), then a cot is the answer.

'Night-time parenting'

A method advocated by Dr William Sears and his wife Martha in their best-selling book *The Baby Book* and through their practices and courses, 'night-time parenting' is simply about feeding 'on cue' — that is, when baby asks for a feed — and carrying baby about in a sling as much as possible during the day. Feeding 'on demand' is also advocated by breastfeeding advisors. This, the Sears say, gives baby the message that 'there is no need to fuss — day or night'. According to them, baby should sleep wherever he does it best. However, many parents may not be able or willing to adopt this practice.

When sleeping with baby is risky

Many more parents sleep with their baby than is generally acknowledged, and researchers have investigated the benefits and risks. These are some of their findings.

- If a baby is put to sleep on his front rather than his back, his risk of dying from SIDS is increased, no matter where he is sleeping.

- A sofa is the riskiest place for you to sleep with a baby. There is a high risk of the baby suffocating in this situation, often because he is wedged between the back of the sofa and your sleeping body.

- If you smoke, the risk of your baby dying has been found to be increased.

- If either parent has taken drugs or consumed a large amount of alcohol, the risk of the baby's death from suffocation or SIDS is increased.

- If either parent is extremely tired then there is an increased risk that the adult may suffocate the baby.

- If the baby's head is covered or the baby is under a quilt or doona, then the risk is increased.

Sleep and the risk of SIDS

Since the late 1960s, SIDS (sudden infant death syndrome) has been the term used to describe the sudden, unexpected and unexplained death of a baby; before that time it was called 'cot death'. In Western society it is the major cause of death in babies aged between one month and one year, and it is most common between two and four months. The reason for SIDS being the cause of so many fatalities is that other diseases and conditions which affect young babies have been successfully treated and prevented in Western society. SIDS has been recognized since biblical times, yet it continues to confound medical researchers.

Since researchers discovered that babies who were put to sleep on their backs rather than their tummies were at a greatly reduced risk of SIDS, the number of babies dying has reduced considerably.

never

* Never put your baby down to sleep on his stomach.

* Never let your baby sleep with his head covered.

* Never allow your baby in a smoke-filled environment.

Avoiding sleep problems

Babies this age do not have sleep 'problems'; it is the parents who have the problem — they are not getting enough sleep because they are being woken by their baby's needs during the night. If your six-month-old baby falls asleep at roughly the same time every night, on your shoulder or lap, and stays asleep for a long period — eight hours or more — then you do not have a problem.

A parent-friendly sleep routine — that is, less disrupted sleep for parents — is more likely if you follow a few simple routines from the beginning.

The bedtime routine. This is the most important. There is no right or wrong bedtime routine — a baby may sleep better tightly wrapped or loosely covered; he may sleep in your room, in your bed or in another room — it just needs to be consistent. You can start to establish a bedtime routine for your baby from a very early age. It can be a happy family time that you and your child look forward to. It may take up to an hour, but it can be one of the most precious times you spend with your child. It may involve a bath, a massage, a feed, then gentle songs, and finally, a cuddle. You may find that a soft night-light near baby's bed and soft music playing

The unhappy hour

At the end of the day, around 5 to 6 pm, when many workers are finishing up for the day and heading for a relaxing 'happy hour' get-together with friends, babies can be at their most fractious. In their first year babies have growth spurts generally around the ages of six weeks, three months and six months. At these times they are often more grizzly than at others.

If you find your baby is unhappy at the end of the day, there are some strategies you can try.

* Carry your baby with you in a sling.

* Have baby near you at all times by carrying him in a baby seat.

* Plan for this time and finish all your tasks so you can sit down with a drink and your baby — a rocking chair is often the ideal place to sit with a baby.

* Give your baby his bath at this time.

are enough to help baby fall asleep, or he may fall asleep of his own accord. Be sure that, wherever your baby sleeps, it is relatively quiet and dark or very softly lit. It is important that baby goes to bed at the same time every night, give or take 15 minutes.

Wake your child at around the same time every morning. This also helps regular sleeping patterns to develop. Of course you can't expect your baby to sleep for six or eight hours and wake up happy if he needs 12 hours a night, so you need to be aware of how much sleep he needs.

Make sure your baby's sleeping area is a comfortable temperature. An ideal temperature is around 21°C (69.8°F). A room that is too hot is a SIDS risk factor and just as uncomfortable as one that is too cold.

Keep loud noises down. If the television is on, make sure it is a low hum in the background; if there is music playing, make it soft and sleepy and not loud and exciting; if there are older children or other people in the house, make sure their noise cannot be heard by your baby.

Experiment with soft noises. You can buy recordings of womb sounds and mother's heartbeats and see if they help your baby to sleep. There are also beautiful recordings of lullabies. Alternatively, try a ticking clock, the filter in a fish tank or the sound of a little indoor fountain.

Try some soothing techniques. Try different soothing methods to find out what works for both baby and you. Rocking, stroking, patting, singing, and giving a dummy are strategies which work for many babies. Taking baby for a stroll in the pram or a drive in the car also works for some parents, although beware of the pitfalls of establishing these habits.

Adjust your bedtime. Be prepared to change your own bedtime to suit baby's. In the early months it may suit you to go to bed when baby first falls asleep, even if it is around 7 or 8 pm. If baby usually sleeps for four or five hours at this time, you too will enjoy a good block of sleep. If you are working, you may need to do this to keep up your energy levels. A parent who is at home with baby may choose to nap in the middle of the day instead.

Relatives or friends. Family members who offer to take baby for the night so you can get a good night's sleep are worth their weight in gold. A baby who is breastfed can be fed expressed milk, and both parents can catch up on their own sleep 'debt'.

What wakes a baby

Your baby is not able to wake himself up; however, other things may. Sometimes it will be something you can't do anything about, such as his own limbs twitching or waving; at other times you may be able to change the situation.

Wet or dirty nappy. Having a wet or soiled nappy bothers some babies and not others. If a wet nappy doesn't bother your baby but changing it will make him wake up screaming, then it is better not to change the nappy. Be sure to use a good layer of nappy rash cream at the last night-time change. If baby's nappy is soiled, however, you will need to change it.

Hunger. A young baby cannot hold enough food in his stomach to last six or eight hours; he needs to be fed when he is hungry for the first few months. Feeding in bed makes this easier, and breastfeeding makes it even simpler.

Baby with a cold. When baby's nose is blocked, he will wake up. You may find a couple of saline drops, or mother's breastmilk, in his

nostrils will clear his nose; however, if this does not work, you will need to consult a doctor. Over-the-counter preparations are not suitable for babies.

Teething. Some babies are more upset by the arrival of teeth than others. If baby is showing signs of teeth (see 'Teething' on page 172), even if they have not yet appeared, then you may need to give him some paracetamol, but check with your doctor first.

Uncomfortable clothing. Your baby's skin is very soft and sensitive, and some synthetic materials are not comfortable. The design of some clothing is also restrictive. If you think this could be the problem, try cotton clothes.

Sudden loud noises. A door banging, a dog barking nearby, a burglar alarm or a doorbell may each be loud enough to wake a sleeping baby. Ordinary everyday noises will usually have no impact at all, as baby used to hear these sounds when he was in the womb.

Development

Your young baby will benefit in every way — physically, emotionally and intellectually — from exercise and play. And there is no doubt that incorporating daily routines into his life at an early age will prepare him for an active and social life as he develops.

Exercise and play

Forget about enrolling in baby gym classes. The activities described below are incredibly simple, and easy for you to do with him every day as you interact with him through the routines of feeding, bathing and nappy changing. Most of the time you will unconsciously encourage him to exercise — even a nappy change or a bath can present a wonderful opportunity to get those tiny muscles moving. You'll also find yourself incorporating playtime into exercise time and vice versa, so the experience will become enjoyable and stimulating for your baby. For all their simplicity, these activities will encourage your baby to think, move, communicate, socialize and imitate.

From day one your baby is stretching his body, arching his back, moving his arms and legs, and attempting to turn and lift his head for a better view of the world. When you cradle him in an upright position with his head against your shoulder you'll be amazed at the amount of energy he invests in attempting to lift his head. In the early days he will tire after a bath and a feed, so it is detrimental to everybody to try anything too ambitious. It's the same with play, as he is still coming to terms with his new environment. Your face-to-face interaction and gentle voice are enough to keep him amused until he is more aware of his surroundings, and you become attuned to his likes and dislikes.

Exercise fun

Exercise makes babies more flexible and coordinated, and increases muscle strength and tone. It also encourages body awareness. It is advisable to supervise all exercise sessions with your baby. Remember that all babies are different and respond differently to ways of being handled. Talk or sing to your baby throughout your 'exercise' sessions.

Tummy time

From the age of six weeks, when a baby can hold his head up, it is recommended that he spend a reasonable amount of supervised tummy time during the day when he's awake. It's the perfect way for your baby to gain upper body strength — resting on his stomach and propping himself up with his arms helps develop the arm and neck strength needed for crawling. It also discourages a condition known as positional plagiocephaly, also referred to as flat head syndrome. This syndrome has become more common since it has been recommended that babies be placed on their backs to sleep to reduce the risk of SIDS. (If a baby spends most of his time on his back or with his head in one position, the weight of his head can temporarily flatten his skull, which is soft and malleable.)

Some babies cope better than others with the tummy position. Make sure you are always with your baby when you place him on his tummy, and when he begins to get agitated, gently roll him over. Keep track of the amount of time he spends on his tummy, and slowly increase it so that by three months he is spending more than a few minutes each session. If he resists tummy time, encourage him with interesting toys and objects. A play mat with a plastic mirror or toys attached will help keep your baby occupied. As he gets older and stronger, place a favourite toy just out of his reach so he will make an effort to get to it.

Kicking and stretching

Set aside some time for exercise and bottom airing during a nappy change. Ensure your baby is lying on a soft towel in a warm safe place — for example, on the floor. Remove your baby's nappy, clean his bottom and then give him the opportunity to kick and stretch. Let him exercise his leg muscles until he has had enough. Kicks without a nappy also allow his bottom to dry naturally and help prevent nappy rash.

Gripping exercises

Gripping exercises encourage development of fine motor skills. They also help to strengthen a baby's hands and upper body. When

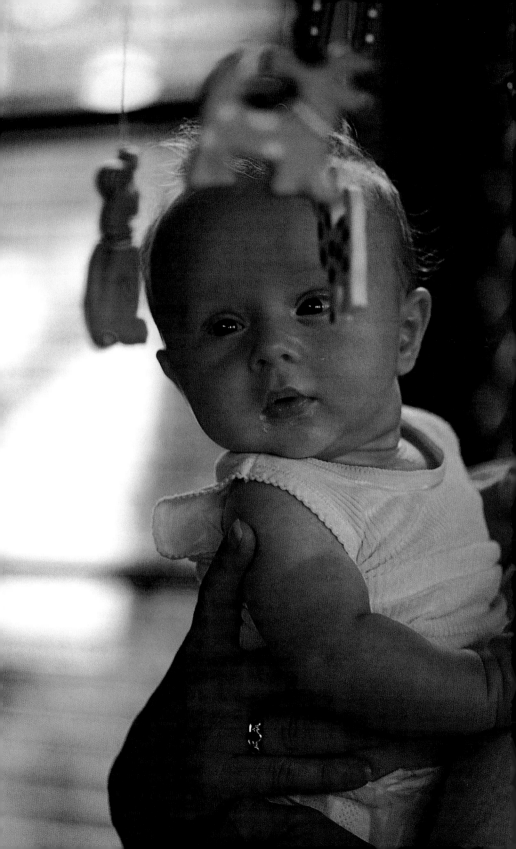

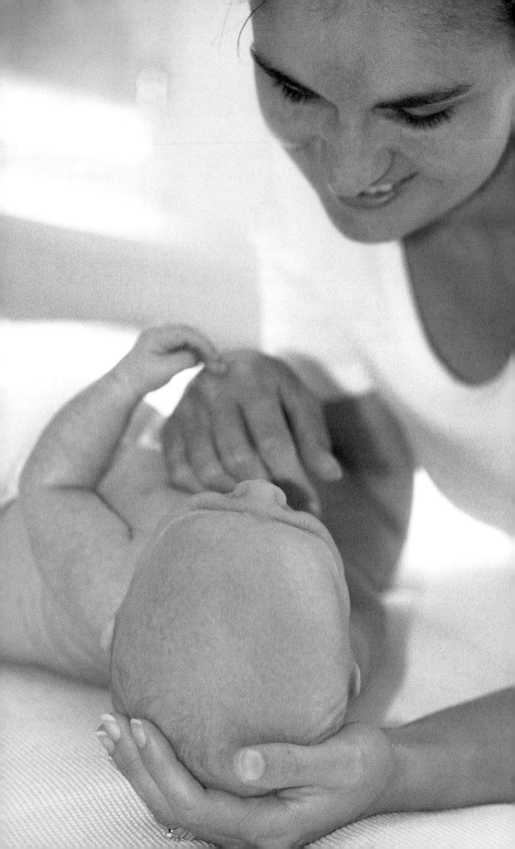

your baby has tummy time, place some easy-to-grab toys close by to give him the chance to practise reaching and grabbing. Change the toys often so your baby doesn't become bored.

Sit-ups

When your baby has some head control, at around three months, let him practise baby sit-ups. While he is lying in your lap or on the floor between your legs, hold onto both his hands and gently pull him into a sitting position. Then lower him gently to his back. Do this several times if your baby enjoys it. By the time he is five months old, you should be able to pull your baby up to the standing position. This is great for the abdominal and leg muscles.

Push-me-pull-me

While your baby is on his back, gently raise his arms above his head and then lower them. After several repetitions, move to the legs and, one at a time, gently bend his knees.

Roll-me-over

Between three and eight months your baby will learn to roll over from back to front and back again. Rolling helps a baby's perception, and he'll be able to see those things he missed out on while on his back. You can help him by gently rolling him onto his tummy and then returning him onto his back.

Play fun

Babies love to play, and you can initiate simple, fun games in the early months to encourage him to interact as a happy social being. Again, these games are simple and usually require few 'props'. Do not throw your baby into the air or pull him up by one arm as these activities could cause harm.

- A newborn baby will focus on your face at a distance of about 20–30 cm (8–12 in), so hold him there while you chat or sing to him.

- From around three months, he will be able to focus on objects further away, so you are no longer restricted to face-to-face games. He is now ready to enjoy mimicking games. Try poking your tongue out at him, and watch as he attempts to do the same. It's also fun copying your baby's 'goo-ing' and 'gaa-ing' and then hearing his response.

- The older baby might love to play with noisy items that can be hit or pushed.

- Mobiles are popular for many reasons. They give your baby something to look at, especially if they are brightly coloured, and feature a variety of shapes. For the younger baby, a mobile with a contrasting black, white and red pattern helps him to distinguish between colours.

■ Gently jiggle your baby on your knee, while singing simple songs or reciting nursery rhymes.

■ 'Peek-a-boo' is as popular as ever, and even though you may become bored with the repetitive nature of this game, your baby will love seeing you cover your face again and again and again once he makes the connection that you're only hiding behind your hands.

■ It's very important to encourage healthy physical contact between you and your baby. Lots of cuddles and gentle stroking reinforce the fact that he is safe and loved. Blowing raspberries at your baby is also a lovely way to make physical contact in a playful context. Blow them on his tummy or in the nape of his neck and enjoy his delighted response. At around three months, try tickling his toes.

■ Also around three months, or once your baby can be seated comfortably in an inclined position in the stroller, take him on lots of walks to view the wider world.

■ Your baby will be mesmerized by his reflection from around four months. Prop him up with pillows in front of a full-length mirror, so he can wonder who that other baby is!

■ Because your baby will place most items in his mouth, an effective method of exploring objects, from the age of four to six months keep a supply of clean, safe teething toys such as large plastic keys on a plastic ring and squeezy plastic blocks.

■ Give your older baby everyday objects — such as spoons, plastic plates and cups — to play with so he becomes familiar with them.

■ Try games which progress like a short story with a beginning, middle and climax. These include 'This Little Piggy' and 'Round and Round the Garden'. For a happy response, walk your fingers up your baby's tummy and tickle him under the chin.

■ Babies love colourful board books, especially if they are very tactile.

■ Read to your baby to lay the foundations of literacy early.

■ Talk to your baby and be amazed at his delighted reaction as he attempts to 'talk' back.

Crying and comforting

Crying is a perfectly normal part of your baby's development; a baby who cries a lot is not a 'bad' baby. The key to success, and your own peace of mind, is to remain patient and calm as you attend to his needs. You should also be careful not to judge yourself too harshly through what may be trying times. Your baby's crying is not something upon which you should measure your success as a parent. Your baby's crying is literally a cry for help and has nothing to do with your parenting skills.

What is your child trying to say?

There are no neat solutions on how to comfort a crying baby, if only because there are so many 'maybes' to consider. Maybe he's tired? Maybe his nappy's wet? Maybe he has a tummy ache? Maybe he just needs to be cuddled? The list goes on. After a while you will most probably be able to differentiate your baby's cries, although at first you will be relying on trial and error.

Crying times

As he recovers from the birth and gets used to his strange world away from the warmth of the womb, your baby's crying will increase in frequency. By six weeks, it's reasonable to expect him to cry for around 30 per cent of his waking hours, which is about 2.75 hours a day. For most babies the crying eases off from 12 weeks, although some continue longer. It could be that you are 'blessed' with a baby who just likes a good cry; around 20 per cent of babies fuss and cry for more than three hours a day on at least three days a week.

It is common for babies to cry in the late afternoon and into the night, typically from 5 pm to 9 pm. This can be stressful for parents who are exhausted from meeting the challenges presented by the arrival of their new baby. There are a number of theories as to why babies cry at this time of day. The most common explanation is a drop in mother's milk supply, which fails to meet the demands of a hungry baby. The hungry baby also tends to gulp air in his haste to feed, which results in wind. And after a long day, a baby is often tired and overstimulated. As a parent, you'll cope better by accepting these regular crying episodes. A baby tends to tune into an anxious parent and responds

in a similar fashion, so take the relaxed approach — it's more likely to have a calming effect on your baby. Also, when you hear your baby's cry (after a minute or so you should know whether it's a false alarm and whether he'll settle by himself), go to him straight away. Next, look for signs that he is becoming distressed, such as squirming and arching his back, yawning or turning away, frowning or grimacing. By attending to him immediately you could well nip the problem in the bud.

Comfort checklist

These are some of the more obvious triggers which might cause a baby to cry.

* Wet or soiled nappy

* Discomfort (tight clothes; too hot or too cold)

* Tiredness

* Hunger

* Wind

* Colic or reflux

* Illness or pain (e.g. earache, tummy ache, diarrhoea, nappy rash)

* Fear (caused by a loud noise, bright lights)

* Boredom or loneliness

* Anxiety (a reaction to an anxious parent)

Avoiding problems

After a while you will discover your baby's likes and dislikes. It could be that he hates being naked, and whenever you undress him, he becomes distressed and inconsolable. Or that he cannot tolerate bathtime or being swaddled. It is wiser to desist rather than persist with these activities. You can alleviate your baby's distress while changing his clothes or a nappy by partially covering him with a soft blanket so he doesn't feel as vulnerable. Similarly, rather than give him a full bath, wash him in stages (see 'Sponge bath for a young baby' on page 78).

Crying and colic

A baby with colic, a gastrointestinal disturbance, displays several characteristics. His cry is more high-pitched than usual, and he tends to draw up his legs and become red in the face. Colic tends to strike in the late afternoon or evening. Its cause is not known, but it is not advisable to use medicines without consulting your doctor. The following soothing techniques may help calm a baby with colic (see also 'Colic' on page 59).

Soothing techniques

If you've run through the 'Comfort checklist' opposite, but still can't find a reason for your baby's crying, try one or several of the following techniques to soothe your baby (see also 'Avoiding sleep problems' on page 102). Remember, too, that less is best. It's advisable to spend at least ten minutes on a technique, as changing quickly from one to another may cause your baby to become more distraught. For example, hold your baby firmly in a comfortable position — with his head over your shoulder — and allow him to cry. Don't put a time limit on him: it could take a while for him to calm down. You could also try this approach while lying next to your baby. Other strategies include:

Holding, cuddling and carrying

Human beings naturally crave physical contact. When you pick up your baby and hold him close to you, you are making him feel secure and loved. You are not spoiling him. When he is cradled safely in your arms he can feel your warmth, smell your familiar scent, hear your breathing, heartbeat and soothing voice, and make out your features. It often helps to take the baby into a quiet, dimly lit room, away from any stimulation. Your baby might

also prefer skin-to-skin contact. Make sure you are in a comfortably warm room before you remove his clothes, except for his nappy, and lay him against your skin (or have his father do it so baby is cradled against his bare chest). This is all many babies need to curb the crying. If your baby is hard to settle, you might find it easier to carry him around in a baby pouch, so your arms are left free. If having your baby with you for long periods isn't a problem, this could be an easy solution to calming a clingy baby.

Rocking

Repetitive rhythmic movements are soothing to many babies. If your baby is having trouble going to sleep, gently rock him in your arms in a horizontal position. If he is wide-awake and fretful, he might react more positively to being held in a vertical position where he can look around. Never rock a baby vigorously as this could be dangerous and have the same harmful effects as shaking a baby.

Change of scene

Go for a drive or take your baby for a walk in the fresh air. The comforting vibration from a moving vehicle is often enough to relax a baby to sleep. And getting out of the house and going for a drive through quiet streets could also benefit a stressed parent.

Massage

See 'Baby massage' on page 80.

Comfort sucking

If your baby's fingers or fists are always finding their way into his mouth, that's great, as he is providing his own comfort. If you think he needs to suck but can't find his fingers, try giving him a sterilized dummy. At this young age, there is nothing wrong with a dummy, although it is recommended a baby be weaned off it after six months when the urgent need to suck abates. Do not dip the dummy into honey or anything sweet as this could cause tooth decay.

Soothing sounds

Just as rhythmic, repetitive movements comfort babies, so do sounds with the same pattern. It's possible to buy CDs and electrical products that simulate a range of soothing sounds, such as a gentle flowing stream, waves breaking on the shore, birds in a rainforest and a human heartbeat. Likewise, the sound of your voice singing a lullaby, a slow lilting piece of recorded music, or the sound of a domestic appliance — for example, a tumble drier — could have a calming effect on a crying baby.

Routines

A regular routine may do more to provide your baby with feelings of stability and security than any of these techniques. Establish it at home in a familiar environment. A repetitive daily pattern which includes sleeping, feeding, bathing and nappy changing is comforting to a baby and helps him to anticipate what will happen next. It also offers security to the sensitive baby who is distressed in unfamiliar surroundings.

Feeds

Offer your baby the breast. Even if he was only fed half an hour before, it could be that your baby is still hungry and requires a top-up feed. Make sure that you are relaxed about feeding your baby at such short intervals, then find a comfortable place where you can feed him without being distracted.

Swaddling

Your baby has just spent nine months cocooned in a warm and watery world. And then he is thrust into an environment with virtually no physical boundaries, so he feels vulnerable and exposed. You can help him feel more secure by swaddling him — that is, wrapping him firmly but not too tightly in a light cotton or muslin wrap. Avoid a blanket as it's too heavy.

Swaddling your baby

What you'll need

❏ Cotton or muslin wrap

1. Fold a cotton or muslin wrap into a wide triangle.

2. Gently lower your baby onto the wrap, so his neck is level with the top edge (do not wrap the sheet around the baby's head).

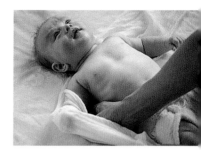

3. Hold one of baby's hands up and under his chin and bring the wrap across the same arm and across his body.

4. Tuck the corner of the sheet under the baby.

5. Repeat this process on the other side, ensuring your baby has enough freedom to move his hands away from his mouth. Don't persist with swaddling if it causes your baby to become more distressed.

never

Never shake your baby.

A baby's head is much larger in proportion to his body. If an angry or frustrated adult shakes a baby, it can result in brain damage, even death. When the baby is shaken the skull can stretch and the brain moves about, causing blood vessels between the brain and skull to shear off, bleed, swell and eventually atrophy.

An adult may become upset and frustrated because the baby is not able to communicate what is wrong, and he or she is unable to soothe or comfort the baby.

If at any time you feel so frustrated that you are tempted to shake your baby, leave the room. If there is no other adult around, make sure your baby is safely in his cot and go as far away as you can so you are no longer able to hear his cries. It is far better to let a baby cry hysterically than to shake him. There are lots of positive ways to comfort your crying baby (see 'Soothing techniques' on page 114).

When nothing works

Don't try to be a super parent. If you've attempted everything and you're at your wit's end, it could be time to ask for extra help.

- If it's possible, ask your partner to rearrange his or her working hours, so he or she is around when your baby's crying is at its peak.

- Grandparents or siblings may also be willing to drop everything to help out in a time of need. Don't be afraid to ask.

- If you don't have access to extended family or friends, take some time out. To do this, ensure your baby is safe in his cot. Leave the room, close the door and spend five to ten minutes by yourself: make a cup of coffee or tea, have a refreshing shower or call a supportive friend. Then return to your baby's room in a positive frame of mind. If he is still crying, take ten 'mindful' breaths before entering. Continue to remind yourself that the crying phase eventually passes, and that if you can get through this, you can make it through anything!

- Find a parent support group through your community health centre. It's always a huge relief to find there are other parents out there going through a similar experience.

- Post a positive affirmation sign on the fridge, reminding you that the crying won't last forever, even though it will feel like it at the time.

- Beware of well intentioned advice. Most of it will probably be conflicting and confusing. Don't feel intimidated; try what seems right for you and your baby.

- If you are feeling desperate, you must seek professional help. There are many organizations dedicated to helping parents who are experiencing the same frustrations as you. You can call one of the 24-hour telephone counselling services that are listed in the phone book (see the 'Resources' list on page 349).

- If you suspect your baby's problem is a physical one, such as colic or reflux, obtain a referral to a paediatrician from your doctor or child health nurse.

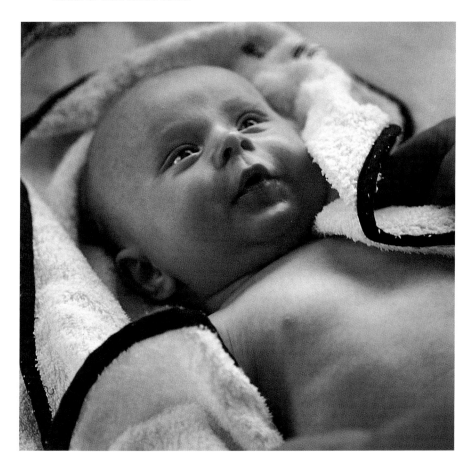

Multiple births

Child psychologist Penelope Leach makes the point that parents of twins and triplets need to remember to emphasize the differences, not the similarities, between their children. Treating each child as an individual is important to their development: 'being fair does not mean treating the children exactly alike but taking equal trouble to meet the needs of each,' she advises.[5]

Birth to six months

Twins and triplets are usually smaller than single babies and weigh less, and many are premature. Babies who are born before 37 weeks' gestation are described as premature or pre-term. Multiples are usually born early because conditions in the uterus become so crowded that labour begins before time.

Many mothers successfully breastfeed their twins and triplets. For these babies breastmilk is even more important in helping them to reach their optimum growth and development. However, breastfeeding multiples can be quite exhausting, and these mothers need extra support and care themselves.

An action plan for parents of twins or triplets

- Be prepared. This is important when expecting one child, but for parents expecting more than one baby it is doubly important. Once you know you are expecting twins or triplets, plan your needs and begin to buy and locate goods and services you will need around the sixth month of the pregnancy. Remember, multiples nearly always come early. There are prams and strollers designed for two babies. If you can't afford one of these, consider hiring one from one of the organizations that support parents of multiples. Also, plan with your partner how you will cope in the early days. Decide on tasks such as shopping, washing, cooking and basic household chores. Discuss night feeding and whether you are both happy to have the babies sleep in your room, an arrangement which will make night-time feeding much easier and more comfortable for you both.

- Seek out the best help in the beginning. These days most parents-to-be of multiples are forewarned, as ultrasound and diagnostic testing is mostly very reliable. So once you have become accustomed to the idea of the birth of babies, rather than one baby, you need to look for expert advice you can trust. Attending meetings of multiple birth and breastfeeding support groups and talking to other parents of multiples is often the easiest way.

■ Have a breastfeeding consultant or advisor on hand at the birth. Someone who is experienced with helping mothers of multiples learn to breastfeed will make the whole process of teaching these new babies how to feed much easier.

■ As the mother is learning, it is better to feed the babies one at a time. After a few weeks tandem feeding, as it is known, will usually come naturally as the mother becomes more comfortable with holding two babies at once. If the babies are being fed by breast and bottle, then one baby can be fed by someone else while the mother breastfeeds the other child. If both babies are bottle-fed, it is important that both babies are cuddled as they are fed, just as they would be if they were breastfed.

■ In the beginning put both babies in the same bed. Twins usually settle better and more quickly if they are close to each other, side by side, as they have been in the womb.

■ Ask for family support. Dad is the ideal support person, and his support is even more crucial when more than one baby is born. But if the father is not around, then the help of another caring relative will make the mother's role so much less stressful.

■ Learn to delegate. Many mothers want to do everything for their babies and often do not believe others, even the baby's father, can

do it as well. This is a recipe for exhaustion, especially with more than one baby. Look for shortcuts and ask others to help out either with household duties or with baby care.

■ Learn shortcuts to quick nutritious meals. If you have another adult in the house, expect him or her to cook the evening meals, at least on alternate nights.

■ Remember that babies don't need a tidy house and an immaculate mother. They need love and care and a mother who has some energy to play with them. Prioritize household tasks and don't do anything non-essential in the first months. If you can, keep one room tidy for guests and always have a packet of biscuits and a quick snack (such as chips and dip) on hand for unexpected guests.

■ If you can afford household help, get it. Cleaning once a week/ fortnight/month, ironing services, Internet shopping, a nappy washing service — all these make new parents' lives easier and more enjoyable.

■ Learn to carry your babies. If you have two babies, have two slings. If both parents each wear a baby in a sling when they need a break, everyone will benefit, particularly if you take a walk together.

■ If your babies are identical, dress them differently, so not only you but also the family can tell them apart. If you really want to dress them identically, then make one thing, such as a hair bow or the colour of their bootees or socks, different so that you are sure to call each of them by their correct name.

■ Check with your social security department to find out whether you are entitled to extra benefits for more than one baby. Some governments provide assistance for triplets and quadruplets but not for twins.

Development

Remember that because your babies were born prematurely they will develop more slowly than babies born at the same time, but full-term.

For each milestone add up to three months onto the dates given for full-term babies, as it has been found that twins develop more slowly than singletons. However, if you are ever in doubt about your children's development, be sure to seek expert help.

Out and about with your baby

It can often seem easier to stay home with baby than plan an outing, particularly in the early days. However, parents who leave home every day with their baby find they are less likely to suffer from depression and feelings of inadequacy, both of which are quite common in the early days of parenting.

Baby's bag

As with everything associated with parenting, the key is preparation. From the moment you come home with your baby, have a bag always ready with baby's needs. Keep this bag ready to go, and every time you return from an outing, restock.

You can buy nappy bags, as they are generally known, in many colours and designs. Some have built-in change mats and extra waterproof bags for keeping soiled clothing and nappies. Some have compartments to hold bottles and formula, your mobile phone and other baby needs. You will need most of these things.

Here is a basic checklist for the average baby.

Nappies. Two or three cloth or disposable nappies. If they are cloth, you will need spare pilchers and possibly a spare fastener.

A bag for soiled nappies.

A small container of nappy cream or lotion.

Baby wipes.

A change of clothing. This should include two singlets if it is cold outside. In winter, include an extra layer of clothing.

Small toy or toys. Babies love rattles and bright things; a toddler will enjoy a set of plastic keys and a toy mobile telephone just like his mother's. A book is also a bonus. Be sure to change these things over or keep them specially for the baby bag.

Hat. A sun hat in summer, a warm beanie in winter.

Feeding needs. If baby is breastfed all you will need is an extra cloth nappy or small hand towel; if baby is bottle-fed you will need a bottle, a separate container of formula and another container of boiled water. Because of the risk of contamination, you should never premix formula for an outing with your baby.

Bib and spoon, solid food. Once baby is eating family food you will need these.

Outings

If you are just going to the park or for a walk in your local area, you do not need to take much, but if you are going further afield, it is a good idea to plan a little more. Take the following factors into account and make your trip a happy one.

- If you're travelling by public transport, consider a backpack so your hands are free for the stroller, or take baby in a baby backpack with a minimum of extras. (Some baby backpacks have a lot of storage but you don't want to load yourself down.) Also, check the timetable and make sure you don't have a long wait for the next bus/train/tram/ferry. Be sure you know the timing of the return trips for the same reason.

- Depending on how long you will be out, take enough baby milk and other snacks if you are not breastfeeding. Be sure to take a bottle of water for yourself.

- Don't forget to allow for the weather — check the forecast.

- If you are travelling by car, include a tape or CD of soothing music for baby and try to travel at baby's sleeping time.

Once you have taken baby out a few times you will learn what works best for you and you can modify these suggestions to suit.

You, sex and your new baby

You need to care for yourself when you are a new mother. This may seem like a tall order when you are tired, emotionally drained and overwhelmed by the responsibility of a small baby, but if you ignore your needs you will be more prone to depression and frustration.

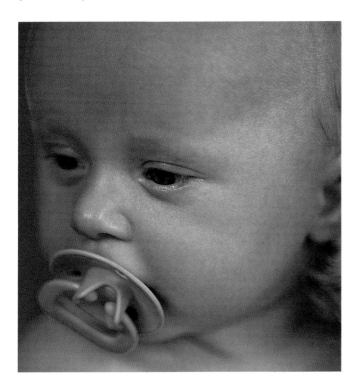

Taking care of you

Ideally you need to be mothered by your own mother, sister, relative or friend. You need someone to make sure you have time to spend with your new baby and that you don't waste precious energy cleaning the house, shopping or doing tasks which someone else can do for you.

If you do not have someone to help out, then minimize your household chores.

■ Keep one room tidy and do the bare minimum in the rest of the house.

- If you can afford it, use disposable nappies or pay for a nappy service.
- Eat sensibly, but eat easy-to-prepare foods and takeaways. Each day make sure you eat seven servings of fruit and vegetables and drink eight glasses of water.
- Take your baby for a walk every day, from the day you get home. Put baby in a pram, and if you feel nervous, just go round the block for the first few days. Gradually extend your outings — it is one of the best sanity preservers — and you will be getting some exercise.
- Take up all offers of help. Try to gently persuade the helper to meet your needs. If you would prefer to look after your baby rather than go shopping, say so. If you would like to go to the hairdresser or the gym and leave the baby with the carer, say so.
- Join a group of mothers with babies the same age. Knowing you are not alone at this time is a great support.

Sex

It is quite normal to experience a variety of feelings about sex after your baby is born. You may feel that you can hardly wait to get your partner into bed; on the other hand, you may think that you will never want to make love again. Your partner may feel that you have been through such an enormous physical trial that he is scared to touch you, or he may be ready for sex at any moment, or either of you could be anywhere in between.

You need to talk about your sexual feelings together, and while the man needs to take account of the woman's physical and emotional fragility in the early days and weeks, he too will need to consider his needs at some stage.

If you are breastfeeding you may not be interested in foreplay, or it may excite you.

A birth which results in trauma or damage to the perineal area can take some weeks to heal and will make sexual intercourse difficult for many and impossible for others.

It may be that masturbation is the answer for you. Talking about your sexual needs and taking account of the stresses and strains of new parenthood, as well as those of the labour and birth, will help you both to re-establish your sex life, in your own time.

Postnatal depression

Between 7 and 15 per cent of women
will suffer from postnatal depression
(PND) after the birth of their baby.
Postnatal depression is not inevitable;
in fact you are far more likely to enjoy
motherhood and your baby than you
are to be depressed because of it.

'Baby blues', the name given to the
hormonal low that many women experience two or three days after
the birth, is not depression. There is no real definition of the
condition. You may experience all the symptoms of major
depression but you may also be suffering from post-traumatic stress
disorder, particularly if the delivery of your baby has been difficult.

It is acknowledged that there is some biological foundation for
the 'blues'. There are also the many necessary adjustments you have
to make in early motherhood, and for some women, there are
additional pressures such as financial or relationship problems.

The key to deciding whether you are in need of help is whether
you are enjoying your baby. If you are not enjoying him, then your
depression is serious. Women suffering from PND feel as if they are
not coping; they also feel guilty that their mothering is not good
enough, although often it is excellent. They are anxious,
particularly about their baby's health, and some suffer sleep
disturbances that are not caused by their baby.

Statistically, women most at risk of PND are likely to be single,
lacking social support or having a baby they did not want.

Support

If you feel you may be suffering PND then
there is plenty of support and help available.
Begin with a visit to your family doctor or
early childhood nurse. (See the 'Resources'
list on page 348.)

Working and parenting

Gone are the days when most families consisted of a father who went to work outside the home and a mother who stayed at home with the children, at least until they started school. These days the mother may work and the father takes care of the children, or one or both parents may work from home or both may go out to work. Entangled in the lives of working parents are the issues of childcare.

Even parents who work from home will find that childcare is an option as their child becomes more mobile, spends more time being active and needs more stimulation.

You may be told that childcare is not good for a child, and you may feel that no one can care for your child as well as you do. You may feel guilty about leaving your child, even for a moment, with someone else, so going to work may be fraught with anxiety. There's not a lot to worry about, as good quality childcare has been found to be an excellent environment for young children.

Research has found that it's not whether you work that is good or bad for children, it's how you parent and how you work. Whether you work or not, you need to give your children the time they need to simply 'hang out' with you as well as time when you focus on an activity together. Quality time and quantity time are both important.

When you consider returning to work, think about your job, because the following points will help you to be a better parent as well as a better worker.

- How demanding is the job? Are you likely to be put under stress often?

- Do you think you can do the job, or do you expect that you will be asked to do more than you have time for? Will you be asked to work overtime?

- How much input will you have into your job? Will you have some say in how you do the job?

- Is the workplace supportive of parents? Do your employers understand that you may need to take time off when your child is sick, for example?

These four points affect how you will feel when you come home from work, and how you feel will influence how you parent.

Childcare choices

Childcare can be expensive, so before you make a choice consider the following points:

- Can you work from home? If so, would you like to? If this can be organized, you may find that having someone in the home to care for your child while you work is the best option.

- Can you and your partner work flexibly so that your child spends more time with each of you and less time at childcare?

- Can you job-share, or work part-time?

Friends and relatives

For many families, the best option is to leave their child in the care of a friend or relative. The child is in familiar hands, particularly if it is a family member, such as a grandmother, who cares for him. The hours of care can be very flexible, and if the child is unwell a family member will often look after him nonetheless. However, if the carer is sick you will need to make other plans. You need to be sure you agree with your carer's approach to raising children. You should also check that the house is made safe for children.

Family daycare

For younger children, many people find family daycare more appealing than a centre. This is usually because, with family daycare, small groups of children are looked after in a home, usually by one adult. These homes are part of a scheme, and the carers and their homes must meet certain safety and hygiene standards. There is no requirement that carers be trained, as they are in a childcare centre, so standards can vary widely. When researching family daycare, ask other families for referrals. Be sure to choose a carer whom you and your child like. You can contact your local council for more information on family daycare.

Childcare centres

Long daycare centres or nurseries, as these services are also called, cater principally for working parents. Generally, they must hold a government licence and meet standards set by regulations that cover the premises, food, hygiene, staff ratios and qualifications, and the programs that the centre runs. Under the 'Childcare checklist' on page 281, you will find points to consider when choosing a childcare centre.

Nanny

A nanny is an expensive option, but if you can afford one it gives you enormous flexibility. You will need to negotiate the hours, wages and services with the nanny or nanny agency. When you choose a nanny, check all his or her references thoroughly, even if the nanny comes through an agency. A good nanny, who has been trained in childcare and who fits in with your family's lifestyle, is worth his/her weight in gold and may become a longtime friend of the family. The downside is that when the nanny is ill, you may have no backup. Also your child will still need to go to playgroup or other activities for contact with other children the same age.

Creche at work

Workplaces with an on-site creche are scarce, but if you are lucky enough to have one, then it is an excellent option. Apart from having that extra travel time with your child, you are close by if the child is sick or needs you for any reason. These centres are run on very strict guidelines and have to conform to regulations just as childcare centres do.

Breastfeeding and working

Many mothers return to work and continue to breastfeed, particularly when their child is under the age of 12 months. If you want to do this, you need to discuss it with your employer and be sure he or she is supportive. In some countries is it illegal for an employer to discriminate against a woman who breastfeeds at work. The best time to discuss this issue is before you go on maternity leave, but any time is better than not at all.

Working mothers who breastfeed need to express their milk throughout the day. To successfully express milk, it is important to practise as early as possible, and to get baby used to accepting breastmilk from a bottle given by someone other than his mother. Refer to 'Returning to work and breastfeeding' on page 52.

Being organized

Once you have made the decision to return to work, you will need to be organized. The parent who goes away from home to work and takes their child to childcare needs to be even more organized than the parent who stays home. When you first return to work, accept all offers of help — it will make your life easier. Here are some other useful strategies.

- Eliminate as many jobs as possible.
- Sort and fold washing as you take it off the line or out of the dryer. Fold nappies into the shape you use.
- Use an Internet shopping service if you can afford it.
- Keep a sponge near the bath and shower, and give them a quick wipe every day.
- Use quilts or doonas on the beds, not blankets, to make bed making quicker and easier.
- If you can afford a cleaning service, it will save you lots of time.
- Do as much as possible the night before.
  - Pack the nappy or change clothes bag.
  - Organize or make lunches.
  - Write notes, shopping and 'to do' lists.
  - Decide what you are going to wear the next day and iron anything that must be ironed.
  - Lay the table for breakfast.
- Give yourself some space: get up at least 15 minutes before your child wakes so you can spend time doing something for yourself — for example, reading the paper or exercising.
- Make the most of the trip to and from childcare. Sing songs together, or if you are on public transport, read him a book.

Be sure to look after yourself by setting aside time for one major activity you enjoy a week — it may be a bath, a massage, a manicure or a couple of hours' shopping. And be sure to include exercise in your own routine, even if it is only a walk at lunchtime. If you don't allow yourself this special time, you're more likely to feel stressed.

Six months to one year

By the end of her first year, your baby will have tripled her birth weight and doubled in height. She will have learnt so much that it will be hard to believe that only 12 months before she was a helpless little newborn bundle.

How your baby grows

The most important thing that you can give your baby is a lot of love and attention. She needs you to spend time with her, to talk to her, read to her, dance with her and play with her. She needs you to look after her physical needs, praise her achievements and provide her with a routine so that she feels safe.

Development checklist

By nine months

**Date you noticed
your child doing it**

Cries differently when she is hungry, uncomfortable or in pain

Lets you know if she is happy or unhappy

Recognizes familiar voices

Can focus on small things and reach for them

If you hide a toy, she will look for it

Explores things by shaking, banging and putting them in her mouth

Babbles away as if talking

Enjoys games which involve dropping things

Responds when you say her name

Understands when you say 'no'

Imitates sounds and facial expressions made by others

Is wary of strangers

Is unhappy if you take something away

Loves tickling games

Will smile at her own reflection in the mirror

Holds out her arms to be picked up

Recognizes the names of other family members

Is unhappy when others are unhappy

May be anxious if separated from parents

First teeth may start to come through

Likes to chew on anything

Reaches for the cup or spoon at mealtimes

Shuts mouth firmly or turns head away when she's had enough food

Can roll from stomach to back, and back again

Can sit without being supported

Pulls up into crawling position; may rock back and forth; may start crawling

Uses pincer grip (thumb and forefinger) to pick up small objects

Can swap something from one hand to the other

Development checklist

By 12 months	Date you noticed your child doing it
Says first words — most likely 'da-da' or 'ma-ma'	
Dances and jigs to music or singing	
Enjoys looking at picture books	
Can clap and wave 'bye-bye'	
Follows conversations	
Likes putting things inside other things (e.g. stacking cups)	
Copies others (e.g. talking on the phone)	
Responds when you say her name	
Offers toys or objects to others but expects to get them back	
Forms attachments to favourite things	
Pushes something away if she doesn't want it	
May stop having one daily nap	
Enjoys finger foods	
Likes opening and closing cupboard doors	
Pulls herself up to stand	
Cruises, holding onto furniture	

Feeding

Some time during the second half of your baby's first year, she will be ready for solids. By offering her a variety of nutritious foods, you are setting her on track to grow into toddlerhood glowing with good health and vitality. This is your golden opportunity to help her establish healthy eating habits for life.

Weaning

You don't have to stop breastfeeding when your baby reaches the 12-month mark. The fact is that many women continue to breastfeed their babies well into the toddler years. The decision to wean should be convenient for you and your baby. Some babies decide to wean themselves by refusing the breast when it is offered. The key to weaning successfully is to do it slowly: decrease the number of daily breastfeeds over a period that could extend to six months. Introduce cow's milk into your baby's diet while you continue to breastfeed, just as you introduce water and diluted fruit juice. As with any other new food, introduce cow's milk at just one meal each day (pour it on breakfast cereal or offer it as a drink) and watch for any reaction such as vomiting, diarrhoea or eczema.

> ### Hint
> If you usually feed your baby to sleep, increase the time between the feed and putting baby to bed, so the feed becomes less important as part of the bedtime routine.

Introducing family foods

Starting solids is definitely a messy experience and it does require patience. But it's also lots of fun helping your baby discover new foods and taste sensations. Some babies will be enthusiastic about solid food from the start, while others may take their time getting used to these new tastes and textures.

Recommendations

The World Health Organisation (WHO) recommends exclusive breastfeeding for six months, with the introduction of solids and continued breastfeeding after this time. The consensus in the medical community is that solids can be safely introduced 'around the middle of the first year'. This guide also applies to bottle-fed babies. Remember that breastfeeding or feeding with a suitable formula remains a vital source of nutrition for the first 12 months and should not be removed from your baby's diet in preference for solids. However, solids are also important as they provide additional nutrients such as vitamin C and iron. They also introduce your baby to new tastes and textures, and help with speech, teeth and jaw development.

When it's too early to start

There are good reasons to avoid giving solids to your baby before she is ready. For instance, there is a greater risk of allergic reaction to some foods. The breastfeeding mother who introduces solids into her baby's diet earlier than recommended may find that her breasts make less milk in response to the decreased demand from baby. And a young baby can be overfed, as she is less able to convey that she is full.

Signs of readiness for solids

It's likely that your baby will let you know when she's ready for solids, so let her be your guide. Once your baby is older than four to five months old, check the following indicators to help you interpret her needs.

- Your breastfed baby is interested in more feeds. Alternatively, she may appear less satisfied with just milk feeds.

- Baby's birthweight has doubled, and she weighs more than 5 kg (11 lb).

- Your baby shows an increased interest in food that others are eating, and tries to grab things and put them in her mouth.

- Baby has the head and neck strength to be able to sit in a supported position.

- Your child no longer displays the tongue-thrusting reflex, which causes her to push solids out of her mouth. This means she is ready to be fed with a spoon.

Six to eight months

There are several reasons why solid foods should be introduced gradually. A 'nice-and-easy-does-it' pace, while maintaining a breast- or bottle-feeding routine, will ensure your baby continues to thrive. And by introducing new foods one at a time you can effectively monitor your baby's reaction: she could be allergic to a particular food or may not enjoy the flavour. If your baby appears to have an allergic reaction to a certain type of food or appears unsettled and in pain, immediately omit it from her diet and seek medical advice. If the taste does not meet with her approval, reintroduce that food at a later stage.

New foods may need to be offered as many as eight to ten times before your baby accepts them. Follow these tips for a stress-free introduction.

- Choose a time when your baby is happy and alert and in between milk feeds.

- Be prepared for a mess. As you feed your baby, a lot of what goes in will probably pop back out of her mouth until she is familiar with the spoon. So, protect your clothes and hers, and be ready with a clean cloth to wipe off any 'leftovers'.

- Before preparing food for your baby, wash your hands thoroughly with soap.

- Your baby may not be strong enough to sit unsupported in a highchair. If this is the case, sit her in a comfortable upright position on your lap.

- Use a small, shallow spoon to feed your baby.

- Initially, offer solids once a day, always after a breastfeed or bottle-feed (never add rice cereal to a bottle). At first, give a half to a full teaspoonful of baby iron-fortified rice cereal mixed to a thin consistency with a little breastmilk, infant formula or boiled cooled water. Cereal is an ideal beginner food for your baby, as it has sufficient kilojoules (calories) and is relatively easy to digest; the added iron is important for brain and nerve development, and also helps maintain a healthy immune system. Increase the amount daily until your baby is happy to eat one to two tablespoons (per day) of that particular food. Let your baby 'tell' you how much

Suitable first solid foods

* Iron-fortified rice cereal, a great beginner food for your baby

* Ripe mashed banana (mixed with a little breastmilk or formula, if you like)

* Stewed apples, peaches, pears, apricots (no added sugar)

* Cooked and puréed (whizzed in a blender so it is soft and smooth) to start with and then mashed pumpkin, potato, sweet potato, carrot, parsnip, zucchini (courgettes), squash, cauliflower

* Mashed avocado

she wants. If she turns her head away or pushes the spoon away, don't try to feed her more.

■ Introduce one food at a time over the next few weeks. For example, give her iron-fortified rice cereal for at least three days before moving on to a new food such as stewed apple. Feed your baby the stewed apple for three days, alternating with iron-fortified rice cereal, before introducing another food.

■ After a couple of weeks, and once your baby is familiar with several foods, begin combining fruit such as stewed apple with the iron-fortified rice cereal.

■ Offer puréed vegetables after about four weeks. There is no need to add salt.

■ It's not necessary to buy commercial baby food; it can be expensive and often contains several foods mixed together. It's also uniformly soft. If you choose to buy baby food, read the labels carefully and avoid foods with added sweeteners, salt and preservatives.

■ Tinned organic baby food is available in the health food section of your supermarket or from health food shops, but it is more expensive than the non-organic.

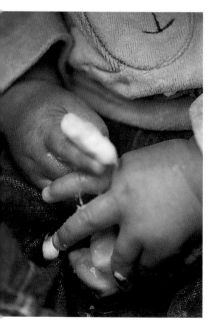

Food ideas

Here are some ideas for suitable foods for a baby aged eight to ten months.

* Oat and wheat-based cereals (oatmeal, barley, porridge, wheat flake biscuits)

* Sliced soft fruit (e.g. bananas and peaches)

* Soft cooked fruit and vegetables

* Minced and finely chopped chicken, red meat and white fish (no bones)

* Grated cheese[†] with vegetables

* Cottage cheese[†] with fruit or avocado

* Chopped tofu[††]

* Plain yoghurt[†]

* Well cooked egg yolk (don't include the egg white until around 12 months)[†††]

* Small sandwiches (no crusts)

* Toast fingers with a smear of cream cheese[†] or avocado

* Rusks

* Well cooked pasta

* Dry plain biscuits (e.g. digestives)

* Mashed beans or lentils

* Well cooked white or brown rice

[†] Small amounts of products derived from cow's milk (such as cheese, yoghurt, custard and cream cheese) can be given to baby before 12 months, preferably from the age of nine months.

[††] Because tofu is a soy-based product, it has the potential to trigger an allergic reaction. Give your baby a small amount, then wait a few days before serving it again.

[†††] Initially, offer a quarter of a teaspoon of egg yolk and wait a few days to check if your baby has a negative reaction before offering it to her again.

Eight to ten months

From around eight months, your baby will be far more interested in what the rest of the family is eating. Now is the time to offer her a wider variety of foods, some in combination. By this time you should also be giving her food which is not so smooth, with soft 'lumps' in it, so she not only becomes accustomed to different textures but also learns how to chew properly. She will also enjoy finger foods where she can feed herself — most babies without

Food ideas

These foods are suitable for a baby aged ten to 12 months.

* Muffins and crumpets, topped with melted cheese that has cooled down

* Chopped cooked vegetables and fruit

* Wedges of soft fruit (e.g. banana) as finger foods

* Rice, sago puddings, butter (thinly spread on sandwiches) and ice cream in small quantities

* Strips of red meat such as grilled steak with the gristle removed, and smooth chop bones for gnawing

* Canned fish such as well drained tuna in brine or spring water

* Baked beans

* Cheese sticks

* Whole egg in custards, omelettes and French toast

teeth can chew efficiently by this stage (never leave a baby alone with finger foods). During this period she may also show a preference for having her food before a milk feed and will begin to fit in with your family meal routine.

Ten to 12 months

From ten months continue to introduce a wide variety of low-sugar and low-salt foods into your child's diet, so that your baby can experience a range of tastes and textures. And have fun combining foods, such as fruit and yoghurt, to tantalize her tastebuds. At each meal you can give your baby cereal or bread and fruit or vegetables, plus a protein food such as fish, meat, legumes or a dairy product.

By around 12 months your baby should be enjoying a well balanced diet that contains foods from the five food groups (see 'The five food groups' on page 145). The size of each meal is comparable to one cup of food. At 12 months your formula-fed baby can change to full-cream milk and should be having the equivalent of 600 mL (1 pt) of milk a day from this and other dairy products. If your baby is still being regularly breastfed, you can offer the occasional drink of milk to get her used to the taste and to using a cup; it's also a good way to introduce dairy products as food.

Your baby's appetite is likely to be different from her little friends and it will vary from meal to meal, day to day. If you are concerned about the amount of food your baby eats, discuss this and her growth and weight gain with your doctor or clinic sister.

Foods to avoid

To ensure your baby's wellbeing, there are certain foods that should be omitted from her diet.

Honey. Babies under 12 months of age should not eat honey as it may contain a type of bacteria that can cause infant botulism. This results in muscle paralysis and requires emergency medical treatment. Children older than 12 months are not affected by the presence of this bacteria.

Choking hazards. Such hazards include grapes, whole nuts, hard vegetables such as uncooked or undercooked carrot rounds, stringy vegetables (for example, celery and string beans), chopped apple, sausages and hotdogs (which also contain excessive salt, nitrates and preservatives), popcorn, corn chips and potato crisps, lollies or sweets (which also contain excessive sugar), seeds, meat chunks and hard beans.

Foods that may cause gastroenteritis. These are foods past their use-by-date, foods not stored appropriately and undercooked chicken. Always refrigerate cooked foods immediately and don't give them to your baby if they have been stored in the fridge for more than one to two days.

Food allergies

There are some foods that may cause an allergic reaction, where the immune system overreacts to an ordinarily harmless food. The symptoms may include a runny nose, hives, rashes, eczema, nausea, diarrhoea, constipation, vomiting, sneezing, sweating or fever, ear infections or shortness of breath. The more serious symptoms are swelling of the lips, tongue or mouth, laboured breathing, asthma and wheezing. If your baby experiences any of these reactions, call your doctor or take her to the casualty department at your nearest hospital.

Allergic reactions are far more likely in your baby if you and/or your partner suffer from allergic diseases. If so, you may want to take extra care in introducing potentially allergic foods, and it would be wise to seek advice from a dietitian or your doctor. The advice is also important if you find you are restricting the range of food your baby eats because of a potential allergic reaction. Avoid these foods.

Peanuts. Babies are highly susceptible to peanut allergy. You can reduce the risk of your baby developing a peanut allergy by not giving her peanut products, including peanut butter, until after the age of three or four years. And then give your child only a small amount to sample. Also, be wary of products that contain traces of nuts, such as biscuits and chocolate.

You should visit a paediatric dietitian, or a dietitian who specializes in vegetarian diets, to help you devise a nutritious diet for your baby. It's a good idea to contact your local children's hospital or baby health clinic for some recommendations.

Recipes for success

Commercial baby foods are very convenient when you are travelling or even just visiting with your baby, but these products often contain several foods mixed together into a uniformly smooth mash. If you prepare and cook your baby's first solids yourself, she will be able to sample the tastes and textures of individual foods. The following suggestions and basic recipes for young babies are quick and easy to prepare; simplicity is the key. You can prepare your own baby food in a blender or food processor, or even with just a fork or a sieve.

An easy way to have a convenient supply of puréed fruit and vegetables on hand is to pour the mixture into a clean ice cube tray, seal the tray in a freezer bag, label it with the food type and the date, and place it in the freezer. Fruit and vegetables can be frozen for up to six months. The small portions can be individually thawed and reheated when it's dinnertime, but note that babies aren't fussy about the temperature of their food, so reheating isn't necessary if an oven or microwave is not available. Be careful when preparing food in a microwave oven, as the heat is unevenly distributed. Make sure you stir the food before giving it to your baby.

As your baby gradually becomes used to a wide range of foods, you can prepare tasty and nutritious combinations for her. Here are some irresistible examples of foods that can be added to the main ingredient.

To stewed fruit (such as apples or pears) add:

- ■ Custard
- ■ Cottage cheese

- Mashed banana
- Plain yoghurt
- Rice cereal
- Boiled short grain or medium grain rice
- Softened and mashed dried fruit, such as prunes or dried apricots
- Minced or chopped cooked chicken (no skin), beef or lamb
- Silken tofu

To mashed banana add:

- A little breastmilk or formula
- Mashed or chopped avocado
- Mashed or chopped paw-paw
- Plain yoghurt
- Cottage or cream cheese
- Cooked egg yolk
- Oatmeal
- Fine flakes of boneless white fish

To steamed and puréed (or mashed) vegetables (such as potato, carrot and zucchini or courgettes), add:

- Cottage cheese
- Grated cheddar cheese
- Plain yoghurt
- Unsweetened custard
- Minced chicken (no skin), minced beef or lamb, flaked fish (no bones)
- Silken tofu

To cooked pasta (such as penne or fusilli) add:

- Plain yoghurt and vegetables
- Spinach and cottage cheese
- Cheese sauce
- Minced or chopped chicken, beef or lamb with a simple tomato sauce
- Boneless flakes of white fish with a simple tomato sauce
- Minced chicken and prunes
- Avocado

To minced or finely chopped beef, lamb or chicken add:

- Mixed vegetables
- Apple sauce
- Plain yoghurt

For the following recipes, the number of serves per dish depends on your child's age and appetite.

Fruit purée

Ingredients

Three apples, pears, apricots or peaches

Method

1 Peel and core the fruit, cut them into slices and place them in a saucepan on the stovetop.

2 Pour in enough water to cover the fruit and bring it to the boil. Lower the heat to a simmer and cover for ten minutes until the fruit is soft and mushy.

3 Or, if you prefer to use a microwave, place the ingredients in a microwave-proof dish and cook on High for about five minutes.

4 If necessary, mash the fruit with a fork and serve. Freeze any leftovers in an ice cube tray.

Homemade rusks

Rusks are a great finger food and they're easy to make.

Ingredients

Wholemeal bread

Method

1 Cut 2.5 cm (1 in) thick slices of wholemeal bread. Remove the crusts and cut each slice of bread into strips about 1 cm (⅓ in) wide.

2 Bake the strips on an ungreased baking tray in an oven on a low heat (120°C or 250°F) for around an hour, or until the rusks are dry and crisp. Turn them occasionally.

3 Cool and store in an airtight container for up to seven days.

Fruity jelly

Ingredients

¾ cup freshly squeezed and strained orange juice or apple juice

¼ cup cold water

1 teaspoon gelatine

Method

1 Place gelatine and water in a small bowl and leave for five minutes.

2 Put the bowl in a larger bowl of hot water and stir the gelatine and water until the gelatine dissolves.

3 Stir in the fruit juice.

4 Pour into a bowl and chill until set.

Fruit custard

Serve this custard with fruit purée, cottage or ricotta cheese.

Ingredients

2 teaspoons arrowroot

½ cup apple juice

1 tablespoon yoghurt

Method

1 Combine arrowroot, apple juice and yoghurt in a small saucepan.

2 Bring to the boil over medium heat, stirring until the custard thickens.

3 Cool before serving.

Egg custard

Serve egg custard with puréed fruit, cottage cheese or yoghurt.

Ingredients

1 tablespoon cornflour

1 egg yolk

2 teaspoons sugar

1 cup milk

¼ teaspoon vanilla essence

Method

1 Combine all ingredients in a small saucepan.

2 Bring to the boil over medium heat, stirring until sauce thickens.

3 Cool before serving.

Baked fish

Ingredients

One small piece from a fillet of a white boneless fish (check with the fishmonger)

Juice of one lemon

Method

1 Place the fish in foil and squeeze a little bit of lemon juice over it before wrapping it securely.

2 Place the fish in an oven preheated to 180°C (360°F) and cook for 15 to 20 minutes.

To serve, remove the fish from the foil and check for bones as you flake it into small pieces with a fork. Provide a vegetable purée accompaniment for a well balanced dinner.

Drinking from a cup

Sucking and sipping are two completely different actions, so your baby will need to practise before she is drinking competently from a cup. You can try this from around seven months, but don't expect your baby to immediately catch on to this complex transition from breast or bottle to cup. If you choose to use a normal cup straight away, you will have to be on hand to wipe up the milk that baby dribbles out of the corners of her mouth and to help steady the cup. A plastic trainer cup with a tight lid and small spout is another option for the child younger than 12 months.

Look for a cup that:

- has a tight-fitting lid with a built-in spout;
- is weighted at the bottom so it doesn't tip over easily;
- is easy to hold with double handles; and
- has a wide base for greater stability.

Initially, you will have to help your baby hold the cup, gradually introducing a few drops of the drink between her lips and stopping frequently to allow her to swallow. The best first drink from a cup is water. If you are giving your baby fruit juice, ensure that it is diluted with two-thirds water. Pear, apple and grape are favourite starter juices. Here's a tip: if you are breastfeeding and are having trouble weaning your baby onto a cup, try giving the cup to her as a toy to play with.

A meal plan

These simple meal plans offer suggestions for each age group.

Around six to seven months

On waking
Breastmilk or infant formula
Breakfast
Breastmilk or infant formula, plus 1–2 tablespoons baby iron-fortified rice cereal mixed with breastmilk or infant formula
Lunch
Breastmilk or infant formula, plus 1 tablespoon mashed or puréed fruit
Afternoon
Breastmilk or infant formula
Dinner
Breastmilk or infant formula, plus 1 tablespoon mashed, boiled or steamed vegetables
Supper
Breastmilk or infant formula

Around ten months

On waking
Breastmilk or infant formula
Breakfast
2 tablespoons porridge or baby muesli (no sugar)
½–1 slice of toast
Breastmilk or infant formula
Mid-morning
Up to 125 mL (⅕ pt) diluted juice (⅓ juice to ⅔ boiled water)
Lunch
Puréed fruit with yoghurt or cottage cheese
Breastmilk or infant formula

Choosing a highchair

A highchair is a handy purchase once your baby can sit up properly without your help. Your aim is to find a safe and serviceable highchair that you can afford. There are basically two styles of highchair — the clip-on model and the freestanding model.

Before you buy a highchair, check it carefully to make sure that it is well designed and safe.

* Check that it is strong, stable and free of sharp edges. Check for any gaps, where fingers or toes could become trapped. If it is a folding model, make sure that the locks work and ask for a demonstration before you buy it.

* If the chair doesn't have a full safety harness (crotch strap, straps over both shoulders and a waist belt), make sure it has the attachment that enables you to fit a harness. Also, look for a restraining device, which prevents a child from slipping out of the chair.

* The tray should be large and securely affixed to the highchair when in use. It should also feature a lip that helps prevent food and eating utensils from falling.

* The seat should be comfortable and (preferably) padded, with the backrest leaning slightly backwards.

* It should be easy to assemble and easy to clean.

* Check that the label features appropriate safety advice. For example, a child should never be left unattended in a highchair and should always be secured in a restraint when seated in the highchair.

* Castors on two of the legs will enable you to move it from room to room. (Do not do this while your child is in it.)

Mid-afternoon

Water

Rusk

Dinner

2 teaspoons lean meat (chicken, boneless fish) or lentils

½ cup steamed vegetables, diced or mashed

Supper

Breastmilk or infant formula

Around 12 months

Breakfast

Breastmilk or infant formula

Cereal with milk and/or yoghurt

Toast

never

* Never leave your child alone in the highchair.

* Never forget to use the safety harness; baby will get used to it.

* Never put the highchair next to windows, unsecured doorways, stoves, appliance cords, curtains or cord blinds.

* Never neglect torn seats, as a baby can choke on padding. Likewise, attend to loose nuts and broken parts.

* Never allow your child to stand up in or climb out of a highchair, as the chair could tip over.

* Never let a baby's hands go near the tray when it is being raised and lowered.

* Never position the highchair near a wall or piece of furniture, as baby may push against it, causing the highchair to fall over.

* Never forget to place the highchair in a safe place out of the reach of children when not in use.

* Never let the highchair rest on the carpet. A plastic mat underneath the highchair could help minimize the impact of spills and food mess.

Mid-morning

Water

Fruit or a small sandwich (with crusts cut off)

Lunch

Sandwich or pasta

Fruit

Breastmilk or infant formula

Mid-afternoon

Diluted juice (⅓ juice to ⅔ boiled water) or water

Fruit or cheese sticks

Dinner

About ½ cup of protein (meat, chicken, fish, lentils, egg)

About ½ cup of vegetables

Fruit dessert

Supper

Breastmilk or infant formula

Caring

Now that your child is becoming mobile and probably adventurous, it's time to childproof your home if you haven't already done so. She'll need clothes that won't restrict her mobility, and once she starts walking outside, her first pair of shoes. This is also a good time to consider updating your first aid skills. Compile a list of emergency numbers that can be posted near the phone or on the fridge, and keep a well stocked first aid kit in an accessible place.

Updating your child's wardrobe

A child continues to grow at a rapid pace in the second 12 months. Your baby will have long outgrown her newborn clothes, and you need to be aware that she will be growing out of most clothes much faster than she can wear them out.

As babies become mobile some time around seven to eight months, the clothes they are wearing need to accommodate their need for movement. Here are a few points worth noting before you buy new clothes for your baby.

- Natural fibres continue to be the best choice. Towelling, denim and corduroy are ideal for a baby who is moving about on her hands and knees. Dark colours and patterns will take longer to look grubby than pastels and white.

- Easy opening between the legs also continues to be important. By the time a baby is six months old, lying down for a nappy change can be a bore, and dressing baby in clothes which allow for quick nappy changing will make life easier for everyone.

- Envelope necks are still a good choice in tops, singlets and t-shirts. Openings and fastenings such as clips, Velcro and press studs are best; avoid ties, tight buttons and zips. Elasticized waist, ankle and wrist bands make dressing quicker and easier.

- Dresses are an encumbrance to crawling and moving about. Until a baby girl learns to walk, she is best dressed in stretch suits, rompers or overalls, ideally with padded knees. If you do put her in a dress, make it short so it doesn't trip her up; put a pair of tights underneath on a cold day.

■ Some clothes can be made to grow with the child. You can cut the feet off stretch suits, remove the sleeves from jackets so they become vests, and add decorative cuffs to rompers and overalls, provided there is still room around the nappy.

■ Hats are important in winter for warmth and in summer for protection. Your baby's head is growing quickly, so it will be necessary to buy one or two new caps or hats.

■ She will need new socks, as her feet are growing as quickly as the rest of her body. For crawling, socks, little sheepskin slippers and bootees are ideal. Even better, some come with grip soles, ideal when baby practises standing up.

■ Babies do not need shoes, even when they first start to walk. In early walking a baby uses her toes to help her establish her balance and understand the texture of the surface she is walking on. Once your baby starts walking outside then it is time to buy her a first pair of early walkers. These should be leather and fit well with enough space for baby's toes to wiggle, between 0.5 cm (⅕ in) and 1.25 cm (½ in), but not enough so that the shoes slip off the foot. The shoes need to be lightweight and smooth inside with no seams; they should also have flexible soles. Baby will grow out of shoes quite quickly and one of the easiest ways to check this is to trace around both feet, cut out the tracings and place them inside the shoes. If they crumple then the shoes are too small (see 'Choosing shoes' on page 204).

■ Don't let your child wear secondhand shoes as they could damage her feet.

Never leave an iron cord hanging down within baby's reach.

Preparing your home for a baby on the move

Before you know it, your baby will be mobile. Once she starts crawling a new world will unfold before her. To keep this magical, exploratory experience free from danger, it's up to you to literally clear a path for her by organizing a baby-friendly home — one that's safe as houses! As she grows the safety zones in the home will need to be extended. By keeping abreast of your baby's development, you are ensuring a trouble-free progression through each phase.

Of course, even in a home planned around children, accidents happen. However, under your ever-watchful eye your child will learn safe behaviour.

First, get down to your baby's level and crawl around on your hands and knees to check out the world from her point of view. This will help you identify potential hazards. You might encounter sharp table edges, an unstable lamp base, breakable items such as glass ornaments, power points, electrical cords and inappropriately located furniture. Note these potential problems so you can rectify them.

This room-by-room breakdown of potential problems and solutions will alert you to the changes you may need to implement to make your home safe for your curious baby.

Teaching your child

It's not too early to teach your child about danger. Use words such as 'hot!' 'ouch!' and 'be careful' to emphasize potentially dangerous situations.

All rooms

When checking the safety of all the rooms in the house, carefully note and consider the following points.

- If you haven't already, now is the time to install smoke detectors/alarms, and to purchase a fire extinguisher and fire blanket (which should be kept in an accessible location). The most important areas in which to install smoke alarms are the hallway, stairwell and near the kitchen.

- Unplug electrical appliances when they're not in use. Make sure the cords are short and do not hang down within a child's reach; run them behind furniture, if necessary.

- In winter use wall-mounted heaters or locate heaters out of the reach of children. Do not use kerosene heaters.

- Install swing safety gates at the top and bottom of stairs.

- If you don't already have a circuit breaker, have an electrician install electrical safety switches — also known as residual current devices — for all power points, except those supplying refrigerators or freezers.

- Insert safety plugs/covers into power points that can be reached by your child.

- Apply safety film and height stickers to glass doors.
- Ensure that there are no railings small children might be able to climb over.
- Make sure curtain cords are secured safely beyond your child's reach.
- Check all furniture and lamps (table and freestanding) for stability and store or replace any rocky ones.
- Place safety latches on all drawers and cabinets at your child's level.
- Provide protective corner covers to furniture with sharp and hard corners.
- Don't put hot drinks where a small child could easily knock them over.

Living room

Insert safety plugs like these in all power points.

- Install safe and secure fireguards on domestic heating appliances.
- Rearrange furniture to avoid collisions — for example, do not place chairs or sofas against large glazed panels.
- Secure any unstable furniture to the wall. For example, if your baby is a climber and decides to scale a bookcase or display unit, it could easily sway and fall if it isn't rigidly attached.
- Keep any alcoholic beverages locked in a cupboard that cannot be reached by a child.
- If you use the living room for sewing, ensure the floor surface is smooth and uncarpeted, so dropped pins are easy to find and retrieve.
- See also 'All rooms' on page 157.

Bathroom

The bathroom is, per hour used, the most dangerous room in the house for children. The most common hazards are:

- drowning;
- hot water burns;
- falls and slipping;
- electrocution;

- dangers from spa baths;
- poisoning;
- lacerations from broken glass or sharp objects;
- children becoming locked in; and
- climbing out of windows.[1]

In the bathroom constant close supervision of your child is essential.

- You should always be present to supervise baby's bathtime. Your baby should not be left alone or with older children in the bath. Make sure you have all the necessary items at hand, including towels. As an extra precaution, either take the phone off the hook or turn on the answering machine.
- Non-slip bath stickers on the bottom of the bath stop baby from slipping. Bath seats are not recommended.[2]
- Provide non-slip surfaces for showers, shower trays and bathroom floors.
- It is recommended that hot water outlets be controlled to a maximum of 50°C (122°F) with thermostatic mixing valves.
- For a young child the water temperature should be no higher than 38°C (100.4°F), and anti-scald devices should be attached to all hot water taps.
- Always run the cold water before turning on the hot, and turn the hot off first.
- All medications, electrical appliances and household chemicals should be secured in a locked cupboard out of baby's reach.
- Unplug electrical appliances, such as hair driers, and store them away when they're not in use.
- Store razors, scissors and other potentially dangerous objects up high and out of baby's reach.
- Mount heaters on the wall and secure all electrical cords out of baby's reach.
- Install emergency release locks on both sides of bathroom and toilet doors.

Adult bedroom

- Keep low bedside tables clear of bottles of pills or any other medication you may use.

- Always keep the lid securely on the nappy bucket; it is a potential drowning hazard. Keep the nappy bucket elevated and out of your baby's reach.
- Your baby should not be able to reach the taps in the laundry tub.
- Keep all chemicals and detergents up high and out of your baby's reach, preferably in a childproof poisons cupboard.
- See also 'All rooms' on page 157.

Outdoors

Of course it's safe to go outside — all it takes is a little preparation. Babies and young children can drown in 50 mm (2 in) of water, so be vigilant about checking for drowning hazards.

- Erect a childproof fence around your property to prevent access to the road and neighbouring properties, which may contain swimming pools or water features.
- Install safety swing gates at the top and bottom of stairs, which should feature balustrades and hand rails.
- Keep the garage and shed locked at all times.
- Make sure the operating switch on an automatic garage door is positioned out of your child's reach. The door should also feature a safety device that renders it inoperable when an object, such as a small child, is encountered.
- Block access from the backyard into the garage and through to the front garden.
- If possible, keep toys, bikes and other play items stored in a shed, away from the garage and driveway.
- Lock power tools and any other dangerous items, including poisons, in a cupboard in a shed or garage, if you have one.
- Cover fish ponds with metal grilles, and prevent children's access to gully traps and open drains.
- Swimming pools should be isolated from all other areas of the property by secure fencing that meets the legal requirements of the local authority.
- Outdoor spas should also feature isolation fencing that complies with the requirements of the local legislation.
- Do not locate the entertainment area — the barbecue and outdoor dining setting — within the pool enclosure.

- Keep garden furniture, and any other objects that could be used for climbing, well away from the pool or spa fence and gate.

- Prevent your child's access to outdoor barbecues and incinerators, and ensure these facilities cannot be operated when they're not in use by an adult.

- Keep pathways clear.

- Install soft-fall materials such as bark chips, not sand, under play equipment.

- Remove low-hanging branches from trees.

- Watch out for furniture or play items left in the sun. Black plastic sheeting — used to cover a sandpit, for example — can heat up and cause burns on contact.

Cleaning the house for baby

There are 'super' mothers, and then there are mothers and their partners who are living in the real world.

Unless you are equipped with superhuman powers, or you have a cleaner, nanny and gardener, as the parents of a new baby it is impossible to maintain a picture-perfect home. Of course, keeping the house clean for your baby is a priority, but you can't achieve miracles — you'll only end up exhausted and at loggerheads over who is and isn't pulling their weight.

However, there are clever, simple ways to get rid of the physical clutter, thereby freeing yourself from its emotional equivalent, and for keeping the house clean with the minimum of fuss.

Order in the house

There's no use running around the house doing a bit here and a bit there. At the end of the day you'll feel exhausted and have little to show for it. To experience a sense of achievement, take a methodical approach to domestic chores so you need never retrace your steps.

You can achieve this by formulating a schedule and sticking to it. The schedule is really just a 'big picture' list that can be broken down into smaller achievable task lists. The list can be used as an effective monitoring tool: it should help you feel as if you've accomplished something, as you tick off the jobs once you have completed them.

Before you start cleaning, target your clutter troublespots and try to clear these areas once a day. For example, get rid of the pile of papers and bills growing on the kitchen table, the basket of clean washing sitting on the lounge, the toys cluttering the living area. Then you can start getting down to business. Consider one or more of the following approaches.

The essentials list

This list covers jobs to be done every day. You could aim to complete half the jobs in the morning and the other half in the afternoon. Modify it to suit your own requirements.

1 Wash dishes as you go, or place them in the dishwasher immediately after use.

2 Empty the dishrack of dishes and eating utensils, or empty the dishwasher.

3 Lightly clean the kitchen sink.

4 Keep benchtops free of clutter and wipe over benchtops, the stovetop, fridge and the handles of the most frequently used kitchen cabinets.

5 Quickly mop or sweep the kitchen floor.

6 Make the beds every morning (it's amazing the difference a neat bed can make to a room).

7 Give the bath tub or shower recess a light wipe over after you bathe/shower.

8 Wash, dry and put away a load of washing.

9 Stack newspapers, magazines and other recyclables in the appropriate recycling bins.

10 Put away shoes.

The once-a-week list

This list features those jobs that can wait until the weekend or an allocated day of the week. Try to get them out of the way early in the day so you can enjoy some leisure time.

1 Change sheets and pillow slips.

2 Air pillows, doona or quilt covers and blankets.

3 Vacuum or mop the most used rooms in the house.

4 Thoroughly clean the bathroom.

5 Change the towels in the bathroom (this could be done every few days, if you prefer).

Spring clean list

These are the spring clean jobs that can only be left for so long before they demand your attention.

1 Clean out the pantry by getting rid of items that are obviously past their use-by date and wiping over the shelves.

2 Also clean out the fridge and freezer and throw away items past their use-by date. Fill a bucket with warm water and detergent, and thoroughly wipe over fridge and freezer interiors, including the shelves.

3 Clean the stovetop and oven. Use a toothbrush to scrub around any hard to get to grooves.

4 Clear out the bathroom cabinets and discard items past their use-by date.

5 Air mattresses and flip them over when you return them to the bed base.

Days of the week

You might prefer to tackle one room a day or one major task a day.

By room

- Monday: kitchen
- Tuesday: bathroom(s)
- Wednesday: bedrooms
- Thursday: living areas
- Friday: study
- Saturday: laundry
- Sunday: take a break

By task

- Monday: dust
- Tuesday: vacuum
- Wednesday: mop, and wipe over all cabinet handles
- Thursday: change sheets
- Friday: wash, dry and iron clothes
- Saturday: clean toilet, bath and sink
- Sunday: take a break

Cleaning products

Here's a list of essential cleaning products.

- General purpose 'spray on and wipe off' cleaner for bench tops, floors, the stovetop, oven, bathroom

- Smooth all-purpose cleansing paste for spot cleaning, pots and pans, the stovetop, stainless steel sink, bathtub
- Furniture polish
- Glass cleaner (either buy one or make your own with vinegar diluted in water — 1 dessertspoon to 500 mL (1 pt) water; use it in a plastic spray bottle)
- Dishwashing liquid
- Dishwasher powder and rinse aid
- Toilet cleaner (biodegradable with vinegar)
- Disinfectant for floors, toilet bowls, sinks, walls
- Bleach for bathroom and laundry use
- Laundry soaker for nappies and hard to remove stains (check label on clothing before soaking)
- Laundry powder

Note: Keep all cleaning products locked safely away and out of the reach of children.

Hints for a clean kitchen

Food preparation areas must be kept spotlessly clean in order to discourage the growth of bacteria.

- Always wash knives, cutting boards and surfaces with hot water and soap before, during and after food preparation,

Cleaning tools checklist

* Plastic caddy for carrying around cleaning products and sponges (this saves you backtracking to the kitchen or laundry and is an invaluable investment)

* Solid, reliable vacuum cleaner with good suction

* Broom with plastic bristles

* Mop

* Squeegee (for the bathroom)

* Mop bucket

* Recyclable cotton rags

* Scourers

* Multipurpose sponges (however, these collect bacteria; as an alternative use a wash cloth that can be washed and reused)

* Rubber latex gloves

* Pots and pans brush

* Bottlebrush for baby's bottles and other narrow items

* Toothbrush for cleaning out grooves in the stovetop and around tap fittings

especially after handling raw meat (whether poultry, red meat or seafood).

■ Keep cooked and any ready-to-eat foods separate from raw meats and their juices. Use separate chopping boards for bread, meat, fish, and fruit and vegetables.

■ Every day thoroughly wipe down food preparation areas after each use.

■ Regularly clean under moveable appliances such as toasters and blenders, and try to clean under the fridge or stove (if it is moveable) whenever possible.

■ Clean up food spills promptly.

■ Keep all perishable food products in sealed containers.

■ Mop the kitchen floor every couple of days and give it a wipe over or sweep every day to remove food particles.

Hints for a clean bathroom

- Rinse out the shower recess or bathtub after each use. This prevents the build-up of grime and soap scum.
- Always wipe around the base of the toilet bowl.
- Use disinfectant to kill germs. Pour a capful into the sink or toilet bowl. Dilute disinfectant in a bucket of warm water and use it to mop the floor.
- Change towels frequently.
- Wash the window curtains in salt water solution before hanging them. This helps prevent mildew.
- Wash shower curtains regularly to avoid the build-up of mould and grime.
- Make sure the bathroom is well ventilated.
- Do a thorough clean of the bathroom once a week.

'Green' cleaning

If your baby is sensitive to dust or suffers from eczema, shop for environmentally friendly, preferably unscented, cleaning products. They usually contain ingredients our great-grandmothers relied upon to keep a clean house: borax, Epsom salts, sodium bicarbonate (also known as bicarbonate of soda or baking soda), cream of tartar, vinegar and lemon.

Instead of using a dry duster, which tends to scatter the dust into the air and redistribute it elsewhere, try a 'wet' duster.

1 Fill a bucket with warm water.

2 Wet and wring out a multipurpose sponge or wash cloth and wipe over the area to be dusted — along the rims of architraves, over the tops of dressing tables, around window frames and along window ledges. This wet method captures dust, hair and other particles.

3 Rinse dust particles off the sponge.

Some uses for natural cleaning products

Here are several ways to use old-fashioned, environmentally friendly cleaning products around the house.

In the laundry

Epsom salts. This works as a fabric softener. Just add 1 tablespoon of Epsom salts to the rinse cycle.

Vinegar. Add ⅓ cup of vinegar to the rinse cycle to brighten whites.

Bicarbonate of soda. Soak dirty white socks in diluted bicarbonate of soda to help bring back the brightness (1 tablespoon bicarb to 5 L or 8¾ pt water). (Try a slice of lemon in a bucket of water for the same result.)

Cream of tartar. Replace bleach with cream of tartar. Mix 2 teaspoons of cream of tartar into 4 L (7 pt) of hot water. Leave clothes to soak overnight.

In the kitchen

Bicarbonate of soda. A multipurpose cleaning product, bicarb is a natural scourer which can be used in paste form to clean pans, sinks and benchtops. Mix it into a paste with a little water to polish the glass on the oven door. To clean the oven interior, apply the paste to the area to be cleaned, turn the oven on to low heat to dry, then remove the dry paste with a scourer. Pour 1 cup of bicarb into your kitchen bin and 2 cups into the waste disposal bin to get rid of nasty odours. To help clean drains, add 1 tablespoon of bicarb to ½ cup of vinegar. Or clean drains with this combination: 1 cup of bicarb, 1 cup of salt, ¼ cup of cream of tartar. Place all the ingredients into a sealed jar and mix thoroughly. Pour ¼ cup down the drain, and immediately add 4 L (7 pt) of boiling water. Leave for one minute before turning on the cold tap. Store the ingredients in a dry place, out of the reach of children.

Vinegar. Add 1 teaspoon of vinegar to a sink full of dishwater, and use it diluted in warm water for cleaning benchtops and glass (1 dessertspoon vinegar to 500 mL (1 pt) water).

In the bathroom

Bicarbonate of soda. Make bicarbonate of soda into a paste, using a little water. Apply the paste to bathroom surfaces with a clean cloth for a fresh result. It can also be used to clean the toilet bowl. Combine it with equal parts of borax and vinegar. Pour the solution around the inside of the toilet bowl, leave it for a few minutes, then flush.

Lemon. For light stains on the sink, rub over with half a fresh lemon. If the stains are stubborn, make a paste of borax and lemon juice and rub it onto the affected area. Leave for ten minutes and rinse off.

Bleach. If you're going away on holidays, pour ½ cup of bleach into the toilet bowl and leave it there until you return (do not use bleach if a tank cleaner is attached to the bowl's interior as the chemicals may react).

How to wash your hands

Use soap and warm running water while washing your hands. Wash for 20–30 seconds, scrubbing the backs of your hands, in between the fingers, under the fingernails and up the wrists. Ideally, dry your hands with a disposable paper towel or, if you're concerned about the environment, with a clean cloth towel.

You should also wash your hands after going to the toilet, changing a nappy, sneezing, coughing, wiping someone's nose, touching sores or skin lacerations, handling animals and pets, changing kitty litter, handling money, touching dirty work surfaces, taking out the garbage, gardening, smoking, drinking or eating, and before handling food.

Always wash your hands vigorously before you eat and insist that other people at the table follow your example.

Vinegar. Wipe soap scum from glass shower doors using a sponge or wash cloth dipped in vinegar.

Personal hygiene

Your good personal hygiene habits influence the rest of your family. To reduce the spread of bacteria, pathogens and viruses causing diseases and food-borne illnesses, always wash and dry your hands thoroughly before, during and after preparing food. When you are preparing meat and then vegetables, wash your hands properly after touching the meat so you won't transfer germs to fruit and vegetables which may be eaten raw.

Effective methods of stain removal

Once you have a baby, you discover a whole new world of stains! The secret is to attend to the stain immediately, before it has time to set. You can either buy products that promise to remove stains (such as nappy presoakers), or try some of the methods outlined here. First spot test the fabric and check the washing instructions on the garment before using them on cotton, wool and linen. Be extra careful if you decide to apply them to synthetics.

Blood. Rinse the stain in cold water, as hot water causes the stain to set. If the colour in the fabric doesn't run, try soaking the stained part in diluted bleach. Or soak the garment in cold water with salt added.

Chocolate. If the chocolate is runny, remove it with soap and water. If it has hardened, scrape off as much as you can and remove the rest with soap and water, or sponge vinegar diluted in cold water onto the stain before rinsing the garment in cold water.

Crayon, indelible marker. Dab lightly with methylated spirits before washing as usual.

Egg. Scrape away as much as possible of the egg. Rinse in cold water. Or try smearing the stain with a paste of cream of tartar and water, with one crushed aspirin added to the paste. Leave for 30 minutes. Rinse in cold water.

Fruit. Rinse the stain immediately with cold water. Then sponge with white vinegar or a paste of borax and warm water, before washing as usual. For fruit juice, smear the stain with a paste of cream of tartar and water. Leave for 30 minutes then rinse well in cold water.

Grass. Sponge the stain with methylated spirits and rinse with cold water. You could also try sponging with vinegar. After washing, dry the garment in the sun.

Grease. Soak the garment in a bucket of hot water diluted with ammonia (be careful of the fumes if you are sensitive, and don't do this with your child nearby). Another option is to place the fabric on an absorbent cloth and sprinkle the stain with cornstarch, which absorbs grease. Wash the garment as usual.

Ice cream, butter and milk. Sponge washable fabrics with lukewarm water, then wash them in warm soapy water (check the care instructions to make sure the fabric shouldn't be washed in cold water only).

Ink. Soak the stain in sour milk (use fresh milk if sour is not available). Alternatively, try sponging the stain with equal quantities of methylated spirits and household ammonia (but be careful of the fumes as they are strong). Rinse in warm water, rinse again in warm water containing a little ammonia, and give a final rinse in fresh warm water. If you don't like the idea of using ammonia, simply sponge on methylated spirits before rinsing the garment in warm water.

Mud. Let the mud dry, then brush it off. Soak the garment in a liquid detergent or a paste made of dry detergent and water. Wash as usual (preferably in warm water).

Pencil. Use a clean soft rubber or eraser to rub off the marks.

Urine and faeces. Scrape the faeces off the garment into the toilet bowl. Place garments stained with urine or faeces in a bucket of lukewarm water diluted with bleach. Leave overnight. An alternative is to soak stained items in a solution of 2 teaspoons of cream of tartar in 4 L (7 pt) of hot water. Leave to soak overnight, then wash as usual.

Old stains. Try softening with glycerine. Dampen the stain, rub in some glycerine and leave for one to four hours (depending on the severity of the stain). Then add a few drops of vinegar and leave for five to ten minutes. Rinse well.

Teething

A baby's teeth are completely formed in the gums at birth. The health of a baby's teeth when she is born has been determined by both the mother's diet and health when she was pregnant.

About 1 in 100 babies is born with teeth. These are early primary, or first, teeth and are called natal teeth. Little yellowy bumps on a baby's gums are sometimes mistaken for teeth; these are known as Epstein's pearls.

There are 20 first teeth and the first to appear are the middle teeth, known as the central incisors, with the two at the bottom being followed by the two at the top. In the average baby, this happens at around six months of age; however, it can happen much earlier or even as late as around a child's first birthday.

Symptoms of teething

Teething has been blamed for all kinds of ills, but the normal symptom of teething is sore gums. These can make a child irritable, dribble frequently and sleep poorly. Teething does not cause diarrhoea or vomiting. If your child is suffering from either of these symptoms she needs to see a doctor. Teething can cause a mild earache: the child may pull at her ears because the lower jaw and teeth share the same nerve as the ear canal. All signs of earache should be checked by a doctor. Teething does not cause a rash on the cheeks — this is more likely to be mild eczema — or fever.

When baby bites

Once a breastfed baby has three or four teeth she is quite likely to bite her mother's nipple, not because there is any evil intent — a baby is not capable of that — but because she has not yet learnt how to use her teeth. For some mothers the biting is so painful that they decide to wean, but this does not have to be the case. A baby will only gnaw on her mother's nipple during a break or at the end of a feed, so be vigilant during a feed and take baby off the nipple before she bites.

Biting can also occur when your baby has a stuffy nose, when she is restless or really doesn't want to feed, or when your supply of milk is slow.

Teething remedies

The best remedies for relieving the discomforts of teething are teething rusks and rings. If your child needs pain relief, use paracetamol according to directions. Occasionally, a local anaesthetic teething gel may help, although it's best to use these sparingly.

From the time your baby's teeth first appear, you need to take cleaning her teeth very seriously. In fact, even before her teeth come through, from around four months, you can accustom her to having her teeth cleaned. Sit baby on your lap facing away from you, gently tilt her head back so you can see her mouth and rub her gums with your clean finger. If she is starting to teethe, she will find this soothing.

After she has grown used to this, use a soft, clean washer instead of your finger and then progress to a soft baby toothbrush. Toothpaste is not necessary until a child is around 12 to 18 months old and the unusual taste, even of junior toothpaste, may put her off the whole process.

Sleeping

By the age of about four to six months, a child is most likely to have developed a regular sleep–wake rhythm; ideally, the ten- to 12-hour sleep will be at night. Of course, daytime naps will still be a part of her routine. Most children require two naps a day at this age.

It is important that parents realize that a child who sleeps through the night is still going to wake at times. Ideally, she will be able to go back to sleep without disturbing her parents but she may well need 'settling'. A survey of Australian parents found that only 50 per cent of babies were sleeping through the night by six months, and that half of these babies regressed and began waking again at night.

It is around this time too that many parents think their child has sleep problems, and they may well be right. However, it is important to think about your child's development before you decide you have a problem. At around the age of six or seven months most babies are sitting up, some are beginning to move about, and they find life and the world around them constantly fascinating and intriguing. They are learning new skills all the time and sleep may not come as easily as it did when they were younger. A soothing bedtime routine may be even more important now than it was before.

Children have problems settling at night for a number of reasons and if parents are aware of the causes they may be able to prevent problems arising or use strategies to overcome the problems (see 'Sleeping' in 'Birth to six months' on page 97).

Night waking

Every baby in this age group will wake up during the night at some point. Some babies will wake more frequently and take longer to settle than others, and for a few their wakefulness at night will cause problems. Some of these babies may not be getting the attention they need during the day, and their night wakings are a way of compensating for this. Babies who are held and cuddled a lot during the day, often with the help of a baby sling, will usually sleep well at night.

Babies who are used to a ritual — which includes physical contact such as feeding, stroking or rocking in order to get to sleep — will usually need these rituals again in the middle of the night in order to go back to sleep. You should try to avoid this happening. You need to end the going to sleep routine with something that does not involve touching and encourages baby to go to sleep on her own. (See 'Daytime naps' below.)

However, this may not happen easily as a baby may need the closeness of you, particularly if you are leading a busy life that means limited daytime contact.

Perseverance with a routine, rather than chopping and changing, is far more likely to result in a baby who sleeps; in other words, be patient and give your baby time to adjust to the new bedtime ritual.

Daytime naps

Parenting is a time of constant adjustment, and it is the adults who are aware of this and adjust their own expectations who enjoy parenting the most. Some babies will nap for 15 or 20 minutes, others for three hours. These daytime naps need to be at about the same time each day, so it is worth continuing to put your baby into her cot for her nap even when you suspect she won't sleep. She may play happily for ten or 15 minutes, and this quiet time on her own helps her to develop self-sufficiency. She may fall asleep anyway. If after 15 minutes she is still awake and grizzling, it is wise to get her up, as a cot can easily become a cage if it is used to contain an unhappy baby.

Between the ages of six and nine months your baby develops the ability to keep herself awake and she can also be kept awake by an exciting or interesting environment. No longer will she fall asleep because she is tired, regardless of her surroundings. This means a baby can become overtired. It also means that there will be times when you will have difficulty getting your child to sleep. In this three- to four-month period anything different can upset sleep

A cot for baby

It might be tempting to buy a secondhand cot for your baby, especially where money is an issue. However, there is often no way you can check the history of a pre-owned cot, and most come without instructions. Because safety standards for cots in many countries are constantly under revision, your secondhand cot may be out-of-date and may therefore pose a potential safety risk to your child.

Most cot injuries are caused by children falling while trying to climb out of their cot. Other injuries occur when a child's head, arms and legs become caught between bars and panels, or her clothing gets stuck on protruding parts.

See 'Straight into a cot?' on page 26 for information on what to look for in a cot before you buy, and follow these tips to ensure your baby's cot, and the surrounding environment, is safe.

* If you have no alternative other than to buy a secondhand cot, thoroughly check it out by referring to the standards set by the consumers' association in your area, or by contacting your government department of fair trading for information on safety standards for cots.

* Even if the cot is new, make frequent safety checks for signs of wear. Remove or repair peeling paint and any stickers that the child could swallow and choke on.

* Move the base on an adjustable cot to its lowest setting as soon as your child can sit up by herself.

* Keep the cot away from windows, heaters and power points.

* Remove items your child can climb up on such as large toys, cot bumpers and V- and U-shaped cushions (these shouldn't be in a cot in the first place as they contribute to SIDS).

* For the same reasons, don't place pillows, comforters, sheepskins, electric blankets or hot water bottles in a baby or child's cot.

* Make sure that if it has castors they are only on two of the legs.

* Do not leave mobiles or toys with stretch elastic in a cot.

routines. Visitors coming to stay, a holiday away, being sick, moving into a bigger bed, one parent being away for a long period — all are common triggers of disrupted sleeping habits for babies of this age.

At around the age of eight to ten months a baby also becomes aware that the important people in her life go away from her sometimes. She does not know that they will come back and she can become extremely distressed whenever her most important carer or carers leave her, even if it is only to go into the next room. This too can be a cause of unhappiness at bedtime. (See 'Separation anxiety' on page 184.)

Child psychologist Penelope Leach suggests gently easing a baby of this age into getting used to her cot and going to sleep in it, even if until now she may have slept in your bed.[3] Establishing a gentle wind-down routine, which can be carried through the toddler and preschool years, shows you are serious about bedtime.

The bedtime routine might begin with a bath, followed by a quiet time together reading a story, singing songs or playing gentle finger or toe games. When baby is in her cot you could dim the bedroom light or turn on a night-light while you sing another song or two. Some babies like a gentle pat or stroke, but this should be followed by you spending some time in the room but not touching baby. Some parents sing themselves out of the room, leaving a CD or cassette to carry on singing to their baby.

During this time of learning to give in to sleep, some babies will turn to sucking a finger or thumb for comfort, while others may turn to a blanket or soft toy or use both. Some babies do not need these comforters, but a baby who does will often develop an independent way of putting herself to sleep.

Development

In the next six months your baby will make great strides. She may not be walking but she will certainly be getting about in some fashion. She will start to make talking noises and may have one or two words by her first birthday; she will certainly understand a lot of what you are saying. Your baby will love to play with you, and will enjoy being among people, although if you leave her she is likely to be most upset. She will laugh and pull faces, she will eat solid food, and if you give her the opportunity, she will drink from a cup. By the time she reaches her first birthday, your baby will have become a toddler.

Sitting

Many babies will sit, albeit in a rather wobbly fashion, from around six months, but others won't do so until they are nine months.

Being able to sit unsupported is due to strong neck muscles. Once her neck muscles are strong enough for her to hold her head off the floor when she is lying on her tummy, a baby's muscle control will develop in her upper back. She will enjoy being propped up so she can see more of the world. A portable baby chair is the ideal way to do this, as you can carry it from room to room with you and it provides baby with much better support than a pile of cushions. Of course, it is important to use the safety harness when using a portable chair.

Baby will love being pulled to a sitting position: as her neck strength grows, you will be able to gently pull her into a sitting position when she is lying on her back. She is unlikely to stay there and will probably fall to one side, so be ready to catch her.

Crawling

It is not crucial that babies crawl before they walk. Up to 25 per cent of babies will not crawl at all. Some may sit until they are ready to walk, and others will adopt a form of shuffling on their bottoms to get themselves around. Crawling also has little impact

on walking, and neither crawling nor walking are related to intelligence. 'Clever' babies do not walk earlier than their peers. It is a myth that learning to crawl is important for developing future skills.

A baby who is put on the floor to play on her tummy for some time each day learns first to raise her head in a 'turtle' fashion and then to push up on her arms. The next skill your baby may learn is to stick her bottom up in the air when she pushes down on her feet, but she still has much to learn. A baby needs to develop balance, control and coordination, together with the arm and opposite leg movements that crawling requires before she is ready to move off. Skills that the baby has already mastered, such as rolling over or pushing up on both hands, have strengthened the necessary muscles.

Some babies object to tummy time, and for these babies crawling or moving about will come as a natural progression from sitting. If your baby does not like being put down on her tummy, then you will probably find she is happy with a baby chair or bouncer.

Generally, babies who are going to use this form of locomotion will learn to crawl between eight and ten months. Rarely will a baby crawl before six months, although she may look like she is going to. At first your baby may just rock back and forth. By this stage she has the strength to bear weight on her hands and knees, but her brain has not developed to the stage where it can produce the complex motor sequences required to propel her forward. This could take up to a month.

When a baby has been sitting unsupported for a while it may seem like she is going to crawl at any time, particularly if something out of her reach has caught her eye. At around the age of eight months, babies develop what is known as object permanence, which means they know that things exist even if they can't see them. This is what drives them to look for a toy you have hidden behind your back, or for the toy car you put under a bucket. This ability gives a baby the sophisticated reasoning powers she needs to focus on reaching a target.

Once she starts to crawl she may find herself going backwards and not towards the thing she wants to reach. This is enormously frustrating for the baby and only makes her more determined to go forwards, which she will do in a very short time. All you and other carers need to do is provide a safe and comfortable environment in which your baby can learn to crawl, as well as plenty of opportunities for her to practise. You cannot 'teach' a baby to crawl.

There is no difference between how boys and girls learn to crawl. A study in the United States found that mothers believed that boys were better at crawling than girls and better at making decisions about crawling down slopes. However, when this theory was tested with a group of eleven-month-old babies, the girls and boys performed identically.[4]

Experts are not sure why some babies do not crawl but instead either find some other form of locomotion or simply go from sitting to pulling themselves up to standing. Of the babies who do crawl, large babies may crawl later than small babies because of the weight they have to carry around. Babies who are shy or nervous may also not crawl until around their first birthday. Babies who live in cold climates and must be dressed in thick heavy clothes will crawl later than babies who wear nothing, or next to nothing, most of the time.

When a baby is concentrating on developing her mobility, you may notice that the development of other skills such as language has slowed down. While learning to crawl is physically exhausting, it is also mentally challenging so this can also be a time when your baby wakes at night again. If this happens, baby needs to know that you are there, and that she will be comforted and helped back to sleep.

Helping your baby with crawling

Although you can't teach a baby how to crawl, you can help in other ways.

- Check out your home and try to anticipate any dangers (see 'Preparing your home for a baby on the move' on page 156).
- Fix the dangers you have identified (again, see 'Preparing your home for a baby on the move'). Also, consider possible new hazards. Have you left your briefcase open on the floor? Or has Grandma just put her handbag down? Is the dog eating its dinner nearby?
- Protect baby's knees. Dress your baby in a stretch suit, or pants which go to her ankles, so that she has some protection from hard floors. Some baby pants even have pads on the knees.
- Never leave your baby alone. You never know what she might find.
- If baby does find something dangerous or something you would rather she didn't have, swap it for something attractive but safe, such as a wooden spoon or a set of measuring spoons.
- Don't worry about a bit of dirt. Moving around on her hands and knees is bound to result in grubbiness, even in the cleanest of houses. Dress baby in practical 'play' clothes so she can explore in comfort.
- Once baby is moving, you can hold out your arms and call to her. She will love crawling into your lap.

Standing

As a baby's muscle control moves down her body so she learns new skills. After she has learnt to sit and crawl she will learn to stand, but first she needs to have muscle control of her back and hips.

Babies love to practise 'standing' from a very early age. If you hold your baby by the hands on your lap so that she faces you, she will start to do 'stand-ups'. This usually happens around the age of four or five months — long before baby will be ready to pull herself to standing. Babies love this game and want to play it every time they are held on a lap. They will also enjoy spending a little time each day in a baby jumper — one of those little seats that can be clipped in a doorway, giving baby a chance to test out those leg muscles.

The first part of real standing comes when baby has control of the muscles in her knees and feet. You will be able to pull her to a standing position, and she will appear to stay there, just as she did when she first sat. But if you let go she will fall over; she still has to learn to balance. The next step is to pull herself to standing while holding on to furniture. Now you need to be sure that the furniture in her environment, most likely your family room, is not going to tip over. Sturdy chairs and low tables are fine, but anything spindly or lightweight is better moved to another room, as baby is likely to practise her standing moves at any time and you may not be watching.

Baby walkers

There is growing concern among baby safety experts about the safety of baby walkers. In some countries there have been calls to ban them because of the number of injuries that can be directly attributed to their use.

These injuries happen to babies under the age of 12 months and are often to the head. A baby in a walker can move at a far greater speed than she can under her own steam. Accidents occur when a baby in a walker propels herself across a room and careens into a piece of furniture or part of the room. Worse accidents occur when baby and walker fall down stairs or over the edge of a landing or ledge. For these reasons a baby in a baby walker needs to be supervised every moment she is in it.

Your baby doesn't need walkers. She's much better off exploring at her own pace as her physical skills develop. A walker won't help your baby to walk and may even slow down her development by teaching her actions that are not part of natural development.

Discipline and the mobile baby

Parents want their babies to be happy, to be well behaved and to be liked by others. You do not want to spoil your baby, but be aware that you will often receive conflicting advice about discipline at this age.

Babies who feel secure and whose needs are met will grow into independent and lovable little people: this is the best discipline they can get. By the time a baby has reached the second half of her first year she can certainly understand 'no' and will start to cooperate with adults. However, she cannot cope with an adult's anger when she doesn't cooperate because she simply cannot understand why the adult is angry. If she is punished, she will not understand why that is happening either. Child psychologist Penelope Leach claims that babies of this age who do things that make parents angry or upset are being punished for being babies.[3] Your baby cannot understand the difference between tipping a peg bucket on the floor and tipping her dinner on the floor. Once you know and accept this, you will be better equipped to cope with your child doing the 'wrong' thing. The best discipline for a baby of this age is love and hugs as well as making every attempt to prevent and divert disasters.

Playpens and safety gates

A playpen is a great way to be sure a baby is kept confined in a safe environment and very reassuring for busy parents, but it is not ideal for babies. While a baby is immobile a playpen may have its uses, such as keeping pets away from baby, storing baby's toys in one place and keeping baby away from you while you are engaged in a potentially dangerous activity such as ironing. Why don't you stand in the playpen while you iron? You can also use a playpen to protect items of furniture that you want to keep away from baby.

However, immobile babies don't need playpens and neither do mobile ones. Immobile babies who are penned in usually quickly learn that the best way to get attention is to throw things out of the playpen and then call you to put them back. Mobile babies will very quickly be frustrated by not being able to explore and will soon come to hate the sight of the playpen.

For those who think they may need a playpen occasionally, so they can run to the telephone or tend to a meal, a travelling cot that doubles as a playpen is probably the best choice. For others, gates protect baby while giving her the freedom to explore. These are adjustable so they will fit in most doorways and will allow you to move from room to room without too much trouble.

Separation anxiety

Another major development in the second year of a child's life is separation anxiety. Up until the age of six months or so, your baby is likely to be nice to everyone and she delights in the company of her parents. At some point though this delight will turn to anxiety the moment you leave her. At first this is heart-warming — your baby loves you. But it can become very frustrating not to be able to leave her, even for a moment, without her falling to pieces. She is not doing this to make you feel miserable, she simply has not yet learnt that you will come back.

If your child is in daycare or a nursery, this can be particularly difficult. If she already knows the day carer, then it may not be much of a problem, but if you introduce a baby to a new carer at this age, even if it is her grandmother, the partings can be fraught with anguish on both sides. The best you can do is prepare your baby for your leaving, never sneak away, and greet her upon your return. Be sure that she is well cared for (maybe even make the occasional surprise early return or visit), and then rest assured that she will move onto the next stage in time.

Fun, games and learning

By the time baby reaches the second half of her first year she will be responsive to the people around her as well as her surroundings, and the games you can play with her will provide lots of fun for you both.

Exercise and play

Your baby will continue to love music, words and movement. Babies learn through repetition and your baby will love you to repeat things over and over again. As you are playing with baby she will be learning all the time. You can incorporate some games into your daily activities.

- If you are using household appliances, talk to baby about the sounds they make and point to them as you talk.
- When you are changing baby's nappy or clothes, include a game of 'peek-a-boo'.
- Read the newspaper, letter, email or a book aloud so baby can hear your voice.
- When someone familiar comes to visit, ask baby, 'Where is [Grandma]?'
- If your favourite song comes on the radio, pick baby up, and sing and dance with her.
- When you take baby on an outing, talk to her about what you can see — a bus, a dog, a tree, autumn leaves, the sound of a bird — and point to things. You will find you get a new appreciation of the world around you as well.
- In the kitchen have a bottom drawer or cupboard filled with household objects that are safe for baby to play with, such as plastic storage boxes, wooden spoons, pegs, pots with lids, an egg whisk. This collection will provide baby with hours of fun right where you can see her.
- As baby starts to eat family food, let her experiment. If she wants to feed herself, try to let her. This is how children learn to eat, and they need to make a mess in the process, so be prepared.

Games to play with your baby

Take time to play with baby two or three times a day at least.

- Put a nappy or small towel on the floor and place a toy on it. Show baby how to reach the toy by pulling the towel.

- Draw a happy face on one side of a wooden spoon and a sad one on the other side. Give baby a little puppet show or sing 'If You're Happy and You Know It Clap Your Hands'.

- When baby is sitting in her highchair, tie a few toys or household items onto the highchair with a length of elastic. Show baby how to pull them up when they fall down. (Be sure to take the elastic off when baby is not in the highchair as she may pull them down on herself.)

- Put a funnel and a couple of plastic cups in the bath with baby and show her how to pour.

When baby can move about, try these games.

- Play hide and seek. Hide nearby behind a piece of furniture and call out baby's name until she finds you.

- Get down on your hands and knees, and play 'I'm Going To Get You' as you crawl towards baby.

- Give baby the chance to play outside in the grass. Be sure to supervise her and talk about what she finds.

- Put pillows on the floor and encourage baby to crawl over them.

- Have a non-breakable or firmly fixed mirror at floor level. Baby will be fascinated by her own image.

Games to play with the older baby

- Play clapping games and naming games: 'Put Your Finger on Your Nose', 'Head and Shoulders, Knees and Toes'.

- Have a toy box in every room where baby plays. Encourage baby to put the toys in as well as take them out. Make a game of taking out and putting in.

- Put an empty cardboard box on the floor and encourage baby to push it around and put things in it.

- Have a large piece of paper and a few fat crayons, and show baby how to scribble.

- Put a toy car on a low table and push it towards baby. Show her how to push it back. Put the toy car in a long cardboard tube and show baby how it comes out the other end.

- Be sure to read baby at least one story every day.

Toys for the toy box

Moving about and exploring the world, the people about them and their own bodies is more important than toys for this age group. Many of the things that children of this age enjoy playing with are not toys: kitchen implements such as wooden spoons, brown paper bags, wrapping paper, face washers and sponges, mugs and funnels, your car keys and a leaf on the ground will all prove to be interesting and fun.

Putting things in and out of other objects is as much as fun as playing with the objects. Some days baby will seem more interested in dropping her toys, so you can pick them up and put them into a basket, than actually doing anything with them — this is all fun for her.

So when you are unpacking shopping or unwrapping presents or about to throw away a cardboard tube, consider whether these things may be safe for baby to play with. At this age babies love novelty.

Toys for this age group include:

* Posting toys

* Heavy cloth or plastic books with large bright pictures

* Balls of different sizes, soft and hard, balls that jingle and balls that rattle

* Chunky movables such as little cars on plastic wheels

* Large soft blocks

* Musical toys such as drums

* Toy telephone, toy key ring

* Stacking rings

* Simple puzzles with large pieces

* Buckets, cups, mugs and floating bath toys

* Stuffed toys

Toy safety checklist

Toys can and do injure children, so before you buy or give your child a toy, think of these safety points.

Does it have sharp edges or rough surfaces? These could give your baby a cut or splinter.

Is it washable?

How breakable is it?

Is it age suitable? Read what the label says. Giving a child toys that are meant for older children will not help her development; she is more likely to be bored, and the toys could be dangerous to this age group.

Are there loose parts? These could be choking dangers. If the toy fits into a 35 mm film canister, it is too small for a child under three.

Are there gaps or holes? Check there are no gaps where a finger might get trapped.

Does it make loud noises? Even some toys meant for babies have a squeak that can damage a child's hearing. If in doubt, don't offer it.

One to two years

In the first year your baby grew amazingly and learnt many new skills. By his first birthday, he will be mobile. He may not be walking but he will certainly be able to get about in some way. He will have boundless curiosity, and your life will change as you reorganize your home and baby's environment to accommodate him.

How your child grows

While some babies develop their physical skills faster than babies of the same age, others will develop their social skills or their mental skills faster. Your baby has his own personality and will develop his skills at his own speed with you as carer, supervisor and fellow playmate. If you are at all worried about your child's development, seek professional advice and reassurance.

Development checklist

**Date you noticed
your child doing it**

Can say between eight and 20 words you can understand

Uses expressions such as 'uh-oh'

Can make you understand what he wants by pointing or saying one word

Will identify a simple picture in a book

Plays 'peek-a-boo' for hours

Can understand and follow simple instructions, such as 'Find your shoes'

Likes taking things apart

May be very unhappy if separated from main caregiver
(this is more likely in children who are mainly cared for by one person)

Likes giving you objects

Will play alone for a little while with toys or things from the kitchen cupboard

Recognizes himself in photos and in the mirror

Enjoys sitting on your lap for a story

Will copy sounds such as animal noises

Loves an audience, especially if they clap!

Moves about well

Can stand alone and sit down

Likes pushing and pulling things

Takes off hats and socks

Likes to carry something when walking

Will roll a ball when asked to

Can turn the pages of a book

Stacks one block on top of another

Can hold crayons and scribble

Likes to hold his own spoon when eating but has trouble using it

Likes closing doors and pushing buttons

Walks without help

Waves goodbye

Claps hands

Development checklist

Around 24 months

**Date you noticed
your child doing it**

His vocabulary has grown to a few hundred words

[ ]

Speaks in sentences of two or three words — for example,
'Max have apple'

[ ]

Talks to himself

[ ]

Has favourite toys

[ ]

Likes to 'sing'

[ ]

Enjoys simple rhymes and finger games

[ ]

Will say 'please' or 'thank you' when prompted

[ ]

Likes to copy you

[ ]

Will say 'no' and shows other signs of independence

[ ]

Finds it difficult to share

[ ]

Patience is not a skill he has learnt yet — he wants things now!

[ ]

Gets angry and frustrated, and has tantrums

[ ]

Will act shy

[ ]

Comforts someone who is distressed or pretending to be distressed

[ ]

Refers to himself by his name

[ ]

Enjoys picture book stories

[ ]

Tries to do things by himself

[ ]

Likes simple pretend play, such as dressing up, playing with
a doll or talking on a phone

[ ]

Has difficulty remembering rules

[ ]

Can get aggressive when frustrated and may hit or pull hair

[ ]

Likes running but isn't as good at stopping

[ ]

Can drink through a straw

[ ]

Feeds himself with a spoon

[ ]

Is learning to wash his hands

[ ]

Has endless curiosity and will get into anything and everything

[ ]

Is able to stack up to four blocks

[ ]

Can throw a ball

Opens doors, drawers, cupboards

Can bend over and pick up a toy without falling over

Walks up steps with help but needs to be taught how to come down again!

Feeding

Your child needs food that provides energy and essential nutrients for good health and vitality. If you introduce him to a wide range of healthy foods from the major food groups now, he will become used to variety in his diet, and you are less likely to end up with a fussy eater. By making the best choices for your child now, you are paving the way for his healthy and active future.

A healthy diet

It can get very complicated trying to work out a balanced diet, particularly for a young child. It is better to stick to a few basic guidelines. When you are preparing a meal, it will save time if you make your toddler's food part of the family meal. Once you get into the habit of doing this, life will be much easier. You can use these simple principles in all the recipes you cook for the family.

Fresh food — the fresher the better. In many societies women shop each day for their family's food. That can be difficult if you live in an isolated area or do not have access to a wide variety of good shops that stock fresh foods, but you can still hold the concept of fresh food as your aim. There are dozens of ways to do this. For example, make your own pasta sauces instead of using store-bought sauces in jars, and stew your own fruit for fruit desserts instead of using frozen apple pies. When you prepare the food yourself, you know exactly what it contains.

Low animal fat. This doesn't mean low-fat foods. Toddlers need fat in their diets, unless they are extremely overweight (in which case they need a diet designed by a dietitian). Chicken without the skin is low in fat. Lean cuts of meat are the best source of iron, and zinc, another key nutrient in lean meat, is particularly important in a toddler's diet. Avoid processed meats, such as salami and corned beef, which are also high in salt.

Little or no salt. You can add salt to your own meal using chutneys, sauces and pickles, or you can add salt to the pot after you have served your child's portion. But don't add salt, in any form, to your child's food. You can't always tell which processed foods are high in

salt. For example, a bowl of cornflakes has more salt than a small packet of potato chips. By sticking to the fresh food rule and looking for salt-reduced foods or foods with no salt, you will be able to keep your child's salt intake down. Many traditional societies eat no salt, apart from that which occurs naturally in food.

Little or no added sugar. It's sad but true: we don't really need to eat any sugar at all! The problem is that sugar appeals to the tastebuds. There are, however, ways to avoid adding it to the foods we prepare, leaving it to the adults at the table to add their own, if they prefer. Don't let them do it in front of your child, as he will have trouble understanding why Grandma can have four teaspoons of sugar in her drink while he's not allowed any! Foods high in sugar include sweetened fruit juices (as an alternative squeeze your own fresh juice), soft drinks, flavoured mineral water, ice cream, chocolate, biscuits, health food bars and some breakfast cereals.

At this young age, it is best not to ask your child what he feels like eating or drinking, as he will only become confused and might not provide the answer you want. But it is a good idea to let him 'graze' on small nutritious snacks throughout the day. Never try to feed him when he is overly tired, and limit his intake of drinks, other than water, between meals.

Snacks for any time of day

Here are some nutritious ideas for snacks your child will enjoy.

- Fresh fruit cut into bite-sized pieces: kiwi fruit (Chinese gooseberries), bananas, watermelon, pears, rockmelon, strawberries
- Raisin toast with a smear of margarine
- Pikelets, plain or with jam
- Blueberry muffins (or variations)
- Wholemeal toast fingers or crumpets with melted cheese
- Pita bread, Turkish bread or lavash accompanied by hummus (a chickpea dip) or tahini (sesame seeds and lemon dip) — either make your own dips or buy good quality ones from the supermarket by checking the list of ingredients for preservatives or dairy products

- Cooked and chopped vegetables: zucchini (courgettes), broccoli, carrot, sweet potato, potato
- Frozen orange segments, pineapple rings
- Frozen yoghurts
- Milky freezes (place milk in ice-cube trays and freeze, then remove and serve in a cup)
- Sliced cherry tomatoes accompanied by sticks of cow's cheese or small slices of crumbly fetta cheese
- Wholemeal sandwiches or lavash wraps with a variety of fillings such as mashed egg (avoid if your child has an egg allergy), cheese and tomato, baked beans, canned sandwich tuna and salad
- Bowl of cereal with milk
- Baked potato in its jacket with toppings such as melted cheese or baked beans

Recipes

Here's a selection of recipes your child will enjoy any time of day.

Chezz's banana smoothie

Serves 2

The secret to the success of this smoothie is the preparation of the banana. Apparently the smoothie is thicker and, as a result, more delicious if the banana is peeled and frozen at least half an hour before it is used. Mangoes also work well for this smoothie, either as an accompaniment or added to the smoothie. Or add canned peaches or apricots for a delightful tangy taste.

Ingredients

1 banana

1 dessertspoon plain yoghurt

1 teaspoon honey (optional)

1 medium-sized glass of milk

Method

1 Blend the ingredients until they are thick and creamy.

2 Pour into a glass and serve.

Earl's scrambled eggs

Serves 1–2

Who says you need cream for delicious scrambled eggs? Here, milk is the substitute. Just make sure you don't use too much. Before serving, drain any excess liquid from the frying pan. Serve with toast, toasted crumpet, toasted Turkish bread or toasted English muffin.

Ingredients

1 egg, lightly beaten

Dash of milk

Pinch of chopped fresh chives

5 g (⅙ oz) butter

Method

1 Pour the egg and milk into a mixing bowl, throw in the chives and whisk lightly until just blended.

2 Add the butter to a frying pan. Place pan over medium heat until the butter melts.

3 Pour the egg mixture into the pan and allow it to cook until it just sets around the edges.

4 Gently stir the egg mixture with a wooden spoon until it is firm but creamy.

Jody's muffins

Makes 12 muffins

Muffins are easy and quick to make. Just be careful not to overmix the ingredients or you will toughen up the finished product, which should be light and moist.

Ingredients

1¾ cups plain flour

¼ cup caster sugar

1½ teaspoons baking powder

1 egg

¾ cup milk

85 g (3 oz) margarine, melted

Method

1 Preheat oven to 220°C (425°F). Lightly grease a 12-hole non-stick muffin pan.

2 Sift the flour and baking powder into a large bowl. Add caster sugar and salt (if desired) and combine. Make a well in the centre of the mixture.

3 In a separate smaller bowl, whisk together the melted margarine, milk and egg.

4 Add this to the flour mixture. Fold in gently until the ingredients are just combined (about 30 seconds).

5 Spoon the mixture into the muffin pan.

6 Bake for 15 minutes or until the muffins are golden-topped and spring back when lightly pressed. Turn out onto a wire rack to cool.

Alternatives

1 Use self-raising flour instead of baking powder and plain flour.

2 For cheese muffins, add ½ cup grated cheese before adding liquid.

3 For fruit muffins, add ¼ to ½ cup dried fruit before adding liquid.

Jody's banana muffins

Makes 16 muffins

Ingredients

225 g (8 oz) self-raising wholemeal flour

140 g (5 oz) raw sugar

1 teaspoon baking powder

2 eggs, lightly beaten

½ cup milk

115 g (4 oz) butter, melted

3 small bananas, mashed

Method

1 Preheat oven to 180°C (350°F). Lightly grease a 12-hole non-stick muffin pan.

2 Sift and mix the dry ingredients in a large bowl.

3 In a smaller bowl, lightly whisk together the eggs, milk and butter.

4 Make a well in the centre of the dry ingredients, and add the liquid and mashed bananas one at a time until the ingredients are well combined.

5 Spoon the mixture into the muffin pan. Bake for 25–30 minutes, or until the muffins spring back when lightly touched.

Holly's pasta with easy-peasy tomato sauce

Makes 4 small serves

This is too easy, but to make it more interesting (with more variety and nutrition for your child), add a spoonful of mashed, drained canned tuna (preferably in springwater, not oil or brine), just cooked (not mushy) vegetables such as diced zucchini (courgettes), diced carrot, diced butternut pumpkin, finely chopped English spinach and finely chopped Italian parsley.

Ingredients

1 tablespoon extra virgin olive oil

1 garlic clove, crushed

400 g (14 oz) diced 'Roma' or plum tomatoes (check label for no added sugar or salt)

250 g (9 oz) penne or farfalle (bowtie pasta)

1 dessertspoon shaved Parmesan cheese (optional)

Method

1 Heat the olive oil in a frying pan over medium heat.

2 Add the garlic and cook, constantly stirring for two minutes. Add the tomatoes and stir through. Reduce heat to low and cook for a further 5–10 minutes, occasionally stirring.

3 While the sauce is cooking, add the pasta to a large saucepan of salted boiling water. Cook it for around 10 minutes or until al dente.

4 Drain the pasta in a colander and return it to the saucepan.

5 Add the ingredients from the frypan and stir them through.

6 Add the vegetables and any other ingredients, such as tuna.

7 Spoon a small portion into a bowl. If desired, sprinkle Parmesan cheese over the top.

Greta's rice pudding

Serves 4

This takes a while to cook, but the result is a delicious dessert. Alternatively, refrigerate it overnight and serve it with fresh or canned fruit in its own juice the next day for breakfast.

Ingredients

½ cup arborio (short grain) rice

4 cups milk

2 dessertspoons caster sugar*

1 teaspoon vanilla essence

1 teaspoon butter (optional)

Pinch of cinnamon (optional)

* If this is too much sugar for you, halve the amount in the recipe.

Method

1 Preheat the oven to 180°C (350°F).

2 Put all the ingredients in an ovenproof baking bowl and stir.

3 Place the bowl in the preheated oven and bake for around 1½ hours, stirring every 15 minutes to make sure the ingredients don't stick to the bowl.

4 Remove the rice pudding from the oven when it has the consistency of creamed rice.

5 Do not let it dry out. Cool the pudding slightly before serving it warm.

Josh's fried rice

Serves 2

Fried rice is so versatile because you can add so many nutritious things to it — for example, add broccoli, green capsicum, spring onions, zucchini (courgettes) and squash for extra flavour.

Ingredients

½ tablespoon canola oil, enough to coat wok

1 egg, lightly beaten

½ onion, diced

½ red capsicum, diced

1 small carrot, thinly sliced (or diced)

100 g (3½ oz) cooked, skinned chicken, cut into small bite-sized pieces

1 cup cold, cooked rice

¼ tablespoon low-salt soy sauce

Method

1 Heat half the canola oil in a wok or frying pan.

2 Add the egg and, as it sets, scrape it towards the centre of the pan with a metal slotted spoon to let the uncooked portion run to the edge. When almost set, break the egg up so it resembles a scrambled egg and remove it from the pan to a plate.

3 Heat the rest of the oil in the pan and make sure it's coating the base and sides. Add the onion and stir-fry it until it is translucent.

4 Add the chicken, capsicum and carrot, and stir-fry for 1 minute.

5 Add the rice and stir-fry until the rice is heated through.

6 Add the egg and soy sauce.

7 Heat through and serve.

Caring

Children don't grow as quickly in their second year as they did in their first. Once your child is moving about, comfortable and easy-to-wear clothing will make life easier. You will need to buy new clothing as your child grows, as buying clothing that is too large makes moving about very awkward for the child.

Clothing update

Separates are ideal for this age group because your baby will still be wearing nappies but stretch suits are no longer appropriate. Both boys and girls will feel comfortable in tracksuits. Some little girls will want to wear dresses and, if this is the case, short skirts with leggings underneath on cold days are best.

At some time in the next year most children want to put on and take off their own clothes — some will want to do it anywhere, anytime!

It is in both your and your child's best interests to provide clothes that are easy to pull on and off. Pants with elasticized waists and t-shirts with easy necks are a good option. Buttons and zips will make life difficult and ties are not appropriate, as they could become a safety hazard.

The nappy-changing dance

Once your child can move about, he will hate wasting time while his nappy is changed. It is up to you to make change time as fast and efficient as possible. Clothing that comes off and goes on easily, such as pull-up pants and pop studs, is ideal. If you have everything you need nearby, including a stand-by set of new clothes, then you can start.

Sometimes it works if you create a diversion. You might sing a song that has lots of animal noises such as 'Old MacDonald Had a Farm', turn on a special musical toy, or give your child a toy that you keep on the change table for him to play with.

Many parents become adept at putting a nappy on a standing child. This is sometimes all it takes, as he may simply hate being made to lie down.

Pyjamas can become an issue around this age. In summer a nappy and a t-shirt will do in most climates, but in winter, when a child is likely to kick off his bedclothes, a sleep suit that is warm enough to sleep in without blankets may be the answer. Active sleepers may also need to wear a pair of comfortable socks inside the suit.

Choosing shoes

We tend to take our feet for granted, underestimating their contribution to our physical wellbeing. Yet the human foot is one of the most complex parts of the body and, if neglected, can contribute to many problems in adolescence and adulthood.

Each foot comprises 26 bones and a network of ligaments, blood vessels, muscles and nerves. The feet of a young child are soft and malleable, so any undue pressure may result in deformity. In the first year of life the feet grow at a rapid rate, and by 12 months a baby's foot reaches almost half the size of his adult foot. Not until his late teens will his feet be fully developed.

There's no need to buy your child shoes before he starts to walk. The pressure of the shoes on his small developing feet will do more harm than good. But once he starts walking he'll need a pair of shoes. It's a good idea to leave his feet bare when indoors so his muscles and bones can develop and strengthen, and he can learn to grasp with his toes. Outside, shoes are necessary for stability and to

protect his feet from rough surfaces and dirty areas where going shoeless could put him at risk of injury or infection.

Buying shoes can be a costly exercise, but you are guaranteeing your child a healthier future by investing in good quality footwear. It is far better to buy your child a well made, properly fitted pair of leather shoes three or four times a year than to buy two or three pairs of ill-fitting shoes. Thongs and slip-ons are not suitable for this age group as your child's feet are not well enough developed to wear them safely. Any open shoes, such as sandals, should have a heel strap.

The not-so-good news is that because a child's feet grow so quickly, and in spurts, you will need to update your child's shoes and socks every three to four months. Between the ages of one and three years, it will be necessary to check the size of your child's feet every three months. Foot care specialists, such as podiatrists and chiropodists, do not recommend 'hand-me-down' shoes.

If it's possible, seek out a specialist children's shoe shop where the fitters are knowledgeable and experienced. It's also best to shop later in the day rather than early, as the feet usually swell slightly as the day progresses. You should look for lightweight, flexible, well ventilated shoes that allow room for growth. Take this checklist along with you.

- Make sure the fitter measures both feet for width and length, because no two feet are ever the same. The depth of the shoes should also be checked to ensure the top of the shoe isn't pressing down on the toes or toenails.

- The shoes should be secured by laces, buckles or Velcro. For the young toddler (nine to 18 months), leather or canvas shoes with laces are more secure.

- You need a flat shoe — no heels — which keeps the foot secure, so the rule is no slip-ons (these are shoes without laces, buckles or Velcro fasteners).

- Favour shoes made from natural breathable materials, such as leather, suede and canvas, or the newer mesh materials. Unless they are worn with cotton socks, synthetic shoes made of nylon, rubber or plastic can trap perspiration which, in turn, increases the chances of toenail problems and conditions such as athlete's foot.

- The insole, which is inside the shoe, should be made of an absorbent material.

Home safety update

* Now your child's on the move, he will be dipping into everything, so constant supervision is vital. Even when your child is asleep, check on him, and always make sure no items that could choke or suffocate him are within reach.

* Reinforce warnings — such as 'that's hot', 'don't touch', 'take care' and 'ouch' — so that he gains an understanding of words and phrases that teach him caution.

* If you haven't already, now is the time to place safety latches on all the drawers and cupboards that contain potentially harmful products such as dishwashing powder and plastic bags, or implements such as knives, skewers, toothpicks and any object that could cause choking. Always reserve a special cupboard or drawer for your child and fill it with items that can be used as musical instruments, for shop games or measuring and pouring fun.

* Avoid toy boxes with heavy lids. Use baskets in the rooms where your child plays.

* Cover electrical outlets with safety caps.

* Place electrical cords out of reach: run them along the wall or behind furniture.

* Check that your child's collection of toys is child-safe (see 'Toy safety checklist' on page 233).

* Never leave a nappy bucket on the floor or in a place where your child could fall into it.

* Likewise, erect secure gates and fences around fishponds and swimming pools to ban your curious toddler from gaining access.

* Place safety gates at the top and bottom of stairs.

■ There is no need for an arch support as toddlers younger than 16 months have flat feet. The arch only becomes fully developed by the age of six to eight years.

■ The shoe should fit the natural shape of the foot and leave enough space around the toes so there is room for them to wiggle. Rounded toe 'boxes' are recommended. Fitters usually ensure there is about 18 mm (¾ in) of growing room (that is, the size of an adult thumbnail) between the end of the longest toe and the end of the shoe.

■ Shoes should fit around the heel so they are neither too tight nor too loose.

■ Check your child's socks are not too tight, and there are no loose threads that could become caught on toes and toenails.

- Before you buy, let your child walk around the shop in the shoes so you can detect any obvious problems.
- Make sure the shoes are flexible — you should be able to bend them to 40 degrees in one hand.
- The soles should be non-slip; grooves and little bumps are best.

- To be on the safe side, always buy a longer rather than a shorter shoe.
- If you can afford two pairs each time, then buy them. The shoes will have a chance to dry between wears.
- Take a pair of your child's socks with you to the shoe shop so he can wear them when trying on new shoes.
- Don't shop for shoes with a hungry or tired child.
- To keep your child amused while shopping, bring a toy.
- Once you're home, for the first week or so keep an eye on your child's feet for red marks, blisters or other signs of irritation. If you've purchased sandals, insist your child wear socks with them for the first few days to soften the leather and thereby prevent the area around the heel (heel counter) rubbing against his heels.
- If your child's shoes wear out unevenly or too quickly, he might have a standing or walking problem. Other indicators of possible problems are night cramps, 'growing pains', fatigue, tripping, walking pigeon-toed (in-toed) or a clumsy gait. Similarly, if you have trouble finding shoes that fit, and your child's feet are prone to calluses, sores or other problems, contact your doctor for advice and a possible referral to a foot care specialist.

Teething

Between the ages of 12 and 24 months, most children will acquire their full set of primary teeth. Following the front teeth, the incisors will appear, then the first milk molars, the eye teeth and the other molars. There are 20 first teeth and they are often referred to as 'deciduous'. These teeth are softer than the second set of teeth which, on average, start to come through when a child is about seven years old. The first teeth play an important role in guiding the second teeth into place and in the development of speech, so don't neglect them.

Taking care of your child's teeth

Decay in these 'baby' or first teeth is often caused when the baby falls asleep with milk, either breastmilk or infant formula, pooling around his teeth. Milk contains milk sugars and these are the culprits. Dummies can also cause decay if they are dipped in something sweet.

Until your child is able to manage and manoeuvre a toothbrush by himself, you will need to clean his teeth for him, every day. He will probably not be able to do it properly himself until the early years of primary school. He should have his own toothbrush and, if he has a soft 'junior' one, he can practise cleaning his teeth before or after you clean them.

Avoid giving your child food that contributes to tooth decay. Sweet, sticky foods that adhere to the teeth — such as fruit bars and straps, jams, peanut butter and fruit juice — are common causes of tooth decay. Young children do not need soft drinks. Water is the ideal drink for them, particularly after food. Fluoride is important for healthy teeth. Many water supplies have added fluoride, but if this is not the case where you live, your dentist will be able to advise you about supplements.

Knocked out teeth

If your child has an accident and a primary or 'baby' tooth is knocked out, it is important to find it so you can be sure it has not been inhaled or swallowed. However, primary teeth cannot be re-implanted. The gum will be bleeding. If your child suffers a dental accident, make sure you take him to the dentist, otherwise there may be long-term problems.

First visit to the dentist

A child needs to make his first visit to a dentist at about the age of 18 months. Ideally, the first visit should be when you go to the dentist for a check-up so that he can see that you are quite happy to sit still while someone looks in your mouth.

If your child's teeth do decay, it is important to take him to the dentist as soon as possible.

Sleeping

By the time a child reaches his first birthday, most parents expect that the night-time sleeps will allow them a little time to themselves and that they will not be disturbed frequently during the night.

Sleep needs

On average, toddlers sleep between ten and 12 hours a night. Of course, this will vary according to the individual child's needs. At the age of 12 months your baby will probably be having two naps during the day. This need for sleep will gradually reduce until, by the age of two years, he will need one nap around the middle of the day, either just before a late lunch or in the early afternoon. In reaching this stage your child may reduce each sleep or give up the morning sleep and go through a cranky period; much will depend on the time he wakes in the morning.

Routine

A bedtime routine continues to play a very important role in getting a toddler to sleep. By this age a child will not drop off to sleep, even if he is tired, and he will often wake if he is disturbed. Your toddler needs a quiet, dimly lit and regular sleeping place, and he needs to feel secure enough to fall asleep.

A toddler can cope with an irregular routine, late nights and being taken out often by his regular carers, but his sleep pattern will no doubt be irregular too. By the time the child reaches preschool or school age and needs to wake up at a regular time each morning, this could be a major problem.

Most parents decide to put their toddler to bed at the same time every night, and work their daytime routines around his naptimes and mealtimes, which should ideally be at the same time, every day of the week.

Naps

One-year-olds who wake early in the morning may be ready for a nap around mid-morning, but those who sleep late may not nap

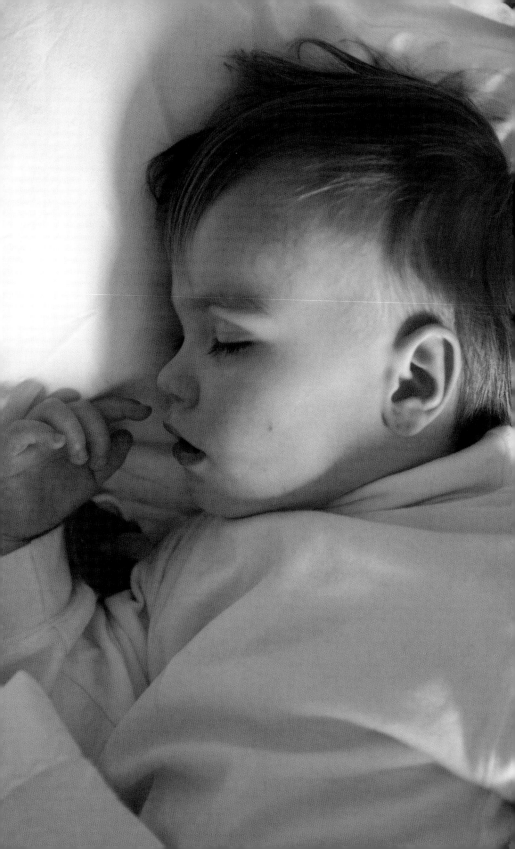

Quiet time

As well as naps, your toddler needs a quiet time during the day. Watching television is not a good solution (see 'Your child and television' on page 234). Reading together or doing puzzles, drawing, making something, or quietly playing on the floor with favourite toys are activities that should be incorporated into your child's day.

until after a late lunch. Two short sleeps a day are generally better for all concerned than one long one of three or four hours. Often parents find they have to wake a sleeping toddler after an hour or so. This toddler will usually be cranky and uncooperative, but in the interests of other commitments — such as everyone having lunch, collecting other children from school and shopping, for example — there may be no other option. If your child is in childcare, he will be expected to sleep and eat at around the same time each day, so if you can keep as closely as possible to this routine when your child is at home, sleeping problems are less likely to develop.

Sleeping problems

Not wanting to go to bed is perfectly normal, even for a tired toddler. There might be a lot of activity in the household, so the toddler finds it difficult to accept that he is not going to miss out by being put to bed.

By the time a child is a toddler he can make himself stay awake, even if he is tired. He can also make you feel frustrated when your attempts to put him to bed after his quiet bedtime routine result in persistent calls for you to return or cries at your departure.

This is when many childcare experts will recommend a version of leaving baby to cry, commonly known as 'controlled crying' (also known as 'controlled comforting'). This is a strategy for helping adults to cope with crying children that has been in and out of fashion since the early part of the 19th century. At its most extreme, it means leaving the child to cry until he falls asleep from exhaustion. Usually, the parent offers comforting words then leaves the child to cry for a short period, say, five minutes, before returning to offer the same comforting words. The carer then leaves the child for longer and longer periods. The idea is to discipline the child to go to sleep while still letting him know that you are there to comfort him but that you mean business. Consistency is the key. Some methods include complicated charts for you to fill in, showing how much time you have spent comforting and hopefully giving you signs of progress.

As well as their toddler's bedtime, most parents also have other things to cope with: feeling tired after a day's work, the need to prepare an evening meal, household chores to perform, perhaps work or study after dinner, or simply the desire to relax together and talk. There may be other children who also need attention. A strategy such as controlled crying can be tempting. For many parents it doesn't feel like the right thing to do. It certainly sells books and is promoted by health professionals taking a clinical approach, but it is likely to make you feel enormously guilty. Mothers are programmed to answer their baby's cry; in fact, once they are mothers, many women will find that any baby's cry alerts them. If you succeed in ignoring your own baby's cry, you are desensitizing yourself.

Letting your toddler get out of bed after the bedtime routine has failed to put him to sleep in the time allowed will only prolong the problem, so you need another solution. Every family will work out a solution that suits them, and some parents may resort to using controlled crying.

Other strategies that are less stressful for both you and your child do exist. These include:

Dummy or cuddly. Encourage your child to suck a dummy or have a cuddly. Either object alone may work for some children, but for others you may need something else as well. Neither a dummy nor a cuddly is harmful, and toddlers who suck dummies do not do permanent damage to their teeth.

Music. Finish the bedtime routine with a quiet song or story CD, and gradually leave the room as the CD continues to play. If you also use a night-light, this can work well. The trick is to put the CD on, give your child a good night kiss and cuddle, and stay for a few moments. As the child settles you quietly do a few things around the room, gradually leaving the room, but staying outside the door. If there are protests, you move back inside but don't speak. This routine may take some time to work through but, in many instances, the child will be asleep before the end of the CD. Eventually you will be able to put a CD on, say 'good night' and leave quite soon afterwards.

Be a boring parent. The object of this is to show your child that you are still there, that you love him, but that now is sleep time. Go through the usual bedtime rituals, say 'good night' and leave the room. Once again a night-light is a valuable prop. If he cries out, wait a few seconds. If he continues to cry out, return to the room, say 'good night' and leave the room again. Don't leave him to cry. Once he starts again, return to the room and repeat the good night message. This can take some time, and may take a week or so of protracted good nights before it works, but if you give up you will have to start all over again.

never

Never give a bottle at bedtime. Most toddlers will not want to drink water, and so a bottle at night is likely to contain milk that can pool around the child's teeth and lead to what is now known as 'bottle-feeding caries (cavities)'. If a child already has a bottle at night, then the solution is to gradually dilute the contents until it is just water. Otherwise, it is better to avoid this strategy altogether.

Waking in the night

Toddlers are not able to make themselves wake up in the night; if they do wake, as with most adult wake-ups, it is beyond the child's control. If your child wakes in the night, he will probably need comforting and help in going back to sleep. He may need a nappy change. Attending to his needs and, at the same time, being a boring parent are the best strategies for you to follow.

Night-time fears

It is quite normal for a child to wake up feeling afraid in the middle of the night. The cause is usually some form of nightmare, and a child can wake up terrified. Obviously, comforting is the most important response and the sooner you reach your child and reassure him, the sooner he will go back to sleep.

Waking too early

If your child wakes at first light, one preventative measure that may work is a heavy blind that blocks out the daylight. However, this may not succeed for long and you may need to provide a couple of toys and books at the end of the cot. Most toddlers are at their most active at this time of day, and often the only solution is to go with the flow and let your child come into your bed or take it in turns to get up.

Development

Some children will begin to walk before their first birthday, others not until well into the second half of their second year. Every child is an individual and will learn this skill at his own pace, given the right environment.

Learning to walk

In order to walk, your baby has to coordinate muscle strength, balance and mental readiness. So trying to teach a child to walk before he is ready will only waste your time and energy, and frustrate both you and your child.

By the time your child is crawling or mobile, you need to be sure that your home is as safe as you can make it. This includes ensuring that baby's cot meets safety standards, as a cot is often the first place where a baby pulls himself to standing. The furniture throughout the house needs safety corners, where necessary, and it must be steady and well balanced with no handles protruding at toddler head height. You should put away any breakables so baby has the space he needs to learn to walk as safely as possible (see 'Home safety update' on page 206).

Standing

Before he can walk, a child must go through a number of stages. The first of these is pulling himself to standing. At this stage your child has more strength in his arms than in his legs, and he uses his arms to pull himself into an upright position. He may have preceded this first 'stand' by crawling over objects such as cushions on the floor.

From this stage he may progress to climbing stairs if they are nearby. He will love this, and will go on climbing until he reaches the top or you stop him. The big problem for crawlers and early walkers who climb stairs is coming down. Left to his own devices, a child of this age will usually turn round and come down face first.

While a stair gate is an excellent way to impede crawling, when you are not there to supervise or a stair gate is not in place, it is also very important that a child knows how to come down stairs. You can teach your baby to come down stairs by turning him round and guiding first one foot, then the other, down the stairs. Baby will soon get the idea, although you will probably need to go through the exercise a number of times.

The first time your baby pulls himself to standing he could be in his cot, holding onto your pants leg, or gripping a piece of furniture. He will feel very pleased with himself and a round of applause from those watching will make him feel every bit as clever as he is. A new world opens up when baby finds himself standing. Now he can reach objects on low tables, on sofas and any other piece of furniture that is at his chest height. You may find that you need to remove remote controls and find a higher home for them. Also, the video player and sound systems can suddenly become vulnerable to inquisitive exploration. Objects that can be lifted and banged down again are also tempting for your child, so rather than trying to ban baby from enjoying things at this level, provide him with toys and safe objects that he can play with. While he is standing in this way he is building the strength in his legs, ready to move onto the next phase.

'Cruising'

The next phase is 'cruising'. This may happen almost immediately after baby has pulled himself to standing, or a few days later. In 'cruising' a baby uses his hands to guide his body around furniture and any available legs. He will slide along the furniture with both hands, then his feet will follow. At the next stage he will reach out with one hand then move a foot, then another foot and in this way 'cruise' around the room. This takes quite a deal of effort, as your baby's little legs need to build up the strength they need as he is learning. As his confidence grows, baby will take the next step and he will actually reach between pieces of furniture, so that there is a moment when there is nothing to hold onto.

During this stage your baby will frequently 'plop' down onto his bottom. He will continue to do this when he begins to walk. Even if your baby's little bottom is not padded by a nappy, this dropping to the floor will not do him any harm; in fact, it is a valuable part of learning to balance. So unless he is likely to hurt himself (usually by an accidental meeting with something on the way down), it is usually not necessary to prevent this sudden sitting down.

When baby reaches this stage you can hold out a hand to him, so he can grasp it rather than a piece of furniture. Once baby appears to be steady on his feet, you can encourage him to take a step on his own before he reaches the outstretched hand. Baby will love to walk with you holding both hands, or between two older people, but it is important to stop these walks as soon as baby has had enough. He may signal this by simply sitting down.

Walking

Gradually your child's confidence will build and he will start to take a few independent steps. Some children find the slowness of early walking frustrating, and will drop to their knees and crawl because they know they will reach their goal sooner. Others will persist until they can walk. At this stage, many children get enormous pleasure from a 'push-along' toy such as a brick or toddler cart. These are solid flat carts on four wheels with a sturdy handle that comes to baby's chest height. Many hold building blocks, but they may also be used to push along favourite toys such as teddies. Baby can grab onto this instead of a piece of furniture and will soon learn that when he takes a step the truck will move. This truck is far preferable to a baby walker (see 'Baby walkers' on page 183) and will provide hours of pleasure. The contents are an added bonus. (Protecting, or better still, removing any furniture that is likely to be damaged by a fast-moving brick truck is a precaution some parents may need to take.)

Once baby is walking without a prop, you will notice that he still has a long way to go when it comes to balance. He will use his arms and hands to help balance himself and will waddle about. The more he practises, the smoother his walking will become.

Once he has found his feet he will take great delight in 'running away', but he won't go far. Research has found that toddlers seldom go further than 60 m (65½ yd) from their safe base. In a crowded place this will mean losing him, so you will need to keep a check

Helping your new walker

* While it is perfectly normal for your baby to sit down abruptly when learning to walk, it is important to protect him from falling against hard objects. If he bangs his head or gets a fright, he may just go back to crawling.

* If the floors are slippery, this can make early walking difficult. Rugs with non-slip undermats or socks with grip feet will solve this problem.

* Sickness can set back your child's walking practice as can an emotional shock, such as the arrival of a new baby. As soon as he has recovered from the illness, your child will resume his walking practice.

on him either by following close enough to grab him or by using reins. In a park you may be able to let him go as far as he feels safe before he turns to come back to you, which he is likely to do slowly, inspecting the things he missed on the way out. However, if you get up and move towards him he is likely to move away — keeping that safe distance is fun.

Not until a child is three is he able to follow. If you get up to move to a different place or to go home, your toddler will ask to be carried. This, says child psychologist Penelope Leach, is a survival instinct and one that is also found in the monkey world.[1] The toddler who raises his arms and calls 'up', or who sits down and cries is not trying to be difficult; he is simply not able to understand that by following you he is staying close. He thinks you are leaving him, and his survival instinct wants you to fix it. Parents who understand that carrying their child, or letting him ride in a stroller or backpack, is the only way to solve this dilemma, have a happier trip home than those who try to make a child do something he can't understand.

Early speech

From the age of six months your baby will be chatting in a language that may seem totally alien. Then, one day, you will be amazed to find that the unintelligible starts to make sense, as your child begins to comprehend the meanings of words and their role in communication.

His constant interaction with other people and the environment encourages the development of language skills, so he will eventually be able to string several words together and communicate his wants and needs more effectively. With your encouragement, which will allow his early speech to bloom, by the time he turns two he will be asking simple questions and responding to your questions with simple replies.

Flat feet, knock-knees and tip toes

When your baby first starts to walk, ideally in bare feet so he can use all his muscles, he will have flat feet and knock-knees. In fact, his first steps will be with straight legs. These flat feet and knock-knees do not strengthen for several years and are perfectly normal in toddlers.

Although it may sometimes be necessary to dress your baby in socks (ideally with grip soles to avoid slipping) for warmth or safety, shoes are not necessary and may slow his progress. As your baby learns to walk, the muscles in his feet and ankles are being used in new and different ways, and the best way to do this is with bare feet. A pair of soft leather shoes is an alternative to socks or conventional shoes when safety is a priority (see 'Choosing shoes' on page 200 for advice).

Some babies only walk on their toes in the beginning. Usually these babies soon progress to using the whole foot, but if this does not happen quite soon, then a check-up with a paediatrician is advisable.

Language and speech

Language is our ability to communicate with one another, which we may achieve through gestures, sign language, writing, computerized communication devices and, most commonly, speech. Speech is the oral form of language.

It's natural to communicate with each other. From the moment your baby is born, you unconsciously and effortlessly lay the foundations for early speech. You make eye contact with your baby and respond to his gurgles and coos with your own baby talk. You pull faces, poke out your tongue, laugh and smile at your child.

Hearing, listening and talking

Your child is like a sponge — he is soaking up everything he sees, hears, feels, touches and tastes in the world around him.

Every day he hears noises — a dog barking, the radio, traffic, birdsong, an ambulance siren, music, people talking, a plane flying overhead. As his world begins to take shape, these all become familiar sounds, each with a meaning attached. They help your child make sense of his environment.

Eventually, with your help, he will be able to attach words to these sounds. But the journey to speech is complex. Before he can speak, he has to understand what is being said. Then, later on, he has to learn to pronounce the words, make sentences with them and learn to listen to other people's words. With your positive encouragement, he will be more eager to use words and communicate with others. But while your enthusiasm is vital, don't overload your child with words. It's no use teaching him to copy sounds before he understands their meaning. You can help him develop his language skills by:

- talking naturally, using simple language;

- avoiding baby talk, such as 'choo choo' for a train or 'moo cow' for a cow;

- naming things correctly — 'dinner', 'lunch', 'bathtime' and 'bed' — so he becomes aware that there is a proper name for everything;

- not correcting his attempts to talk. If you are using the correct pronunciation and talking clearly and slowly, your child will eventually tune into this;

- listening to your child and always giving him the chance to speak without any interruption; never ignore or dismiss his attempts at talking;

- pausing frequently so your child has a chance to understand you and to reply;

- responding to two-syllable sounds, such as 'da-da', as if you are having a normal conversation. You can also imitate the 'da-da', to help him learn this new sound;

- lengthening your child's words and phrases into sentences;

- repeating the description of the daily routines, such as bath- and naptime. This gives your child the building blocks for later learning. Repeated positive experiences, such as a story or song before bed, not only help your child develop a sense of security, but they also give him the chance to hear words again and again;

- always looking at your child when you're talking to make it easier for him to work out meaning from your eyes and gestures;

- adding non-verbal cues (simple gestures) to your verbal directions to help him understand what is being said. For example, when you want him to come to you, hold out your arms and call out, 'Come over here.' As his language skills develop, the gestures won't be necessary; and

- having your child's hearing tested if you find you have to repeat instructions frequently, and he seems not to be hearing what you are saying unless he is looking directly at you at close range.

Talking to your child

The most important thing is to talk *with* your child, not *at* him. In the end, it's all about communication, so just enjoy being with him. It's essential for you to maintain a positive attitude so that your child feels comfortable talking to you. His temperament will affect the amount of language he uses and how he uses it.

Most young children utter their first words between the ages of 12 and 18 months. Then, before they turn two years old, there is a noticeable increase in their language development. They begin to join words together at around two-and-a-half years of age.

Encourage your child's talking.

- Play alongside him, then copy some of his actions as well as his sounds and facial expressions. You can also show him new actions and play games such as 'peek-a-boo'.

- Chat to him about routine activities. For example, talk to him while you stack the dishes in the dishwasher or hang the clothes on the line. If he's digging in a sandpit, comment: 'Wow! You're digging a hole with the spade. It's such a big hole. I wonder what will happen if you keep digging?'

- Discuss familiar items around the house and make a game with them. Introduce your child to phonics, or speech sounds, by personalizing household items and toys — for instance, a soft toy that goes 'g-g-g-g!' or a clock that makes the sound 't-t-t-t!'.

- Show your child that a single word can be incorporated into a sentence. For instance, if your child says 'cat', respond with, 'Yes, it's a big cat.'

- Talk about practical activities. These could be activities such as bathtime, bedtime, dressing and undressing. For example, when your child is getting dressed, talk about colours, patterns on clothes, zippers and buttons. As you help him dress, describe the process: 'Okay, arms up and I'll put on your singlet. Ooh, over your head it goes and out pops a little head, and now I can see two little arms poking through the armholes.'

- Point to body parts. Simple nursery rhyme games such as 'Head and Shoulders, Knees and Toes' are a fun way to teach your child the names for the different parts of his body.

- Involve him in activities. These activities should encourage listening and learning skills, as well as developing fine and gross motor skills. For example, use finger games, soft dolls, stuffed toys, balls, blocks and activity boards.

- Create an 'ice box'. Place some ice in a container and get your child to touch it. While he is touching the ice, talk about how it feels by using words like 'wet', 'cold', 'icy' and 'brrrr'. You can also play the same game using all sorts of materials. Try feathers, fur and leaves, for example.

- Look at letters, magazines and newspapers together. You provide a good role model for your child by reading for your own pleasure. Even though he can't read, show him letters and postcards. Browse through magazines together, pointing out photos or illustrations of interest. He will soon learn that words and pictures go together.

- Read a book together every day. Take him to the local library and choose a book that is appropriate for his age. If you're having trouble deciding which books are suitable, ask the librarian for suggestions. Read stories in a way that encourages him to participate — for example, repeat rhymes and refrains so he can copy you.

- Tell stories about you and your family, or make up stories with your child in the lead role. For example, 'There once was a brave prince named [use your child's name here], who loved going to the park and playing on the swings.'

- Talk at the dinner table. Describe the food and point out simple adjectives such as 'hot' and 'cold'. Make your child aware of the smells and tastes of different foods.

- Name items used in daily routines. When he's washing his hands, use the relevant words, such as 'clean', 'dirty', 'soap' and 'water'.

- Socialize. Visit friends, join a playgroup and go out with other parents and their children. Your child will learn about language by being with other children of various ages.

- Build up a repertoire of familiar songs and nursery rhymes such as 'Round and Round the Garden, Like a Teddy Bear' and 'I'm a Little Teapot'. Songs with actions encourage your child to join in.

- Be a successful listener.

- Play with words with mix-up rhymes — for example, 'Funny bunny in the honey. That's so yummy!'

- Vary the tone of your voice when speaking to your child. Try whispering or speaking in a squeaky mouse voice.

- Describe what you see when you go on a walk.

- Ask questions.

From one to two

At around 12 months your child may be saying several words, usually with meaning; 'no!' and 'mine!' are common early words. Your child may also be able to understand and respond to simple commands such as 'Where's your nose?'. Warnings such as 'That's hot!' and 'Don't touch!' also become meaningful to the adventurous toddler. As the months pass, your toddler's vocabulary will grow steadily. Soon he should be able to point to body parts and name them. By the time your child is two, he could be asking questions such as 'More bikkies?' or 'Go Nanna's?' He will enjoy listening to simple stories and songs sung by you, often the same ones over and over again.

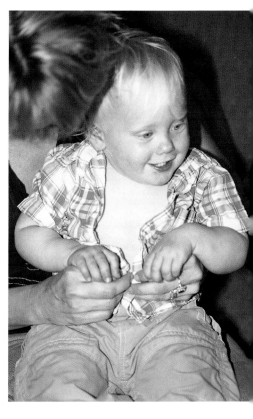

But my child's not talking yet

Every child has an individual rate of development. Sometimes a child will put language development on hold while he concentrates on learning gross motor skills such as walking. It's also important to remember that his speech won't always be grammatically correct and that this is perfectly normal. When they are learning to talk, all children occasionally misunderstand what is said to them, utter strangely worded sentences and put speech sounds in the wrong spots (or leave them out altogether).

Baby talk

The arrival of a new baby brother or sister can be a traumatic event for a toddler. All of a sudden there's another little person in the house who is receiving the hugs, kisses and attention that used to belong exclusively to him. This can be confusing, and cause him to feel he no longer has an important role in the family. In a desperate bid for your attention he may resort to baby talk. It is his way of letting you know he feels isolated and abandoned. So how do you deal with your child's baby talk?

* Don't admonish your child for this regressive behaviour.

* Do give him more hugs and kisses than usual.

* Do let him help care for his sibling. For instance, involve him in bathtime and nappy changing by letting him pass you the barrier cream or soap, or helping you gently dry the baby.

* Do try to find a few minutes to play with him or read him a story when the new baby is sleeping. The time together without any interruptions will boost his self-esteem and strengthen your relationship.

* Do encourage him to talk like a big boy by praising him when he acts his age.

The baby talk will eventually disappear from his vocabulary when he gets used to his baby brother or sister.

Don't worry if your child isn't chatting away like his best friend at playgroup who's the same age. It doesn't mean he has a speech problem. However, if you haven't heard your child 'speak' by the time he's 18 months old, you may want to spend some time with him, simply interacting, to encourage him to talk.

When to worry

If you are worried about your child's language development, seek the advice of your doctor or child health nurse. If your child appears to stutter, they will most likely organize a referral to a speech (and language) therapist. Likewise, a husky, hoarse voice is not normal and requires a professional assessment. If your child is withdrawn, refuses or is unable to make eye contact and respond to what you say by echoing all or part of it back to you word for word, it is advisable to seek the help of a professional who can assess his communication skills.

You may feel concerned if your child:

- does not appear to be listening to you — he doesn't seem to enjoy sounds and doesn't respond to them;
- has trouble sucking, chewing, swallowing or biting; or
- isn't using 'real' words by 18 months.

Twins and triplets

Twins and triplets are individuals, even if they are identical, and they will usually develop very different needs, including sleep.

More than one baby is always extra work for the parents, but one of the big bonuses is that as they grow they will amuse each other and play together, although they may not develop at the same pace. However, it is just as important for twin and triplet parents to set aside time to play with their children, even though they do need to be more organized than parents of single babies. If one baby is asleep, be sure to make this a special time with the other child.

As with all babies, parents need to be one step ahead and to ensure that the babies' home environment is as safe as they can make it (see 'Toy safety checklist' on page 233).

It is quite common for multiples to start talking later than singletons the same age. Being born prematurely affects speech development, but multiples have the added problem of needing individual time with older people and adults in order to learn how to communicate. Furthermore, twins often develop a unique form of communication between themselves and work as a team in communicating with others. So late speech development is not unusual with these children.

Fun, games and learning

Your child has reached that delightful age where he is looking for action! You can help by introducing him to new, fun experiences and situations where he is involved with other toddlers in a stimulating environment.

Choosing a playgroup

A playgroup provides you and your child with the perfect opportunity to make new friends. One of the most attractive aspects of a playgroup is its informal nature, which lets you and your child relax in a friendly environment. There should be no pressure on your child to perform or to be involved in a structured activity. A playgroup gives him the opportunity to learn through play. Hopefully, there's a local playgroup in your area that meets the needs of its own members. Your child will benefit from being with other children. In their company he will learn about sharing and cooperation and thereby improve his social skills; he will also learn simple rules and routines, and improve his problem-solving abilities. In short, he will learn more about his world.

A playgroup also works wonders for parents. You will benefit from talking to other parents of children who are around the same age, sharing experiences and ideas.

If there isn't a playgroup in your area, or you have tried one but found it did not work for both of you, there is the option of forming your own local group. If you know of a playgroup association, ask them to provide you with guidelines for getting started. Create a flyer and distribute it locally, making sure you send a copy to the local baby health centre. If you're a working mum and your child is in the care of a family day carer, nanny or grandparent, you may like to arrange for them to visit a selection of local playgroups to check out which one best suits your child and his carer.

Play

Never underestimate the value of play. Through play your child learns to concentrate, use his imagination, sample ideas, develop his language skills, practise grown-up behaviour, and to organize and gain a sense of control over his world. By playing games with him, you encourage his curiosity and expand his opportunities for emotional growth. He will also love to help you in your daily tasks, which teach him about cooperation and sharing as well as help develop fine motor skills.

As his ability to manipulate his hands and fingers becomes more complex, he will enjoy activities that involve pushing, pulling, poking, hammering and digging. There's no need to organize highly structured activities. At home, create a junk box of items, such as plastic containers, old socks, tissue paper, measuring cups of different sizes, a turkey baster, egg carton, clothes pegs, plastic bottles, containers with lids that are easy to open and close, and paper cups (keep small, easy-to-swallow objects out of your child's reach).

When you're out together, take the time to be with him and to show him the world. Play could take the form of a walk in the park where he stops to feed the ducks, pat a dog, kick some leaves, pick berries, observe a goldfish in the pond, see the other children playing and play with them on the play equipment. These real-life experiences teach your child far more about the world than a pressured one-on-one 'play' session. Also, your child may not be ready to share his toys with other children (this is a social skill you will need to help him with), and he may not yet be interested in interacting with them either. This is a completely normal part of your child's social development. So be patient and gently reinforce the importance of sharing without making an issue of it.

Modelling dough

Make up some modelling dough for your two-year-old. When it is not in use, store it in an airtight container. Here's a simple recipe.

Ingredients

½ cup salt

1 cup flour

2 tablespoons cream of tartar

1 cup water

1 tablespoon oil

Food colouring

Method

1 Mix the salt, flour and cream of tartar together in a saucepan.

2 Add the water, oil and food colouring.

3 Stir everything together, then cook on a medium heat for around 3–5 minutes until the dough is malleable.

4 Supply plastic biscuit cutters, blunt plastic toy knives and rolling pins, and your child will be busy with the modelling dough for hours.

One- to two-year-olds like to alternate active, noisy and busy periods of play with quiet, restful interludes. When you go out, whether it's to the park or into the garden, bring along a few items for quiet times, such as books or soft toys.

You can help your child enjoy play by:

- giving him simple games, activities and materials that lead to learning;

- taking an interest in his discoveries;

- trying to see the world through his eyes and, because of this, providing him with experiences that enhance his knowledge of it;

- being patient with his weaknesses and praising his strengths;

- not having unrealistic expectations; accept your child for who he is and allow him to develop his potential at his own rate; and

- giving him age-appropriate activities. Don't push him out of his depth.

Keep in mind that each child is an individual and what works for one may not work for another.

Games

Here are some fun games to play with your child.

Crawling. If your child is still crawling, get down on the floor and crawl around with him — he will love having you at eye level.

Water play. You and your child can play with water in the kitchen sink. Give your child plastic dishes and cutlery, a sponge or cloth and dishwashing gloves just like the ones you use. (*Note:* If your child is using the sink, be sure he is standing on a stable chair with arms. Stay in the room to supervise.) Also, float a variety of sponges in a basin of water and let your child experiment by squeezing them or soaping them up. Pop objects on top of the sponges and explain why sponges float. In the bath, provide a set of measuring cups so your child can pour water from one cup to another. Let him blow bubbles using a straw; let him help you count the toys as you drop them into the bathtub. Make a puppet from a face washer. In an outdoor wading pool use a variety of containers that can be filled and emptied — sponges, squirt bottles, funnels and sprays. (*Note:* For bathtime safety ensure your child is in no danger of touching the hot water tap and that he doesn't stand up in the bath.)

Sand play. Use measuring cups, tipper trucks, spades and buckets. Poke holes in a plastic container to create a colander that he can pour sand out of. (*Note:* Cover the sandpit at night to keep out rain and animals.)

Stacking blocks. Your small child will need your help with this activity, as he can successfully stack three blocks at around the age of 18 months. If you build a tower, let your child knock it down.

Dancing. Dance to music together and encourage your child to sway and wiggle.

Reading. When he is around the age of 18 to 20 months, help him to turn the pages of a book as you read to him.

Building. Show your child how to take simple things apart and fit things together.

Colours. Look for colours around your house — for example, look for all the things that are blue or red.

Balls. Kick a ball together or, if your child isn't yet walking or is not interested in kicking, sit down opposite him and roll a ball back and forth.

Sorting. Show him how to sort objects and shapes.

Colouring. Colour with crayons.

Puppets. Make a friendly puppet out of a wooden spoon by drawing a face on it. Add wool for hair and fabric for an outfit. Give the puppet to your child.

Rattles. Make shaking toys, such as a plastic bottle filled with beans or rice. Don't forget to put the lid on securely once you have filled it.

Mirrors. Play with safe mirrors. Stand or sit with your child in front of the mirror. Talk to him, make funny faces and sounds, and encourage movement.

Housework. Let your child help you. If you're sweeping, provide a smaller broom for your child to sweep with.

Containers. Give your child a container, such as a shoebox or clean ice-cream container, and a few toys that are easy to grasp. Show your child how to place the toys in the container and then take them out. Once he catches on, your child will love doing this by himself.

Cupboard. Choose a low, easy-to-open cupboard to house your child's kitchen playthings. Fill it with plastic containers and pots and pans that can be used as instruments and stacking toys.

Cardboard box. Find a cardboard box that's big enough for your child to sit in, or one that can be turned into a cubbyhouse. It can also become a car, a bus, train, boat, plane or shop.

Songs

Your child doesn't care if you can't sing, or you think you can't sing. Make up your own tunes and words. For example, 'Daddy loves baby [use your child's name here], Uncle Tom loves baby, Grandma loves baby, Grandad loves baby, We all love baby!'

Then there are the traditional favourites such as:

- 'Old MacDonald Had a Farm'
- 'Humpty Dumpty'
- 'Incy Wincy Spider'
- 'Row, Row, Row Your Boat'
- 'I'm a Little Teapot'
- 'The Wheels on the Bus'
- 'Mary Had a Little Lamb'
- 'Baa, Baa, Black Sheep' (substitute your child's name for the little boy/girl who lives down the lane)
- 'If You're Happy and You Know It Clap Your Hands'
- 'It's Raining, It's Pouring'

Fingerplay

Try this favourite fingerplay game, guaranteed to get lots of giggles.

'Where is Thumbkin?'

(Sing to the tune of 'Frère Jacques')

Where is Thumbkin?
(Put one hand behind your back)
Where is Thumbkin?
(Put your other hand behind your back)
Here I am
(Bring your hand forward in a fist and pop up your thumb)
Here I am
(Bring your other hand forward and pop up your thumb)
How are you today sir?
(Wiggle one thumb to the other)
Very well I thank you
(Wiggle the other thumb in response)

Run away
(Wiggle your thumb and put your fist behind your back)
Run away
(Wiggle your other thumb and put your fist behind your back)

Do this for every finger, using a different finger for each verse.
1 Thumbkin is the thumb.
2 Pointer is the first finger.
3 Tall man is the second finger.
4 Ring man is the third finger.
5 Pinky is the little finger.
For more fun, draw a happy face on your child's thumbs with a
ballpoint pen so he can join in!

Toys for a one- to two-year-old child

Here is a list of some toys that are fun and educational for a child
this age.

- A simple to work 'Jack-in-the-box' (the box should open
  easily enough for your child to do it alone. Make sure the toy
  is safe and his fingers can't get jammed)
- Stacking rings
- Snap-lock beads
- Bath toys (e.g. small boats)

- Toy telephone
- Dolls (when he is ready for more sophisticated play, a doll that can be dressed and undressed)
- Stuffed toys
- Nesting cups
- Large puzzles with knobs that make them easy for your child to use
- Sorting and posting toys
- Ride-on toys
- Plastic tea set
- Push toys (e.g. a block wagon) are good for walking practice
- Push-along cars, trucks and trains
- Pull toys such as a toy animal that he can pull along behind him with a string
- Large crayons and drawing paper
- Pots and pans, plus wooden spoons to hit them with
- Board books and big picture books
- Balls
- Shape toys, such as diamonds, balls, cubes and stars
- Big wooden beads
- A sturdy tipper truck
- Modelling dough (see the recipe supplied on page 227)
- Alphabet or number blocks (for a child aged 18 to 24 months)
- Barn and farm animals
- Basic puzzles (for a child aged 18 to 24 months)
- Bucket and spade
- Children's musical instruments (e.g. tambourine and drum)
- Other music toys, such as a child's cassette player and cassettes, and CDs for children
- A peg board and hammer
- Threading toys

Toy safety checklist

Before you give your child a toy to play with, run through this safety checklist first.

* Is it safe?

* Is it age appropriate? Check the label.

* Is it unbreakable?

* Is it washable?

* Is it too big to swallow?

* Does it have any sharp edges or other pointy bits?

* Does it have any strings, cords or ribbons longer than 15 cm (6 in) attached?

* Is it made from non-toxic materials?

* Does it run on batteries or electricity? (Batteries are dangerous if sucked.)

* Does it have any small gaps that can pinch fingers?

* Does it make loud explosive sounds that could damage a baby's hearing?

* Avoid toys that are smaller than a 35 mm film canister as they are potential choking hazards.

Your child and television

Never use the television as a babysitter. Research shows that children who are high achievers in school have families who limit the amount of time they spend watching television, and censor the type of shows they watch. It's recommended that, when your child does watch television, you watch it with him. This allows you to talk about the program so it becomes a shared learning experience. Also, get into the habit of recording the programs you want to watch, so you can watch them when your child is asleep.

Choosing the right books

If you had little contact with children's books before you became a parent, knowing what books to read to your child can cause a dilemma. Returning to those books you loved when you were a child is always a good start, although you may not be able to find them or remember them without your own parents' help.

To discover what's new and popular, ask a children's librarian and visit a children's bookshop, or a bookshop with a sizeable children's section and helpful, knowledgeable staff.

By the time a child is one year old, he may already be familiar with nursery rhymes, jingles, and naming books and board books with single pictures and one word per page. In the second year, children for whom books are a part of everyday life will want to handle their own books. They will want to turn pages and will make sounds as they are 'reading'. Books need to be as readily available as other toys, and parents need to understand they will suffer the same wear and tear. This sometimes means that favourites need to be replaced.

In this second year, your child will be ready for theme books. These are different to storybooks, which require the mental ability of being able to follow a plot. A theme book may have the same

child on every page doing different everyday things, or it could be about sizes or shapes or noses or eggs. Following on from theme books are descriptive books. These are often about an activity, such as going shopping or spending a day at the park, and will have the same characters on every page. Lift-the-flap books are also popular with this age group.

Water awareness

You can't teach a child under three to swim. Drowning is a major cause of accidental death in this age group. It is possible for motivated parents and swimming coaches to teach an individual child skills, but there is no guarantee that the child will use these skills if he falls into cold, unfamiliar water.

If you are aware of this, you and your baby can relax and enjoy the positive aspects of toddler water familiarization classes, which can have social, emotional and physical benefits. Your child will be playing next to other children in a relaxed environment where fun should be the main goal. He will also be exercising his body in a weightless, watery environment. At the same time, he will be concentrating on all that is happening around him, learning more about the world. Ideally, the classes will also help him develop confidence and independence.

You can also gain from this experience. It provides another opportunity for you to bond with your child, with the added bonus that you will have the chance to meet other parents of children the same age.

Before you and your toddler head off to the pool, it's important to prepare him. He needs to feel relaxed in the swimming pool and comfortable in a group class. It's advisable to start 'practising' several months ahead. At home during bathtime gently drip water over your child's forehead (don't continue if he doesn't like it). Eventually, after several weeks, you may have progressed to a small cup of water, which you can also pour over his face. Warn him that you're about to pour by counting to three and exclaiming: 'Pour!' Only do this a couple of times each bathtime and never use shampoo or soap. Remember to always keep bathtime fun.

If your child is scared of the water, there is no point pursuing classes. It's no use forcing him into the water if he's not happy and willing to go. Wait a season and try again, all the while maintaining non-threatening bathtime activities. While the age at which a child becomes water competent varies, sooner or later every child who has the opportunity will become familiar with basic water safety.

When choosing a swim program for your child, make sure the classes meet the following standards.

Qualified teachers. Check that the teachers hold a relevant certificate and are experienced.

Class ratios. You will be in the water with your child in a class that should have no more than six children to each teacher.

Water temperature. Warm water is important for very young children. They won't stay in the water long if it is too cold.

You can find water awareness or familiarization programs through private swimming schools, local swimming pools, school programs or holiday programs run by the relevant government organization.

Gym for little ones

Even before your child is on his feet, he will be eager to explore his environment. There are many ways you can encourage him to become involved in the physical activities that help promote rhythm, coordination, flexibility, body strength and movement without having to enrol in a baby gym class.

Why not kick a ball together? Dance together, play gentle wrestling games, play in the pool together, have 'races' with each other, go to a park with age-appropriate play equipment, and encourage (supervised) climbing and jumping, sliding and swinging. On a rainy day create an obstacle course inside, using boxes with the tops and bottoms cut out and a table and chairs covered with blankets. Your child will love negotiating his way through the course. Another easy game is tossing beanbags into a laundry basket or box.

Formal baby gym programs are designed to promote the physical, social, emotional and cognitive development of the child. They usually comprise a series of structured classes. Many programs use tools such as exercises and dancing to music. These classes are usually devised for infants from six weeks through to early school age. As with water awareness classes and playgroup, they are a great way to meet other parents. However, some instructors are better trained than others. Look out for instructors with early childhood or recognized physical fitness qualifications.

Children's play equipment for the garden

Whether your garden is a small paved courtyard in the inner city or a big suburban block, here are some guidelines for making your backyard as safe as possible for kids.

- It is a safe place to run around, with the play area separate from the driveway.
- If there's a shed in the yard, it's securely locked with all dangerous items stored out of reach of children.
- All gates have childproof latches.
- The children's toys are stored separately.
- It has safe play equipment that can be used for a range of physical activities.
- There is a soft surface (not sand, which compacts and becomes hard, but bark or rubber) underneath the play equipment to cushion falls.

- If it has swings, they have been professionally installed. Make sure there's enough space around them so your child can swing safely.
- Your backyard has a safe uncluttered path that is wide enough for ride-on toys. A gentle slope may be okay with parental supervision, but a steep slope is a danger zone.
- Water features, such as fountains, are set higher than a toddler can reach (not less than 1 m or 3 ft) and are completely surrounded by childproof fencing.
- A wading pool is kept empty when not in use and in full view of adults when it is being used. Similarly, in-ground and above-ground swimming pools always pose a danger to young children and, tragically, many drownings occur in the moments when caregivers are distracted. Ensure your pool has isolation fencing that meets the appropriate standard, with a secure magnetic self-latching gate. Never leave a young child unsupervised in a garden with a pool.
- It has a shady spot for adults where they can sit and watch the children play.
- Make sure your garden is fenced off and that everything is safe. (*Note:* Young children have no fear, so it is never safe to leave them outside without adult supervision.)

Add some fun to your garden

A safe garden is of crucial importance, but it can be restricting without the addition of some magical elements. For a start, everyone loves secret nooks and crannies, so a garden with an element of a 'secret' garden will appeal to all children. You can help create a children's wonderland in your garden by providing various spots of interest and activity. Here are some ideas.

- Create a 'stepping stone' pathway with timber logs cut into 3 cm (1 in) thick slabs. Make sure there's a surprise at the end of the pathway, such as a garden with gnome or fairy statues.

- Reserve a part of the garden for a selection of pretty flowers such as pansies and violets, and fragrant herbs, including orange or lemon thyme.

- Pick a sunny plot with good soil and drainage, and create an edible garden together.

- Give your child a set of small tools — such as a trowel, fork and hand rake — so he can help with the planting and nurturing of easy-to-grow vegetables such as dwarf beans, snow peas, lettuce and cherry tomatoes.

- Add a sandpit, but make sure it is shaded by a tree, small pergola or shadecloth.

- A cubbyhouse will provide hours of fun. Children usually appreciate a cubby that's child-sized. Also, let them help when you build or assemble it, as they will then feel actively involved in its construction.

- A multipurpose play unit which features swings, monkey bars and climbing features will get much more use than a single-purpose one. You can check the equipment is safe before you buy it, as it should comply with the appropriate safety standards.

- If there's a large strong tree in the garden, make a swing from a section of tyre (not the steel-belted variety). When hanging the tyre, place a strong rope through a hole in each end and then knot it using blocks or washers to spread the load. Manila and sisal ropes cost less than synthetic rope, and are less likely to give rope burn, but they are stiff to knot. Polymide or nylon ropes are strong and stretch under strain, but are affected by sunlight. Polyester is strong and not

affected by sun, water or stretching. Note that the thinner the rope, the greater the chance of children suffering rope burn, and that when you double the diameter of the rope, you multiply the strength by four.

- An old wooden table that can be used for painting and other craft projects.

Your child's first birthday party

Some people love giving parties and can't wait to host their baby's first birthday party. Others dread the very thought of the organization and the mess, and would prefer to forget it altogether. Most parents will, at some stage, hold a party for their child, although some may leave it until the child is old enough to know what a party is all about, round the age of three or four.

Guidelines for a smooth party

What do you do for a child's party if it's years since you've been to one and you know nothing about what is expected? Here are some guidelines for holding parties in your child's early years.

Baby's first birthday is really a celebration for baby's parents. Your baby will not know what all the fuss is about. He is likely to enjoy the wrapping paper more than the presents.

Many people celebrate their baby's first birthday with a party for adults or family. A barbecue or lunch is fun for all and a baby who has a morning nap will enjoy the attention. Keep it simple; unless you have home help a fancy lunch will make life more complicated. Ask guests to help by providing some of the food or drink.

Some families have friends with babies the same age, and celebrating their child's birthday with a party for these families is important. If this is the case, be sure to plan ahead.

- Have the party early in the afternoon and make it for an hour.

- Ask the parents as well as the child.

- Check with the parents if their child has any allergies. For example, some children are allergic to strawberries and milk.

- Ask parents to bring a cup or bottle for their child. Provide juice and milk.

- Babyproof the house as much as possible.

- Hang all adult bags and nappy bags out of the children's reach.

Food

- Provide bread sticks, cupcakes and cut up fruit, or little fruits like seedless grapes and strawberries as party food. Avoid junk food.

- Have food and drink for the adults.

Balloons

Balloons are fun and very much a part of most parties. Even babies love balloons — trying to grab them is part of the fun, but they must be supervised all the time. When they burst they can frighten a baby and the little bits are choking hazards.

On the day

- Sit on the floor, or outside on the grass, with the children.

- Make an event of present giving by helping your child open the presents as soon as the guests arrive.

- Read the children a story or sing some songs. Simple nursery rhymes are best — 'Baa, Baa, Black Sheep', 'Incy Wincy Spider' or songs from a favourite CD.

- Serve a cake and help baby blow out the candle.

Golden rules

- Remember no party turns out exactly as planned.

- An extra pair of adult hands will make all the difference.

- Put away favourite toys. Toddlers can find it difficult to share their toys with others.

- Take note of who gave which present so you can thank them.

- Have a contingency plan in case of rain.

- Never take a hungry child to a party.

- Make sure every child wins a prize if you are having games.

- Ensure that the birthday person is made to feel special.

- Keep a birthday party book and stick in it invitations, photos and the guest list for each year.

Two to three years

A three-year-old is an intrepid explorer. The world is a fascinating place and your three-year-old is watching and learning with new eyes — she will make you look at your world afresh.

How your child grows

Toddlers are keen to develop their skills and will spend hours riding a tricycle or making something. Time is a concept they have not yet grasped, so telling them 'next week' or 'tomorrow' is a waste of effort.

Development checklist

Around three years

**Date you noticed
your child doing it**

Most of your child's speech is understandable, although she will occasionally stumble

Talks in complete sentences: 'The dog is eating dinner' or 'The car goes fast'

Enjoys repetitive language, short rhymes

Listens attentively when a short story is read to her and likes familiar stories read in the same way

Will 'read' a favourite book

Loves to sing

Asks questions such as 'why?' and 'how?'

Can stack up to seven blocks

Enjoys playing with modelling dough

Can put together a six-piece puzzle

Draws circles and squares

Can name the common colours, such as red, blue, yellow and green

Can count up to three

Can solve simple problems

Can match things up

Knows that younger children are younger but can't tell the difference between herself and older children

Knows her age

Seeks adult attention: 'Watch me, Mum!'

May show a preference for the parent of the opposite sex

Accepts suggestions and follows simple instructions

Enjoys helping out

Likes to be a clown

Enjoys playing alone but likes other children nearby

Will play with other children sometimes, but still finds sharing difficult

Likes to hear stories about herself

Enjoys playing 'house'

Development checklist

Around three years

Date you noticed your child doing it

Has a full set of teeth

Puts on shoes and can dress herself in simple clothes

Tries to catch a ball; can kick it and throw it

Hops on one foot

Can walk on tiptoes

Is able to pedal a tricycle after being shown how

Walks on a line

Can feed herself with a spoon and fork

May use the toilet independently and wash her hands

Can get a drink

Wants to help prepare meals

Can jump over a very small hurdle

Feeding

Most children experience a fussy eating phase. It seems they live on little else but the air they breathe, but still they continue to grow! Usually, there's nothing to worry about. Throughout the day your child picks at this and that, and still manages to achieve the nutritional quota. However, if your child appears unwell, is lacking energy and complaining of tiredness, there may be something wrong and a visit to the doctor is recommended.

Fussy eaters

Rather than setting rigid mealtime rules for your child, it might be a good idea to impose some rules on yourself — relax, take it easy and remember that toddlers don't intentionally starve themselves. If you are struggling with your own weight issues, try not to impose the stringent rules and regulations you set for yourself on your child. Let her assert her independence by making her own decisions, within reason, about who she plays with, what she wears, whether she will wash her hair, and what food she will eat or choose not to eat. Your role is to help her take control by guiding her gently in the right direction.

As you read this book you may have realized that your child's reaction has a lot to do with your attitude. There's no point getting angry just because your child has an aversion to broccoli, or all vegetables for that matter. What you need to do is forget the battle and get clever. Find foods that are going to bring the same nutritional benefits to your child's diet as vegetables, or camouflage the green stuff, so she doesn't realize she's eating it. You can make sure she is eating enough from all the food groups by offering her a selection of fresh fruit, lean meat, dairy products, grains and legumes. Then work on a plan to hide her greens — for example, purée vegetables into a pasta sauce, add them to white sauce or make soup with them.

Tips on how to deal with the fussy eater

Here are some other tips on how to coax your fussy eater to the meal table.

- Eat as a family around the table, not in front of the television, as often as possible.
- Children love routine, so keep mealtimes regular.
- Make eating fun and relaxed. Let your child help with the preparations. She can help set the table, gather some herbs from the garden or mash the potatoes.
- Check that your child is sitting on a comfortable chair and that she can easily reach the table and the food on her plate.
- If it's nice weather, occasionally eat outside or throw down a rug and have a picnic or a barbecue in the backyard.
- Offer your child more than one option, and don't force her to eat a specific food.
- Don't worry if your child spills or drops food. This is a clumsy time in her life because her fine and gross motor skills are still developing.
- Give vegetables funny names and be prepared to play 'Mr Aeroplane' as you zoom 'Ms Carrot Head' towards your child's mouth.
- Arrange the meat and vegetables on the plate so they resemble a funny face. Encourage your child to eat the face, piece by piece.
- Small serves are better than large serves, which can appear overwhelming to your child.
- You could also place a large serving plate, featuring a selection of appetizing finger foods, in the middle of the table to allow your child to choose what she likes.
- A tired child has no appetite. Don't force the issue if she'd rather be in bed.
- Don't bribe your child with a sweet reward for eating a certain food she doesn't like. You will find that she still dislikes the food she is being forced to eat, and will come to associate fatty foods, such as cake, with being a good girl.

- Children's tastes change. One day she'll love something and the next week she'll hate it. So be careful not to stock up on this week's fad!

- Children are great imitators, so if your child sees Dad, Grandma, a favourite cousin or best friend eating a different food, she might be influenced to try it herself.´

- Praise your child for trying a new food, but don't worry if she leaves it.

- Offer a variety of foods from all the food groups and also offer foods from different cultures such as fetta cheese, baked ricotta, tabouli, felafel, olives and sun-dried tomatoes.

- Keep offering your child new foods until they become regulars at mealtime.

- Give your child small quantities of a new food on the same plate as the familiar food.

- Avoid sugary drinks such as fruit juice and cordial. They fill your child up with empty kilojoules (calories).

- Don't give sugary foods as a meal replacement. They always come after the main course.

- Watch out for sore throats, teething problems and upset tummies, which might be affecting your child's appetite.

- Your fussy eater won't be rushed. Be patient and let her take her time at the dinner table.

Caring

You can continue to dress your child in the types of clothes she has been wearing since she reached toddlerhood.

Clothing update

If your child starts to use the potty or toilet during the day, take it into account when dressing her, as you don't want her to have difficulty with her clothes when she is in a hurry.

Children grow at different rates, and you may be surprised to find that the clothes you bought your toddler a month or so ago are now too small. At the beginning of each season you can buy clothes that are a little too big, but if you buy two sizes too big you may find they hamper your child's movements as well as make her look a little odd.

Remember to keep a check on her shoes and socks, too. Her feet will be growing as much as her body, so she may need new shoes every couple of months.

Hair care

It takes a lot of time and practice for a child to master the skill of hair brushing and combing. You should start showing your child how to do it properly now, and she will be ready to do it all by herself around the age of seven.

Bathtime

It may also take a while for your child to enjoy having her hair washed. You can make this experience fun by employing a few clever tactics.

- When it is hair-washing night, do the wash as soon as she hops in the bath.

- Swimming goggles can be put to good use at bathtime if your child's eyes are sensitive to shampoo suds. Have her hold the goggles over her eyes while you use a plastic cup to rinse the shampoo out of her hair. Turn the event into a learning experience by counting each time you pour fresh water over her head, and encourage her to count, too. You might find it takes 20 cups of water or less to get rid of the suds. If you don't own goggles, substitute a face washer folded and pressed over her eyes, or shop around for special bathtime visors, which are stocked by pharmacists and some specialty shops.

- With your help, let your child lather up the shampoo on her hair. This gives her some control over the situation and teaches her another skill that requires coordination.

- Lather your child's hair so it pokes out in spikes, then give her a mirror so she can see the hilarious results!

- Rinse her hair with an assortment of cups, bottles and even a watering can. Pretend your child is a flower, and every time her head is watered she grows just that little bit taller!

- If your child still can't bear the thought of having her hair washed, the best option is to keep her hair quite short so the experience is quickly over and done with. For girls, at least, this strategy might be enough to coax them back into the bath!

Combing and brushing

- Give your child a doll with hair that can be combed and brushed so she can start to practise on a passive model.
- After you wash your child's hair with shampoo, finish off with a conditioner so that brushing or combing is not a painful experience.
- Use a wide-toothed comb to combat knots and to make the experience more enjoyable for your child.
- Stand in front of a mirror when you are combing or brushing your child's hair and tell her how nice she looks.
- Give your child her own comb and brush, and keep them in a special place, such as a painted box decorated with stickers and glitter.

At the hairdresser's

Some two- and three-year-olds fear the hairdresser more than the dentist. They find it hard to understand that their hair will grow back and that it is not going to be lost to them forever. Because scissors are involved, they might also believe that the 'cutting' will hurt them. You can alleviate their fears by using strategies to make the event terrific rather than terrifying.

- Take along distractions — drawing materials, books, dolls, trucks — anything to keep your child occupied while her hair is being cut.
- Let your child watch the hairdresser cutting your hair. If she sees Mummy or Daddy having a haircut, she may realize it's not going to hurt after all.
- Turn the haircut into a special occasion. Give her a big cushion to sit on, swirl the protective cape over her shoulders as though she is a princess warrior — for a boy it could be a save-the-world superhero cape — and stay by her side for support during the haircut.
- Let her watch her hair being cut in the mirror.
- Congratulate her on a job well done and praise her appearance when the haircut is completed.

Safety: what to watch for

Children of this age are particularly prone to accidents because their behaviour is so impulsive.

Safety in the kitchen

If you haven't already, now is the time to check the kitchen for danger spots and ensure that they are made safe for, or inaccessible to, your curious child.

* Use a safety gate at the entry point(s) to the kitchen to keep your child out of the danger zone, but still in your line of vision. Limit the entry points to the kitchen to one.

* A toddler is insatiably curious. If she can't see what's on top of the stove, her natural instinct is to reach and grab! To prevent this disastrous scenario, fit a stove guard that blocks access to the front and both sides of the stove. If the stovetop is part of a freestanding stove/oven unit, ensure that is anchored to the wall. Add an oven lock to prevent your child pulling open the oven door. And always point pot handles to the back of the stove.

* Ideally, the kitchen drawers should be located away from the stove and oven, and be fitted with child-resistant locks.

* Place child-resistant locks on kitchen cupboards that contain dishwashing liquid, other cleaners and medications.

* In the perfect home, the kitchen is positioned to provide a clear view of the outside play areas, so you can keep an eye on your child in the backyard while you're preparing meals.

* Make sure hot and cold taps are clearly marked. Install a thermostatic mixer or tempering device, or turn the hot water down to 50°C (122°F) to help prevent scalds.

* Buy electrical appliances with curly cords. If your toaster or kettle doesn't have a curly cord, push it to the back of the bench, out of reach of little hands.

* Electrical outlets are best positioned away from the sink area. At least six electrical outlets are recommended for a kitchen, each placed on the wall, 25 cm (10 in) above the bench.

* Store fire control devices, such as a fire extinguisher and blanket, near the exit to the kitchen. Fit a smoke alarm near the entrance to the kitchen.

■ Your three-year-old will be fascinated with water, so she must be supervised at all times around ponds and pools; empty your wading pool when it is not in use, and never leave your child alone in the bath.

■ Plastic bags, and other items that could suffocate or strangle your child, should be kept well out of reach.

■ If your child has a first tricycle, make sure she wears a helmet whenever she is riding.

■ Her sense of balance and coordination is still developing, so she could easily fall from high play equipment or household furniture. Supervise, and provide a soft undersurfacing to any garden play equipment.

- Playing outdoors is fun. In the summer months be sure to protect your child's skin with a hat and high-protection suncream. In the hottest part of the day playing indoors is preferable.

- A two- or three-year-old cannot perceive the dangers of traffic. Always supervise by holding your child's hand when you are walking near a road, observe sensible road safety rules yourself, and be sure that your own garden has safe, secure fencing with self-latching gates.

Pets

Pets can be very important to a child, who will learn valuable messages about caring, friendship and responsibility as she grows. Animals are not a risk to a child's health if you follow a few simple rules, and teach your child how to care for them and how to behave safely around them.

The most common age for a child to be attacked by the family dog is two years old. This is not surprising if you look at the two-year-old from the dog's point of view. At this age a child's curiosity can lead her to poke the dog's eyes or pull its ears, interfere with its food and perhaps even try to take a bone. Research has found that although it is important to choose a breed that fits in with the children as well as the family's circumstances, when it comes to attacks the breed doesn't matter — it is the way the dog is treated.

Dogs attack in order to defend what they see as their own — their food, territory or young. They will attack when they are afraid, teased or in pain. A dog must know who is the boss. A dog that is friendly and gentle with an adult may not behave in the same way with a toddler.

If you have a dog, it is important that you teach your toddler to respect it. This means leaving the dog alone when it is sleeping, eating and playing with other dogs. You also need to supervise the dog and toddler when they are together.

The most common places for a child to be bitten by a dog are the face or neck: this is due to the child's height in relation to the dog. If your child is ever bitten by a dog she may require a tetanus injection, so it is worth taking her to the doctor.

If you have a cat, you should teach your toddler to respect it too. Cats are usually more adept than dogs at getting away from small children, but they will also lash out if they feel threatened,

and the toddler may suffer a nasty scratch. Cat scratches can easily become infected because of the bacteria in the cat's claws. It is important to flush the area with water, and then apply an antiseptic. If it is a bad scratch, a visit to a doctor would be a wise precaution.

If you have a cat and a children's sandpit, you need to be wary of the cat using the sandpit as a litter box. Covering the sandpit after use is the best precaution.

Birds are only of interest to a toddler while she can watch them — she is really not capable of handling them gently. It is possible to catch a flu-like illness, known as psittacosis, from a bird, by breathing in the dust containing dried bird droppings. If you have a bird, it is important to keep its cage clean and to take care when you are getting rid of the droppings. Birds are better kept in cages outside.

Talking about sexuality

From the moment she is born, your child is a sexual being. And how she is taught to experience and think about sensuality and sexuality is likely to have implications throughout her life.

A responsible approach

These days sexuality educators encourage parents to treat sexuality as part of their total existence. If your child is taught that sex is a

Body parts

The earlier you start using the proper names for the parts of the body, the easier they are to explain. Children can become confused when genitals are given pet names, especially if it's a pet term known only to the family. This can cause communication problems if your son is in the care of others and hurts his penis in a fall, but refers to it by another name when describing the injury! If a child has access to the correct words, he can understand his body and more easily explain himself if problems arise. It's also healthier for his self-esteem to avoid baby talk. By talking frankly and honestly about genitals yourself, your child will not regard his genitals as being significantly different from any other part of his body. It may be easier to talk to boys about their genitals because the male genitals are more exposed and therefore easier to label, whereas girls' genitals are more enclosed and may require more description.

natural part of everyone's lives, she is likely to grow up feeling good about sex, and she will be equipped with the skills and confidence to protect herself from being abused or exploited. A child who is comfortable with the topic of sex is more likely to approach her parents when she has worries or needs information.

By being available to discuss sexuality with your child, you are letting her know sex is not taboo, that it is really no different from any other issue she might approach you about. As informed and responsive parents, you are also in a position to clarify any misinformation that your child might gather from other children (especially older ones), television or other family members. On the other hand, parents who do not talk about sex with their child are likely to convey a negative message, which could cause their child to look elsewhere for answers and information.

Finding the right time

There may never be a 'right time' to talk about sex. The first step you can take as a parent is to analyze your attitude to your own sexuality. After all, you can't expect your child to feel good about herself if you don't feel comfortable with yourself and your body. The next step is to concentrate on becoming an approachable parent, which means being open to your child's queries on any topic, and feeling comfortable and confident with your replies.

Your child may not bring up the subject of sex until she is older, but at least you will be prepared if you think about it now. Here are some suggestions for when the time comes.

- Answer questions about sexuality when they are asked, and don't send your child to the other parent.

- Children need to know sex is private, and they also need to be aware that a man and a woman have a sexual relationship, not just for making babies, but also for the sake of their own relationship.

- Keep the answers simple, honest and short. Children don't need a thesis on the subject!

- Sometimes, when you answer questions, ask a few of your own, particularly if you are concerned about the nature and origin of your child's questions.

- Don't assume your child isn't interested in sexuality if she doesn't ask questions. Introduce the topic where appropriate. For example, if you visit the house of a pregnant friend together, ask your child, 'Did you see her big tummy?' and continue from there.

- In the end, the message is about love. Let your child know how much you love her and that you believe in her. This will help her believe in herself and feel confident about all aspects of her life, including her sexuality.

'Doctors and nurses'

Preschool children play 'Doctors and nurses' to figure out gender differences: they note each other's physical attributes, including the genitals. This is natural curiosity, although some parents might misconstrue it as being primarily sexual.

It is wise not to overreact if you discover your child involved in sexual play. By showing anger, disgust or imposing a punishment, you are teaching your child to associate sexual behaviour with guilt, shame and confusion. A more positive option is to respond in a calm manner and use diversionary tactics such as taking your child for a walk to the park, or baking a chocolate cake together.

Some parents are also embarrassed about masturbation. But there is no need to be — masturbation is natural, and by the time a child is ready for school she has usually learnt that it is inappropriate to touch her genitals in public. If the touching appears to be obsessive, there may be other factors at play and professional advice may be required.

Exposure to nudity

When you allow your child into the bathroom with you when you are naked, you are showing her that the adult body is good and nothing to be ashamed of. You are also giving your child the chance to ask questions, especially if you talk about parts of the body. If you don't feel comfortable allowing your child to see you naked, still endeavour to give your child the message that her body is 'OK' and 'special'.

Sleeping

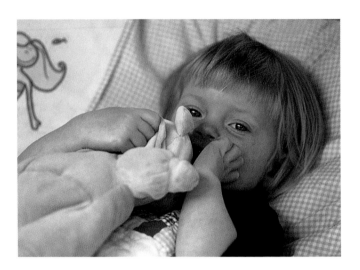

Children who have learnt how to go to sleep by themselves by this age will often talk themselves to sleep and may run through some of the things that have happened in their day. If you are still having difficulty getting your child to sleep most nights, then you probably need to adopt a new tactic. Turn back to the section on sleep in the 'One to two years' chapter for some suggestions (see page 212).

Night-time problems

This is the time to make sure you have firmly established good sleeping patterns and a bedtime routine. If your child has established bad habits, such as sleeping in your bed every night or falling asleep in front of the television, she can wreck the whole family's sleeping patterns and cause lots of stress.

Night terrors

After a tough or stressful day a child may experience night terrors. These are frightening for both the parents and the child. A sudden scream in the middle of the night will bring anxious parents running to find a child possibly hysterical and absolutely terrified. You will need to be calm and to comfort your child until she settles down again.

Night wandering

Night wandering is another problem that may arise. The toddler who can climb out of her bed may wander into your bed some time in the night. Climbing out of bed is dangerous in itself, and once she is free to roam around the house that too is a problem. It is far better to prevent her from wandering in the first place.

A child who wanders in the night was probably ignored when she cried out, so one of the best ways of ensuring the wandering does not occur is to settle her every time she cries for you. Another option is to dress your child in a sleeping bag at night. You can also avoid the climbing by making sure the rail is too high for her to get a leg over, and there are no props such as large soft toys to help her.

If she does appear next to you or in your bed, the surest way to make sure she does not reach her goal is to take her back to her own bed, gently and firmly. A child who wanders is obviously not ready to move from a cot to a big bed. Save this move until the fascination of coming to you in the night has worn off.

Development

If parents don't understand something about child behaviour, their toddler will inevitably do lots of things they may find difficult to live with. Many of these behaviours resurface in a similar form when the child reaches her early teens, but for different reasons.

Why toddlers behave the way they do

While many toddler behaviours are antisocial, a child who has plenty of practice mixing with other children — at playgroup, at daycare or childcare, or on outings with other children — will work out how to get on in a social group.

Discipline

Children need to learn self-discipline in order to function in society, and they will learn this from their families. Children must have limits set for safety reasons. There are times when you will need to take action to discipline your child, and your approach will depend on your own attitudes, experience and upbringing. This action needs to be coupled with love, affection and understanding.

Today's parents want to teach their children to be honest, to respect the feelings and property of others, to love their family and their home. They want their children to be polite, generous, sociable and self-reliant.

It is during the second year that discipline can become an issue for parents. You need to talk about your own expectations and to reach a consensus about how you are going to handle or, better still, prevent unacceptable behaviour.

Once a toddler is fully mobile, the horizon of new and exciting things to explore widens. Sometimes there will be so much to see and do that a toddler will work herself into a state of frenetic energy or excitement that could lead to a tantrum. If you see this coming, you can prevent it by diverting your child's attention.

Sometimes a toddler will appear to 'tease' you by attempting something that she knows will provoke a 'no'. This behaviour usually requires you to stand your ground gently and firmly, and weather the storm that may include a tantrum. You are setting limits, and your child is testing them.

Attention deficit hyperactivity disorder

Attention deficit hyperactivity disorder (now commonly referred to as ADHD) is a growing problem among young children, particularly boys. It is important to know that preschoolers and toddlers behave in many of the ways that older children who have ADHD do. These behaviours are a perfectly normal part of their development. ADHD can occur in the very young, but it is rare and needs very careful assessment.

Many children are constantly on the go, so what's the difference between these children and those with ADHD? Children who are most often diagnosed with ADHD are:

* restless to the point where they cannot be controlled;

* unable to maintain a normal attention span; and

* tend to be overly impulsive.

Usually part of the treatment is a course of Ritalin, a drug classed as a stimulant; it is not without side effects. Back in the 1970s, an American doctor called Ben Feingold devised a diet to treat the condition, then known simply as hyperactivity. The diet excluded artificial colours and flavours, some preservatives and natural salicylates (salts). It was controversial at the time. By the 1980s the American National Institutes of Health found that, in the majority of children, the diet did not help the condition.

It is suggested that if your child has ADHD you need to:

* remind yourself what is considered normal behaviour for this age group; children are (usually) naturally curious, active and sensitive — they (especially boys) don't like to sit still. This is normal behaviour, but some parents who prefer children who are 'seen but not heard' might think differently.

* read about the subject widely;

* ask for a detailed assessment (this means at least two or three sessions with a paediatrician); and

* ask for a second opinion if you are not happy with the results.

An assessment should include questionnaires to be filled in by you and other carers.

Most of a toddler's behaviour arises from an emotional tug-of-war — her need to be independent battling her fear of loss of security when she leaves the shelter of her parents.

A child of around two years of age is totally self-centred and will continue to expect you to meet her every need. When this doesn't happen, a tantrum may result. A child this age needs to learn to make choices too and this can be difficult: a biscuit or a banana? going or staying? These choices cause inner conflict because the toddler wants it all.

If you adopt the policy of being positive rather than negative — praising good behaviour, ignoring or avoiding unacceptable behaviour — and provide the safest possible home environment for your child to make her own discoveries, you will have fewer problems with your toddler's behaviour. A toddler needs her parents to:

- remind her that she is special but not the centre of the world;

- make it clear she can't get her own way all the time;

- help her learn to tolerate frustration and to cope with her feelings; and

- ensure that she knows you are there for her and in control, particularly when she is unable to control her own emotions.

Attention seeking

Being able to meet a child's needs can be difficult at times, and at other times simply not possible. However, if you meet your child's needs as much as you can then you are less likely to suffer from attention-seeking behaviour that seems hard to prevent.

The clingy child

When your child is out walking with her prime carer, she may seem clingy when she is really just reacting naturally to you moving away (see 'Walking' on page 217). Once you understand that when a child asks to be carried it is for a good reason — she is either frightened, tired or a mixture of both — you will accept her clinginess.

When meeting someone new, whether it's an adult or a child, children in their second and third year will often act very warily. When you take a child of this age to play or be with other children, it can take some time before she will actually play. Once she does, she is more likely to play alongside, rather than with, the others. When you introduce your child to a new child you need to stay nearby as she will probably be clingy. When she is ready, she will gradually move closer to the other child, or one child among a group of children. If you move away too quickly you may have to start again, so take it slowly and carefully. This whole process can take half an hour or more, but until your child is familiar with the other child or children it is a necessary part of learning to socialize with others.

Stress and anxiety caused by moving house, a new baby, illness or a marriage break-up can affect a toddler and make her more clingy than usual.

Whining and whingeing

Whingers are made, not born. Whingers have learnt that their behaviour gets them what they want. Sometimes they start whingeing because they see an older person doing it. Indeed, many adults whinge without realizing they are doing so.

Here are the best strategies for coping with a child who is starting to whinge.

- Decide what is causing it — for example, tiredness, hunger, not feeling well, boredom.
- As soon as the whingeing starts, try to divert your child's interest onto something else. If you have worked out that tiredness is the cause, deal with that straight away.
- Tell your child, 'I can't hear you when you whinge.'
- Praise your child when she behaves well.
- Make a joke of it if you find yourself or others whingeing.

Fears and anxiety

All children will be afraid of something at some time. Fears are a normal part of development, and if you handle them with understanding, it will help your child to grow out of them.

Some children are naturally more shy and sensitive than others. If your child shows she is afraid of something, you need to respect that fear. It may be anything, from the vacuum cleaner or a flushing toilet to a large dog.

To the toddler the world is a scary place. There is so much to learn and so many unknowns. Dogs are at the top of the list of toddler fears, followed by the dark. Confronting your toddler with her fear will only make the problem worse; it won't help her to conquer her fear. When there really is nothing to fear, it helps to tell your toddler, 'There's nothing to be afraid of, but we won't go any closer because I can tell you are afraid.' Don't say, 'Don't be afraid.'

Independence

Learning that they are independent, separate people is the most important thing children learn between the ages of one and three. Many of the problems that parents encounter are the result of their toddler's struggle for independence while still being a baby in many ways.

Frustration

Frustration is a common emotion for toddlers. A child of this age faces so many mental and physical challenges, it is not surprising that tantrums can arise.

Tantrums

A toddler may fly into a tantrum for any number of reasons: frustration, boredom combined with fatigue, difficulty in communicating, lack of control of the current situation, desperation, and pain or disappointment. Toddler tantrums have been featured so much in parenting books that most parents approach their child's toddler years with trepidation; most have seen at least one bewildered or frustrated parent at the receiving end of a child's tantrum. Psychologist Penelope Leach has a radical approach. She recommends that parents do not anticipate tantrums. They should behave as if they know nothing about them, dealing with them in the course of the day if, and when, they happen as unfortunate episodes.[1]

Here are strategies that you can use for dealing with these outbreaks.

* When your child is showing signs of a tantrum, steer her in a different direction with a diversion or change of scene.

* Keep your child safe while the tantrum is in progress.

* Try not to be affected by the tantrum — don't let your child benefit from it.

* If possible, avoid being embarrassed by the tantrum: either remove the child from the scene or wait the tantrum out.

When you notice your child becoming frustrated, provide a diversion. Here are some strategies you can try.

- Put on some of your child's favourite music and encourage her to dance.

- Begin a new project — modelling dough, water painting or water play are all fun diversions.

- Go for a walk. This works well for adults as well as for children. The walk can be a short one if time is limited, or a longer one to the park or nearby beach.

- Avoid obvious triggers. An overtired and hungry child who is taken somewhere boring — for example, to the supermarket for the weekly shop — or who is made to wait while an adult finishes a task, is likely to resort to a tantrum.

Learning social values

A small amount of aggression in this age group is normal, and all toddlers cling and grizzle at some time. Toddlers learn best when they are loved and feel safe. Patience and praise from parents and carers are very important, as is teaching by example the right way to behave.

Signs of aggression...biting, hitting, hair pulling

Aggressive behaviour is not socially acceptable and needs to be stopped as soon as it starts. A toddler whose feelings of anger or frustration are out of control will resort to aggression if the situation involves another child. An adult needs to either remove the child from the situation or avoid it altogether. If two children are playing in a sandpit, they need a bucket each. If there is only one bucket, an argument may result. If that happens, the adult needs to remove one child.

A child who hits, bites or pulls hair will not learn that such aggressive behaviour is unacceptable if you hit, bite or pull her hair in return. She will not be able to understand why she can't do it but an adult can. You must stop these acts every time, as soon as they happen. You should tell the child that it is not acceptable behaviour. You may even need to remove her from the situation for a time.

Sharing and caring

Toddlers are not capable of understanding the concept of sharing and really do not want to do it. If you understand this, you can help your toddler to learn how to play with others.

- Show her how to take turns.
- Put much-loved toys away when other children come to play.
- Help the toddler to choose toys she is willing to share with other children.
- Don't expect a toddler to share with a new baby.
- Set a good example through your own generosity.
- Praise good behaviour.

Ready for the toilet

Here is a story about a mother who was eager to toilet train her daughter before the age of two. When the child turned 19 months, her mother turned on the pressure. This caused friction. The toddler didn't understand why she had to sit on the potty for so long or why her mother was angry, so she chose to do a bowel motion in a corner of the room away from her mother's prying eyes and mixed-message comments. Her mother became increasingly frustrated by what she perceived to be her daughter's lack of cooperation. There were tears, of course.

Unfortunately, this fictional tale has a ring of truth to it when parents, with high expectations for their child and themselves, attempt to determine the precise time their child should become dry both during the day and at night. The fact is that all children are different, and for every one child who is toilet trained by the age of two, there are many more who are not yet physically or emotionally prepared to tackle this significant milestone.

Like every major developmental achievement, toilet training cannot be rushed, and may take longer than 12 months. It requires perceptiveness, patience and encouragement from you before your child can successfully move forward through this major developmental process.

Change in attitudes

Back in the 1950s, new mothers were advised to hold their babies over the potty from the age of six weeks! It sounds irrational now, but at the time it was considered expert advice. In the 1960s, the 'rules' were relaxed somewhat, with toilet training starting as early as ten months. These days preparation for the potty can begin anywhere from 18 months to three years, with some children not being toilet trained until around their fifth birthday, or later.

It's fortunate that our children don't have to endure the regimented routines of the past. However, because of their own early experiences, many parents may find it hard to shake off the notion that their children should be toilet trained by the age of two. It's important to remember that it really doesn't matter whether your child is ready or not, and that she should not be pushed to perform on the potty — no matter what her age. Your role is to encourage and enlighten, not to wield the imaginary big stick. So what if the neighbours' kids were using the potty at two? Don't feel the need to compete with other parents.

Your child is an individual, and if she's not fully ready by the age of four, she shouldn't be made to feel bad about it. Also, avoid the well-meaning advice of grandparents, as most of them are from a generation when children were regimented into a potty routine from an unrealistic ten months. Their comments may imply that successful toilet training reflects successful parenting and a child's capabilities. And that's not fair to you or your child.

Don't think you're spoiling your child by letting her discover when she is ready to use the potty. Your role is to ensure she grows up with a healthy self-esteem, so gently guide her to potty readiness.

Signs of readiness

Your child may be ready to learn to control her bladder and bowels somewhere around the age of two, but it could be closer to three. Often boys start later than girls. If your child displays three or more of the following signs, she may be ready to start.

* Your child is able to recognize that her bowels and bladder are full and indicates her feelings of discomfort to you.

* She stops what she's doing, appears distracted and makes faces and noises which indicate she is passing a bowel motion. This means she is thinking about what's happening. Gently let her know what is going on in familiar terminology.

* Your child understands what the potty is used for and indicates that she is happy to use it.

* She lets you know she is doing a wee or poo, or that she has just done it.

* You find that your child is staying dry for around two to three hours at a time and may even be dry after a daytime nap.

* She can dress and undress herself.

* Your child is able to understand and follow directions.

* Your child tells you when she is feeling wet and uncomfortable.

* She tells you she doesn't want to wear a nappy anymore.

If your partner is unsure that such a relaxed method is the right approach, visit your doctor together, or show him or her related websites and recommended childcare manuals that deal with the topic. These all agree on one point — to pressure your child into using the toilet will only lead to negative consequences.

If she is forced on to the potty or toilet too early, your child may become so confused and distressed by the regimen that she becomes constipated; she may rebel by urinating or passing a bowel movement in her pants; or she may feel embarrassed and humiliated and so find a 'hiding place' to do her business. It's important that you and your partner agree on your approach to toilet training and that you are both sensitive to your child's needs. Let her make the decision. Let her feel she is in control and not being bullied into using the toilet before she's ready.

It's not easy, but keep this in mind: if your child isn't toilet trained by the age of three, this is no reflection on your parenting skills. Just give her time and eventually she'll make it. After all, as a wise parent once asked rhetorically, 'Have you ever seen a school-aged child in a nappy?'

One step at a time

If you gently guide your child through the toilet-training process, it will be a pleasant, stress-free experience.

Step 1

Some parents prefer their child to use the big toilet from day one, while others use the potty to prepare their child for toilet readiness. The potty is handy because it can be moved from room to room and taken on trips. However, your child can have just as much success using the big toilet provided it's fitted with a training seat and is easy to access via a step-up stool or other firm platform. Shop together for the potty or training seat, and let your child help choose it. After all, it is her very own potty/seat. At home, let her sit on the potty or toilet fully-clothed to see what it feels like. Explain that one day she might like to do her 'poos' and 'wees' in it. Get her into a routine of sitting on the potty or toilet, but don't force her to remove her nappy unless it's her decision. Also, teach her the terminology and use the words you're comfortable with. When she passes a bowel motion, you may prefer to call it a 'poo'; when she urinates, you could call it a 'wee'. Use the words 'wet' and 'dry' to describe the two different feelings in her pants.

Step 2

After your child has had the potty for about a week, move it into the bathroom near to the toilet so your child can see you using the toilet and make the association. If your child is using the toilet, allow her easy access to the bathroom when you're using the toilet. Tell her that everyone uses the toilet — you, her other parent, siblings and grandparents. When you are in there, let her know what's going on. Don't make her feel that urinating is a 'dirty' practice. It is totally natural and we all have to do it. Explain that she's big now and soon she'll be using the potty or toilet.

Children are great imitators, and your child may express a desire to sit on the potty at the same time you're using the toilet. Ask if she wants her nappy removed. Again, do not insist that she removes it, as she may feel threatened and compromised by this action. Keep this routine going for the next week or so until your child is happy to remove her nappy when she sits on the potty or toilet. Avoid placing pressure on her. Let her decide when it's the right time.

Step 3

After several weeks, start emptying the contents of your child's full nappy into the potty or toilet. This makes it fairly obvious that this is what the potty or toilet is for. Explain what you are doing: 'Look, here's your poo and wee and I'm putting it in the potty. Maybe one day you'd like to do a poo and a wee in your potty.' If she is scared by the flushing of the toilet, don't flush the potty's contents away in her presence. She may be confused as to the whereabouts of the bowel motion, or she may feel that she could be flushed away as well! If the flushing sound doesn't frighten her, help her to press the flush button and let her watch the water swirl around the toilet bowl. Explain where the contents are going, so that she is in no doubt.

Step 4

The next step may take time. If your child expresses an interest in using the potty or toilet, remove her nappy and let her play around the house with nothing on. Most children have a bowel movement once a day about an hour after eating, and most urinate within the hour after a large drink.

You may begin to notice that your child has a bowel motion at roughly the same time every day. Around that time, ask if she would like to use the potty or toilet to do a wee or poo. If she's not interested, relax and ask again a little later. Look out for the signs that she is about to urinate or pass a bowel motion, and then lead her to the potty or toilet immediately because, initially, she won't be able to hold on. Try not to rush the process, as you may find your child resists. If this is the case, ease off for several days. You don't want her to feel that potty/toilet time is a negative experience. However, if she seems keen, offer her the potty or toilet once more. If she does a poo or wee, congratulate her but try not to go overboard because she'll wonder what all the fuss is about.

Step 5

If your child enjoys using the potty, try to continue this routine at home. Each time she uses the potty or toilet successfully, praise her. If she tells you she wants to use the potty or toilet, thank her for letting you know. Of course, there will be times when she'll forget or not make it to the potty or toilet on time. This is perfectly normal. Let her know that wetting on the floor is nothing to be concerned about.

Training pants are absorbent, but less absorbent than a nappy. You can either use disposable training pants, cloth training pants or underpants. Avoid using training pants until your child is ready (see 'Signs of readiness' on page 268). It may act as an incentive if you allow your child to choose underpants which feature her favourite television character.

If she accidentally does a bowel motion in her training pants, place it in the potty or toilet to reinforce that this is where it belongs. Avoid returning her to nappies as she is likely to read this as a sign of failure.

Toilet tips

These tips on toilet training may make the whole process easier.

- It's important to be consistent. If your child is in daycare or a nursery, liaise with the carer or carers to make sure you are using the same toilet-training approach. Insist that their routine be based on positive encouragement, that your child is allowed to go at her own pace and should not be forced into a stressful situation where she feels pressured to perform.

- Make sure the training pants are easy to slip off and on.

- Choose easy to remove clothing. Both boys and girls will have trouble with overalls, fiddly buttons and zips. Elasticized shorts, elasticized long pants and leggings are all appropriate. A girl can also wear a lightweight cotton dress or skirt that is easy to lift up and out of the way.

- Initially, you may have to help your child pull her pants down and back up. Practise with her so she becomes confident enough to do it by herself.

- Avoid negative speak. A child's positive self-image is paramount in toilet training. Even if you find it hard to cope with the smell and appearance of a bowel motion, try not to let your child know your feelings. Avoid negative comments such as: 'Yuk, what an awful smell!' Always remain positive.

- Bladder and bowel control may not be achieved at the same time. Your child may gain bowel control before urine control, or vice versa.

- Some toddlers do not like to do a bowel motion in the potty because they are worried that they are losing part of themselves. Tell your child not to worry and put the bowel motion from her pants into the potty or toilet.

- A boy will begin to use the potty or toilet sitting down. When he is confident on the potty, have a male role model such as his father or brother show him how he can urinate while standing up.

- Train your daughter to wipe herself from the front towards the back to avoid possible infection of the vagina.

- Teach your child to wash her hands with soap and water every time she uses the toilet.

- Always leave the bathroom door open so your child can easily get to the toilet.

- Your toddler has a curious mind, so this is no time for modesty on your part. Your child will naturally ask questions which you should answer in a matter of fact way.

By giving truthful answers you encourage her natural curiosity. Do not label going to the toilet or the male and female genitalia as subjects that are secretive, somehow 'dirty' and not to be discussed.

- Children's books with toilet-training themes are handy tools. They use simple terms to help explain the transition from nappies to the potty or toilet.

- Praise your child for small achievements. Let her know you are proud of her.

Dry at night

Just because your child is dry during the day doesn't mean she will be dry at night. Night-time readiness doesn't usually begin until after your child is dry during the day and after a nap, which may occur any time around three and four years. Be aware that many children aren't fully dry until well after the age of six because their bladders just haven't grown big enough to hold all that liquid! A good indication that your child is ready is when her nappy or training pants are dry for more than four to six hours a day. There is no point waking up your child to take her to the toilet in the middle of the night — it won't speed up the process. Leave the time frame to your child as it's her call. Sooner or later her bladder will signal that she needs to go to the toilet and she will wake up and go to the bathroom.

A new baby

If your child is showing signs of readiness for toilet training, it is better to start preparing her, at the suggested leisurely pace, before rather than after the birth of a new baby. At that time you may be feeling tired and preoccupied with the needs of the newest family member.

If you don't notice any progress in your child's toilet training, don't worry. After the new baby arrives, wait a few months for everything to settle down before starting again. Be understanding if your child reverts to wetting herself after the birth of a sibling. She is still a baby herself, and probably feels insecure now that she has to share you with someone else. If she wants to wear a nappy (and it must be her choice) or drink from a bottle again, let her. Avoid chastising her over any toilet accidents and don't put her under any pressure to perform — no matter how exhausted you are from a new round of sleepless nights! Just think, 'The more I pressure her, the worse she'll feel and the worse I'll feel.' So take it easy. You will not only make your life easier, but hers also. Get a plastic sheet and put it under the bottom sheet, but on top of the mattress and mattress protector. It's a handy investment that will help avoid stains and unpleasant odours, and it will make any night-time accidents easier to clean up.

You can help your child get back on track by commenting positively after she does a poo, even if it's in her nappy. Explain that you are happy she's done a poo because it's good for her. If she uses a potty, allow her to carry it around and let her use it like a seat. Praise her for small achievements such as sitting on the potty or toilet for a short time.

Be prepared for small steps and you won't be disappointed. These suggestions can also be used if your child is recovering from an illness or reacting to other stressful situations such as starting preschool, parental separation, moving to a new house, or the death of a family member or a pet.

Other problems

A child can become constipated if she is recovering from an illness or feeling pressured into using the potty or toilet. If the bowel motions are difficult to pass, a tear around the anus may form and compound the problem. This situation can be stressful for all involved. You can help by making sure your child drinks lots of water, and eats fruit and a reasonable amount of fibre. If the problem persists, take her to the doctor.

Urinary (bladder) infections are another cause for concern, and also require a visit to the doctor. These are the signs of a urinary infection.

- Your child urinates constantly.
- She feels pain while urinating.
- There is blood in her urine.
- Your child is wetting frequently during the day after the age of two.
- She has odd-smelling urine.
- Your child is five years or over and is still wetting herself during the day.

Dummies, bottles and comforters

Your toddler may still be attached to a dummy or bottle, and will probably have a special soft toy or blanket that she uses to comfort herself.

Dummy and bottle

If you haven't weaned your child off a dummy or bottle by the time she starts preschool, now is the time to do it. At this age dummies and bottles do not do permanent damage to teeth, but most parents would like their child not to be dependent on them by the age of three.

If your child is attached to a bottle and it contains something other than water, make the bottle boring by gradually diluting the contents until it's just water. Do this as soon as possible because anything in a bottle other than water can pool around a child's teeth and cause 'bottle caries', particularly if she sucks on it when she is lying down. The effects can be severe enough to affect all the primary teeth and lead to a round of dental appointments. A child needs to lose her first teeth naturally, if possible, as they are an important guide to the second teeth.

If the bottle is not naturally discarded once it only contains water, then you can try other tactics that also work with weaning children off dummies.

- Tell your child that the bottle/dummy is not good for her teeth and that now she is a big girl. Let her choose a new toothbrush to replace it.

- Cut the top off the bottle teat/dummy so it is useless and give the topless teat or dummy to the child. Once they are 'broken' they are no good.

- Restrict the use of a bottle/dummy to certain times — for example, when watching television or riding in the car.

- Paint the dummy with the same bitter-tasting substance used to put people off biting their nails.

- Lose the dummy.

Comforters

Comforters — often given names such as 'lovies', 'blankies' or 'snugglies' — are an entirely different matter. A comforter is commonly a blanket, nappy or soft toy which provides a young child with comfort when she is feeling insecure, unhappy or tired. A child who has a comforter that helps her to fall asleep, or that reassures her that she is safe and secure occasionally, is helping to build her own resources.

However, a child who often uses her comforter during the day when there are adults to care for her and other things happening around her, may not be getting enough loving and cuddling. The parents of a child who withdraws to rock herself with her comforter on a regular basis need to seek expert advice.

A comforter usually becomes valuable some time in the second half of a child's first year. By the time she is a toddler it is a well established part of her life, particularly at bedtime.

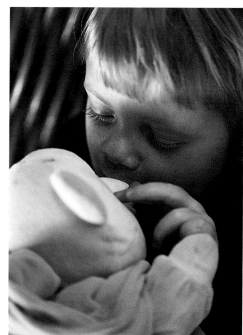

As the comforter grows in importance, it is up to parents and carers to treasure it. There could be a major upheaval if it is washed, lost or left behind somewhere. If a child's comforter is a blanket or nappy, a clever parent will have a couple of spares hidden away. If this is not possible, cutting the comforter in half and storing half is an alternative. If it is a soft toy, purchasing a second identical toy is the best solution. Part of the attraction of a comforter is its familiar smell and, of course, the spare will not smell the same unless you can work out some way to rotate the comforters. It will, however, be better than nothing if the original comforter is lost.

If this happens, you should:

■ remain calm, as panicking will panic your child;

■ acknowledge the loss, letting the child know that you too believed the comforter was very important; and

■ find similarities between the new comforter and the old, and help the child to focus on them.

The arrival of a sibling

Toddlers tend to have mixed feelings about the arrival of a new brother or sister. A toddler who is just leaving babyhood herself when the new baby arrives has to cope with no longer being the centre of your affections all the time. From the child's point of view, there is not an ideal age gap between herself and a new sibling, so you need to make your decision based on your own needs and expectations.

The other point that you need to realize is that you cannot expect a toddler to be excited or pleased about the coming baby — it's a concept the toddler finds hard to understand. You have to accept that a toddler's jealousy is natural and you need to adopt the strategy of helping the toddler to cope with the new arrival. This means doing everything you can to eliminate other stresses before the new baby arrives. These may be starting at childcare or a nursery, changing from a cot to a bed, or using the toilet or potty during the day.

Under the age of 18 months a child is unlikely to understand much of what is happening. However, from the age of around two years, your child will have some comprehension. You can help your child to cope by using some of the following strategies.

- Wait until a month or so before the baby is due before raising the subject. A toddler has no concept of time, so telling her about the baby in the first trimester will have no meaning to her at all.

- Explain that the new baby is part of your growing family. Avoid saying the baby is going to be a friend to the toddler or that you are having another baby because you love the toddler so much. This is not productive.

- Give the toddler some idea of what a new baby is all about. Spend some time with friends or relatives who have young babies.

- Get your partner involved. A father who takes over much of the day-to-day care of the toddler before the baby is born makes the transition easier for her and her mother. He can also enjoy the bonus of spending special time with his child.

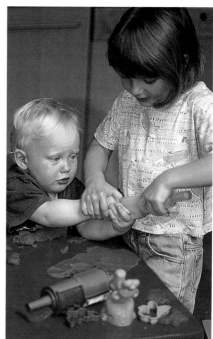

■ Let the toddler become involved in the preparation for the new baby.

■ Involve the toddler in the care of the new baby — encourage her to fetch nappies or just talk to the baby.

■ Create a special time each day for you and your toddler. If you begin this routine before the baby is born, it will be easier to continue with it after the birth.

■ Don't ignore the new baby's cries in order to attend to the toddler. This will only cause distress all round.

■ Make 'no fighting' a rule from the very beginning.

At first most toddlers grudgingly accept the arrival of a new baby. Some are more involved than others, and you need to understand that your toddler will grow to love her younger brother or sister. But it won't happen instantly.

When the new baby moves into the mobile stage, new frustrations will arise for the older child, and you need to be aware of the needs of each child. Expecting a three-year-old to be understanding with a baby brother who destroys her games is unrealistic. It is better to provide a private space for the older child and remove the baby.

Fun, games and learning

Children usually love being with other children their own age. Your child may already be making friends through playgroup or mothers' group, and this may suit both of you.

Is your child ready for preschool?

If you are thinking about returning to work outside the home, you may require a more formal childcare arrangement for your child that offers supervised care for longer periods. Preschools and long childcare centres or nurseries are two options for mothers working out of home. They also cater for mothers at home who feel their child is ready to move into a more structured social environment with children her own age for one or two days a week.

Usually there isn't a lot of difference between the activities offered by preschools and long childcare centres or nurseries. However, a long daycare centre (LDC) or nursery is open from around 7 am to 6 pm and may accept children from the age of six weeks. Preschools often, although not always, adhere to primary school hours — 9 am to 3 pm — and accept children from three to five years.

Whichever form of childcare you choose, it is important to find the centre or preschool that caters for your child's needs, and to feel confident that your child is relaxed about the arrangement and coping with being separated from you for longer periods.

Your child's readiness

Some children resist change and may be terrified of being left alone in a strange place, surrounded by unfamiliar faces and with a new set of rules to learn. You can nip your child's fears in the bud and ensure the transition from home to preschool runs smoothly by always praising her good efforts and helping her to feel comfortable and confident around others. Self-esteem is of paramount importance. If your child feels good about herself, being separated from you for several hours won't be such an issue.

These simple activities should help foster independence in your child, so that she is able to adjust to the preschool environment without too much fuss.

- Read to your child every day. Let her participate in the activity by pointing to pictures and helping to tell the story. Nursery rhymes are also a fun way to get her involved in the action. Through reading, your child not only learns about language, but also about how to use her own fertile imagination.

- Read books on the topic. For girls and boys, look for *Arthur Goes to School* by Marc Brown and for girls, try *A Bit Of Dancing (Three Picture Stories)* by Helen Oxenbury.

- Encourage your child to try new activities in order to expand her personal repertoire of small achievements and so she can socialize with other children. Enrol in a playgroup, music classes, swimming lessons or a gymnastics class for toddlers.

- Do practical fun things together, such as singing and dancing to music and finger painting.

- Encourage your child to help you make the beds, sweep the floor and clean up the mess she has made.

- Play games that involve simple sets of instructions. For example, hide a treat for your child to find, then give her directions and clues which lead her to it. This encourages her to concentrate and follow simple instructions as well as develop problem-solving skills she will be using every day at preschool. Other games which encourage her to follow instructions are 'I Spy' and 'Simon Says'.

- Listen to what your child has to say. It helps you get to know her better and to understand her unique personality. It also sends her the message that her opinions are valued.

- Let your child socialize with children of all ages so she learns to share and to take turns. This will lead her to the realization that occasionally she may have to take 'no' for an answer.

- Don't give in to all your child's demands. By setting limits for your child, you are showing her how society works and the importance of 'give and take'.

- Teach your child good manners. She will soon learn that the words 'please', 'thank you' and 'excuse me' will open many doors!

- Allay your child's fears about preschool or long daycare (nursery) by arming her with valuable information. Don't talk in generalizations, but tell her where she'll be going, what she'll be doing and whom she'll be doing it with.

But is my child up to speed?

You can gauge your three-year-old's readiness for preschool by running through this checklist with its focus on comprehension. Is your child able to:

* speak sentences of three to four words?

* remember her full name?

* ask 'what' and 'why' questions?

* understand and follow instructions such as: 'Put the doll on the shelf'?

* tell a simple story?

* sing simple songs?

* use a variety of verbs that help her to express complete ideas, observations, concepts and relationships in short sentences?

* talk about facts and ideas?

* name one or more colours?

* be understood by the listener when relaying information and ideas?

* tell the difference between 'he' and 'she'?

■ Visit the centre when the children and teachers are there, so she can imagine where she'll fit in. Meet the teachers and make sure she's introduced to several of the children her own age. Arrange introductory play sessions at the centre prior to your child's formal start.

■ Establish a routine from day one at preschool. When you leave her in the morning, always give her a kiss and let her know you will be back at a certain time to pick her up. Do not linger, as this will make the final farewell harder for both of you. Leave immediately after saying goodbye. Be firm but gentle if she is clingy, and find a teacher, activity or other children to distract her.

■ When you pick up your child, note her behaviour. Ask about her day. What activities did she enjoy? Who did she play with? What did she eat for lunch? What books did the teacher read?

Is preschool ready for your child?

By checking out more than one preschool you can make quality comparisons. Even if a particular centre is highly recommended by a friend or relative, it's still a good idea to do your own research because the status quo may have altered since their child was at the centre, and your child may have different needs or requirements from their child. Many preschools have extensive waiting lists, so it is a good idea to plan ahead. Don't wait until your child is about to turn three and then ring around local centres in a panic; contact your local preschools early.

Never feel that you're intruding by asking questions of the preschool or LDC (nursery) staff. They expect parents to be concerned about their child's welfare and would probably be worried if you didn't ask any questions at all. So make it your priority to quiz the head teacher on the centre's policies and philosophies to ensure they sit comfortably with your own personal views.

Childcare checklist

A practical checklist is also useful and allows you to easily compare one centre to another.

The basics

- Is the centre located a convenient distance from your home or workplace?

- What are the opening and closing times, and when are the holidays?

- What are the monthly or annual fees, and are there any other extra costs not included in the fees? What do the fees cover?

- Are the staff experienced and qualified?

- What is the child to adult ratio?

- Does the centre fulfil the quality accreditation requirements set by the appropriate government body? Are they available for you to see?

- Is there a wide range of policies regarding issues such as behaviour management, hygiene procedures and sun sense? Are they available for you to see?

- Does the centre have an orientation day when families can meet the teachers and find out more about what the centre has to offer?

Health and safety issues

- Is there a nurse on staff? Are staff members familiar with cardiopulmonary resuscitation (CPR) and first aid?

- Is it a requirement that all the children and staff are immunized according to the guidelines set by the relevant government body?

- Is the centre secure from intruders? Are there gates across stairways, and are all the fences and gates around the centre childproof?

- Is the playground equipment safe and well maintained? Does the soft-fall material cover the whole area under and surrounding the play equipment?

- Is the centre attractive and cheerful? Is there plenty of room? Is the noise level moderate?

- What is the daily routine for napping, and where do the children sleep?

- Does the centre meet your standards of cleanliness? Are the children's bathrooms clean and is the babies' change table spotless?

- Are there emergency exits, and is there an emergency plan?

- What is the policy for sick children, and for the use of prescription and non-prescription medicines?

- Does your child take a cut lunch or does the centre provide nutritious meals? Is there a weekly menu you can look at?

- Are the children supervised when eating?

Relationships

- Are the parents made to feel welcome, even if they drop into the centre without prior notice?

- Are cultural differences recognized and accepted?

- What is the turnover of caregivers?

- Do the children who attend the centre look happy and content?

- Do the caregivers appear genuinely interested in the children's welfare? Do they make an effort to talk to and encourage the children in a non-patronizing fashion, frequently using their names?

- Are there meetings between staff and parents, and are the staff relaxed about casual chats about your child's wellbeing?

Education program

- Is there a planned educational program for your child which takes into account her individual developmental level?

- Is there a wide range of activities and toys for the children?

- Do the activities change on a regular basis?

- Are there any specialized programs — such as dance, music or art — available?

- Is there a balance in the daily schedule that includes free time as well as scheduled activities?

- Is there flexibility in this schedule to accommodate children's individual needs and abilities? Are children given a choice of activities? Is there an outline of a typical day at the centre for you to see?

Don't forget that choosing a preschool is a bit like choosing a builder: it helps to ask other customers about their personal experiences. So talk to other parents who have children at the centre to find out more about the quality of care.

The importance of creative play

Creative play is your child's way of learning about the world and her own capabilities. It teaches her about decision making, enhances creative thinking and, when she is in a social setting, contributes to her appreciation of her peers. Creative play enables your child to reach personal goals, and gives her the confidence to take the next step. Creative play isn't about forcing your child into a highly structured learning environment. The best thing you can do is provide positive encouragement: be there if she needs you, but don't stand over her; provide the resources for learning through play, but don't take over the games because you think you can do it better. In his book *Touchpoints*, child behaviour expert Dr T. Berry Brazelton advises parents to always be supportive of their children and to allow them to take one small step at a time, with gentle guidance if necessary.

Organize a craft materials box and keep it in an accessible place. Assorted pencils, crayons, coloured chalk, paper and modelling dough in a sealed container are indispensable creative play tools. Allow your child to use them as she wishes (within reason). Keep paints, felt tip markers and safety scissors out of her reach, but in her view, as 'ask me first' items.

Painting

Painting isn't about being neat. It's a messy business where the creative process, not the end product, is the most important element. Your child will need:

- an old shirt or paint smock to protect her clothing;
- newspaper or plastic covering to protect the painting table;
- large sheets of paper to paint on;
- a couple of sturdy paint brushes;
- rags and sponges for cleaning up;
- shallow containers, such as plastic ice-cream containers, for paint and other materials; and
- ice-cream container lids to be used as palettes.

If possible, paint outdoors. If this can't be organized, make sure the floor covering and possibly the walls are also protected from accidental spills. Buy paint that is easy to wash off.

Here's a recipe for a fingerpaint base that can also be used as a paper glue. Just add food colouring to turn it into fingerpaint.

Glue or fingerpaint base

Ingredients

2 tablespoons cornflour

1 cup water

Method

1 In a saucepan, mix 2 tablespoons of cornflour with cold water to form a paste.

2 Turn the stove to medium heat and add 1 cup of water, stirring until the mixture is thick like custard.

3 Store this versatile stuff in the refrigerator, and add food colouring for fingerpainting, or add it to store-bought fingerpaint to boost the quantity. It can also be used as a glue for paper.

For interest and variety, let your child experiment with her painting, using objects such as combs, scrubbing brushes, feathers, leaves and sponges of all different shapes and sizes (cut sponges into shapes such as trees and stars, dip them into paint and then stamp them onto the page). Let your child place her hand in the paint and then onto the paper for handprints. You could even let her make footprints!

For more messy fun, try this recipe for 'goop', an incredibly tactile experience for a toddler. Goop can be squeezed from a bottle or poured into a container so children can dip their hands into it. Because it is rather stringy and blobby, it is heavy enough to run slowly through fingers, and can be used to make patterns on paper and in the air.

Goop

Ingredients

1¾ cups cold water

2 cups flour

½ cup salt

¼ cup sugar

Tempera for colour (tempera is a paint made from pigment ground in water and mixed with an emulsion of egg yolk or a similar substance)

Plastic squeeze bottles (used honey bottles are perfect)

Method

1 Place the cold water into a bowl and sift in the other ingredients, constantly stirring.

2 When it is thoroughly mixed, use a funnel to pour the goop into squeeze bottles.

Drawing and writing

Preschoolers aren't constrained by artistic convention. When they draw they are expressing themselves and giving you an insight into their view of the world. They are also developing the fine motor skills that are needed for writing.

Your child will not begin to draw 'people' until she is three or four, and even then her 'person' will feature a round head with facial features and limbs coming straight from the head. But right now she is focused on lines and curves, sometimes formed into patterns, and sometimes random strokes and swirls of colour. At two she will start making zigzag lines across the page, usually horizontally. By around the age of three she will be creating swirling patterns.

Sometimes your child might decide that her picture is something in particular, probably after she has drawn it. If she tells you she has drawn a fish and a beach, it's unhelpful to ask 'Where's the water?' or say 'Sand isn't green.' Instead, praise your child's artwork with comments such as 'I like those colours', 'You made some beautiful straight lines there' and 'Look at all those circles'. Value her work for what it represents — your child's natural creativity.

You can encourage your child to draw in various ways.

- Look at pictures in art books with her and talk about how the artists made the pictures. Talk about how the pictures make your child feel — happy, sad, scared or lonely. Point out how the colours, shapes and lines make the pictures.

- Organize a permanent drawing table. Tape butchers' paper onto a child-size table and let your child fill it with her scribbles. When it is completely covered, replace it with a new sheet of paper.

- Show your child how to draw circles by standing behind her and guiding her hand round and round to form the shape. When she is 18 months old, her own attempts at a circle will look like a curve that spirals around but doesn't join up; by three she'll be able to draw a loop that crosses over or joins roughly at the same point. You can also show her how to master lines and zigzags in the same way.

Reading

You can now start to encourage your child to select her own books. Help by taking her to the children's picture book section in the local library and browsing alongside her.

- Let your child 'read' to you or to her doll or teddy, using the pictures as cues. You could prompt her by asking, 'What is happening on this page?' Alternatively, get her to describe the actions in the pictures.

- Talk about the pictures — for example, 'Does that teddy look like your teddy?'

- Always look interested, and praise and encourage your child's attempts.

- Ask questions such as 'Did you like the story?' And for more information, add: 'Why?'

- Expose her to different types of literature, such as nursery rhymes, poems and theme books.

- Put aside a special reading time each day — bedtime is ideal — where you get the chance to share a book and snuggle up at the same time.

- Set up a comfortable reading space, especially for your child. It might be a corner of the living room filled with plumped-up cushions or a special spot in her room with a bookshelf and cushions.

- Explain the difference between the illustrations and the writing. 'I'm reading the black letters. They're words.' Follow the words with your finger.

- Point to signs in your local area such as STOP signs, the names of popular fast-food outlets and petrol station signs.

- Start an alphabet scrapbook. Write a letter in a scrapbook. Cut out pictures of things starting with the letter and let your child paste them in the book. Don't worry if it's messy. That's your problem, not your child's!

- When you are out shopping together, point to words such as 'push', 'pull' and 'exit'.

Birthday parties for toddlers

For you, holding a party for toddlers can seem like a daunting task. It needn't be. Here are some tips for holding parties for two- and three-year-olds.

Second birthdays

Some of the children with older brothers and sisters, or those who have been to other parties, may have some idea that a party is special, but don't actually expect much.

Television and computers

There is a place for television in the lives of our toddlers, but not as a regular babysitter. Your toddler's viewing needs to be monitored by you, not just for what she watches but also how much she watches. Most toddlers can quickly master the on–off switch, and so there is the problem that your child may also turn the set on when you are not in the room. This may mean turning the television off at the wall when it is not in use, or simply hiding the remote control. (Check to see whether your television has an electronic lock.)

Most of the time, toddlers need to watch television with you so that you can talk about what is on the screen, and interact together with the games and songs. A toddler who is left in front of a screen for any length of time is at risk of watching something you would prefer she did not see. One program that is not considered suitable for toddlers or preschoolers is the news. The high level of violence and graphic images can affect a child, so it is better for you to record the news and watch it when your toddler is in bed than to allow her to watch it.

An hour or two a day is plenty of television for a toddler. They have so many other things to do with their time. Obesity is on the increase in children, and sitting in front of television, often while eating, is one of the recognized contributors. Children need physical activity every day, and even dancing in front of the television screen, although it is an activity, is not as good as riding a tricycle or running around the park or back garden.

Computers pose a similar problem. To toddlers there is not much difference between television and computers.

Toddlers need to interact with people to learn social skills. They won't do this in front of a computer. As with television, so there is a place for computers, and in families where a computer is part of the family activities a toddler will be introduced to using it gradually. At the age of 18 months, a child will enjoy sitting for a short time on your lap as you write an email, or operate a program, and by three years of age the same child will probably be interacting with software programs or the Internet.

Introducing toddlers to computers is about gradually letting them have a go. Give your child her own mouse and keyboard to play with, and choose software packages designed for your child's age group. This will allow her to experiment, and is a good way to start. It is also important that you share the time spent on the computer with your toddler, but make sure you allow her to experiment at the same time.

Five children from playgroup, mother's group, daycare, nursery or childcare are ideal. Any more and it becomes a big production when you include the adults as well.

Plan ahead

- Be sure to include parents in the invitation, and keep the party time to about an hour.

- If you are having the party at home, keep decorations low-key: decorate a low table or the floor with a brightly coloured tablecloth.

- Consider a park or the beach, particularly if you don't have a suitable outdoor area at home.

- Balloons and coloured lanterns lend a party air. Tie a balloon to the gate if you are having the party at home, to a tree if you are in the park, or to a sun shelter or umbrella if you are at the beach.

Food

- Fruit — on a hot day frozen grapes, slices of kiwi fruit (Chinese gooseberry), orange quarters and strawberries are delicious and fun

- Pretzels, cupcakes or pikelets and ice creams or ice blocks

- Milk or juice to drink

- Food and drink for the adults

On the day

- Bring each guest into the area you have organized for the party.

- Help the birthday person open the presents as soon as the guests arrive.

- Serve the food, and have a helper serve the adults. Read the children a story while they are eating.

- Activities can include a story reading and singing songs together, particularly if a parent plays a musical instrument. Activity songs such as 'Twinkle, Twinkle Little Star', 'Put Your Finger on Your Nose' and 'I'm a Little Teapot', and simple games such as 'Ring-a-Rosie' and 'Follow the Leader', are popular with this age group.

- If you want to give party favours, hand them out as guests leave the party. Make party bags from either circles of cellophane tied with ribbon or brown paper bags on which

you have drawn the first letter of the child's name in bright felt tip pen. Some suggestions for party favours are: paint-with-water books and a large paintbrush; bell bracelets (a couple of little bells sewn onto a bracelet made of wide elastic); little pots of modelling dough and stick-on spots, stars or cartoon characters.

Third birthdays

At this age it is still better if the parents of the invited guests are there as well, so be sure to invite them. It is also reasonable to keep your guest list to five or six. By all means send out invitations, but if you put them in a child's bag at daycare, nursery or preschool you will need to follow up with a phone call. An hour and a half is plenty of time for a party for this age group.

From this age on you can think about theme parties; they give you the opportunity to be creative. So many things lend themselves to this concept, from a favourite colour to a favourite story book or television character. Here are some suggestions.

A red party. Everyone wears something red; serve red food such as jellies, strawberries and ice blocks; play games with a red theme such as 'Hunt the Red Thing' and 'Musical Chairs', but use a final red cushion.

A teddy bears' picnic. Ask everyone to bring a teddy bear; give every bear a prize; serve the food as a picnic and include teddy bear biscuits and honey sandwiches; organize activities such as 'Pass the Teddy' (instead of the parcel), so that everyone gets something when they are 'out', and 'Teddy Bear, Teddy Bear, Turn Around'.

A dinosaur party. For food serve a nibble tray of celery, baby tomatoes, carrot sticks, sultanas, crackers, fresh fruit and a couple of favourite dips; organize 'dinosaur' activities such as fossil handprints in wet sand, 'Hunt the [plastic] Dinosaur' and 'Dinosaur Says', played to the rules of 'Simon Says'.

Fairy party. Everyone dresses as a fairy or an elf. Serve fairy bread and star-shaped biscuits. Involve the children in a craft activity, such as decorating a fairy/elf crown. Make the crowns the night before up to the stapling stage, then staple each one to suit each child's head. Write the child's name on the inside and let him or her add the stars, diamonds and other stickers and glue glitter.

Plan ahead

By the time the children are three they are old enough to wear party hats. If you have time you can make the hats and let your child help by sticking on stickers and painting them with sparkle glue.

Here are some simple hats to make.

Headbands. First, measure your child's head so you know how long the bands need to be, then add 2.5 cm (1 in) to allow for joining or 5 cm (2 in) for tying. Headbands can be made from Christmas tinsel tied in a circle, strips of cardboard or crepe paper.

Crowns. Using the same measure as for the headbands, cut a wide band of cardboard. Then cut triangles along the length of the strip. Decorate them before stapling them onto each band. Have a collection of decorative things which your child can stick onto the hats — for example, shapes such as hearts, stars or moons cut out from cardboard, balls of coloured cotton wool, sticks of glitter glue and rose petals (dried or fresh).

Food

The type of food you serve depends on whether it is a meal, or afternoon or morning tea. Here are some ideas.

- Little sausages or meatballs with tomato sauce for dipping
- Little pizzas — tomato and cheese on muffins
- Pikelets
- Jelly cups — homemade ones are easy to make
- Pita roll-ups — spread each pita bread with smooth peanut butter or hummus, then roll it up and cut it into manageable pieces
- Fresh fruit — slices and chunks of melons, oranges and bananas
- Drink — juice, milk, water

On the day

- Decorate the table with a large sheet of plain paper — brown is fine — and provide fat crayons so the children can draw on it.
- Bring each person to the party space and help your child open the presents.
- Serve the food. Read a story or play a story CD while the children are eating.
- Have a helper serve the adults.
- Sing some songs.
- Play some games and sing — for example, 'Hokey Pokey' and 'Everybody Do This'.
- Have everyone sit in a circle with their feet touching. Roll a ball to the party person, then get them to roll it to someone else. Go back and forth, then try it to music.
- Have some free time.
- Have a birthday parade to the music of 'Follow the Leader'.

Party safety

Inside the house:

* Put away all low ornaments, put safety locks on cupboards, remove any valuables and put safety corners on sharp corners. Put pot plants outside and cover power points with safety plugs.

* Check that the bathroom is reasonably safe as well. Make sure everything is locked away.

* Be sure that guests put their bags out of the children's reach.

* Use a stair gate to keep children in the area you have 'prepared'.

Outside:

* Be sure to have a safe area with a gate between the garden and the street.

* Lock away all garden tools, implements, sprays or fertilizers.

* Check the pool fence and be sure there are no objects such as chairs or benches nearby that could help a toddler to climb over the fence.

* Have sun protection cream and insect repellent on hand.

Common illnesses of early childhood

A to Z medical reference

Use the following information to help you identify illness in your child and whether he needs medical assistance. If in doubt, always contact your doctor and never put your child's health at risk. Remember that your child's symptoms and the manifestation of a disease may vary from the information listed. You know your child better than anyone, so follow your instincts when it comes to what is best for your child's health.

While every care has been taken in compiling this information, you are urged to seek professional advice if you have any doubts about your child's health or condition. If you are not happy with the advice you receive, then seeking a second or third opinion is the wisest course.

Illnesses set in **bold** are listed elsewhere in this section.

Anaemia

When a baby or toddler suffers from anaemia, it is usually caused by an iron deficiency in the diet. When your baby is born, there is enough stored iron in his body to last the first six months, unless he is born prematurely. Some time after your child turns six months, he needs to start eating foods that contain iron, such as cereals and meat. A one-year-old child whose diet consists mainly of milk may suffer from anaemia. The solution is not to give iron supplements, as they can cause their own problems, but to provide the child with an adequate diet. This can be done with the help of a child health nurse, a doctor or a dietitian.

Appendicitis

This condition is very rare in children under two and tends to occur in older children and young adolescents. The main symptom is abdominal pain in the middle of the stomach that gradually moves to the lower right side, where the appendix is situated, and grows in intensity. Other symptoms may include a mild fever or loose stools.

If you suspect appendicitis, then take the child to a doctor or hospital emergency department immediately: an operation may be needed. The only treatment for acute appendicitis is the removal of the appendix.

Arthritis

Red, swollen, warm and painful joints indicate arthritis. Arthritis in children is mostly caused by infection. Any pain in the joints, especially if it is accompanied by the other symptoms, needs to be checked by a doctor as there are several kinds of arthritis children can contract.

- Acute rheumatic fever can affect many joints and is usually accompanied by a fever.

- Allergic arthritis is the result of an allergic reaction to certain foods, insect bites, medication or pollution. It is usually accompanied by hives.

- Infectious arthritis is caused by bacteria and can affect babies younger than 12 months. It is also associated with a fever.

- Post-viral arthritis occurs, as its name implies, after a virus. The symptoms are similar to rheumatoid arthritis. This condition usually gets better of its own accord.

- Rheumatoid arthritis is also known in children as Still's disease. It may affect one or more joints, often the neck. The cause is not known.

Any delay in the treatment of arthritis can lead to further problems. Paracetamol may be prescribed for the pain and an ice pack or a hot pack — whatever is most soothing — may be used initially. Antibiotics, steroids and other drugs may be used in the treatment.

Asthma

Asthma, once an uncommon complaint, is now found in as many as 1 in 5 children. It has become the most common medical condition and, for unknown reasons, affects more boys than girls. In a family with a history of asthma or eczema or hay fever, or a family where either parent smokes, a child is particularly vulnerable. Parents and carers can take precautions such as giving up cigarettes, limiting pets and pollution, and taking steps to keep house dust down (see **Hay fever**). Viruses, food and sudden changes in temperature can also trigger an asthma attack.

The most obvious symptom of asthma is wheezing and laboured breathing, and the sooner this condition is diagnosed, the sooner the symptoms can be relieved. People with asthma have bronchial tubes that are sensitive to irritants. When these are affected, they will inflame and swell involuntarily, becoming narrower; at the same time excess mucus will be produced. All these things affect breathing. This may not happen immediately but may take place over a few hours.

Treatment depends on the severity of the condition and will involve prevention as well as relief of the symptoms. Medication used in the treatment of the condition is usually inhaled through a device called a nebulizer or a spacer. Asthma cannot be cured, but it can be managed successfully, and some children are troubled less as they get older. However, asthma can occur and be severe at any age.

Any asthma attack not responding to the usual medication must be treated as an emergency. Medical help should be sought immediately.

Boil

A large red lump, known as a boil or abscess, is caused when a hair follicle becomes infected with bacteria. The lump fills with pus, which bursts after two or three days and then may disappear, although it may also cause other boils to form. A large boil with several heads is known as a carbuncle, and a boil on the eyelid is called a stye.

Never squeeze a boil. If it is being rubbed by clothing, apply a dressing to protect it. If it is causing pain, medical treatment will relieve the discomfort.

Breathing difficulties

See **Asthma** and **Bronchiolitis and bronchitis**.

Bronchiolitis and bronchitis

Severe breathing difficulties can be caused by bronchiolitis, which is an inflammation of the bronchial tubes, the smallest airways in the lungs. The condition is usually caused by a virus and may be a complication of a cold. It commonly affects babies under the age of 12 months.

A dry, hacking cough, runny nose, fever, loss of appetite and general weakness are the symptoms of bronchitis. If your child is having difficulty breathing, seek medical attention immediately. If your child has less severe symptoms, you should still take him to the doctor. He or she may suggest paracetamol, a humidifier and, perhaps, antibiotics or asthma medication, depending on the specific diagnosis.

Car sickness

See **Motion sickness**.

Chickenpox

Chickenpox (varicella) produces an itchy, blistery rash and is caused by the varicella-zoster virus (VZV). Someone with chickenpox is highly contagious in the one or two days before the blisters appear and until they have all crusted over. Chickenpox can even be caught from touching clothing that has fresh fluid from the vesicles on it. The virus is spread after contact with another person.

In most cases, chickenpox is an uncomfortable infection and the treatment involves relieving the itchiness of the blisters. It is important not to scratch the blisters as they will scar and can become infected. This, of course, is a problem with young children. Keeping your child's fingernails short is very important, and you can also alleviate the itchiness with oatmeal bath preparations and calamine lotion.

Complications of chickenpox include pneumonia and encephalitis, which can be fatal. A vaccine has been developed, and may be part of the immunization schedule in your area or be available on request.

Colds

Baby's colds are seldom serious. Babies, on average, have between five and ten colds a year, but this depends on their exposure. A cold is a virus and babies have the same symptoms as adults — runny nose, swollen nasal passages, sometimes a cough and a sore throat, maybe a headache and a fever. The cold will run its course in the same way it does in adults — from clear to sticky yellow mucus after the first day or so.

Babies cannot blow their noses, so even slight congestion can be a problem. Dry air makes matters worse. So one of the best things for relieving a baby's cold is humid air. Humidifiers, if used safely, are a good way to keep the air in your baby's room humid. Sometimes a gentle saline spray will also loosen the mucus in a baby's nose. If your baby's nose is badly blocked and he is having trouble feeding, the family doctor may show you how to use a bulb syringe to shift the mucus. Over-the-counter nasal sprays are not recommended for babies and young children.

Babies can develop a fever with a cold. If a child less than six months old has a temperature over 37.4°C (99.3°F), it is best to consult a doctor. Other signs of a more serious condition include:

- laboured breathing that is faster than normal;
- unusual irritability or lethargy;
- the number of wet nappies in a 24-hour period is down to three or four;
- the fever has lasted for two days or more;
- baby has an unusual cough; and
- the cold lasts more than 14 days.

It is far safer to take your baby to the doctor's if you are worried than to hope things will get better of their own accord.

Conjunctivitis

See **Eye problems**.

Constipation

Babies who begin life being exclusively breastfed have many advantages. One is that they are rarely constipated, although they may have as few as one motion every five or six days. Babies who are fed baby formula can become constipated, and once a child starts on family foods it is also a possibility, but uncommon. A varied diet with enough vegetables, fruit and cereals plus plenty of water should prevent constipation. If you are concerned that you child may be constipated, seek medical advice. Do not attempt to treat the problem yourself.

Convulsions

A febrile convulsion is a type of seizure that can occur when a child has a fever. It accompanies an infection in a part of the body, commonly the upper respiratory tract, and occurs in children between the ages of six months and five years.

Children are susceptible to convulsions of this nature because their brains are not yet mature. These convulsions are terrifying to the adults caring for the child, but are not usually serious. Around 4 per cent of children will experience such a seizure and most will only ever have one fit.

Triggered by a sudden rise in body temperature, convulsions include symptoms such as loss of consciousness, stiffness, a brief cessation of breathing, passing of urine or faeces. The child's limbs may twitch and his eyes roll back. When the convulsion is over, the child will regain consciousness and may fall asleep.

When a child has a convulsion it is important to seek urgent medical attention. If your child has ever experienced a convulsion, you must lower his temperature the next time he has an infection. otherwise you run the risk of him having another convulsion.

Other causes of convulsion are epilepsy (see **Epilepsy**) and meningitis (see **Meningitis**).

Coughing

See **Bronchiolitis and bronchitis**, **Colds**, **Croup**, **Influenza**, **Pneumonia** and **Whooping cough**.

Croup

Croup is characterized by a barking cough and is caused by a virus. Croup usually begins with cold symptoms, including a runny nose and nasal congestion, and possibly a fever or mild sore throat. Following this, the linings of the voice box and windpipe become swollen and irritated, and this leads to noisy breathing (stridor) and the barking cough.

Croup is usually managed in the same way as a cold, so antibiotics are not effective. Plenty of fluids to prevent dehydration and help move the mucus in the airways, as well as a humidifier, can help relieve the symptoms. If your child is having difficulty breathing or is experiencing stridor, even when he is resting, then it is important to seek medical attention.

Dehydration

Dehydration is a serious condition, particularly for babies whose bodies require more fluid relative to body weight than adults' bodies do. Signs that a child is dehydrated include:

- dry mouth;
- sunken eyes;
- skin that will not spring back when gently pinched;
- no wet nappies for 12 hours, or only two or three in a 24-hour period;
- a sunken fontanelle (soft spot); and
- lethargy or sleepiness.

Urgent medical attention is vital. To prevent dehydration, which can be caused by heat stroke or exhaustion, by diarrhoea or vomiting or when a child has gastroenteritis, encourage the child to drink plenty of fluids or suck on an ice block. Some children who eat family foods but are still breastfed will get great comfort from frequent breastfeeds. The doctor may recommend an oral rehydration solution in addition to other fluids. Soft drinks and diluted cordials do not have the same effect. When dehydration is severe, a child will probably require hospitalization so that fluids can be restored intravenously. (*Note:* Seek medical advice regarding your child's specific fluid intake needs.)

Diarrhoea

The appearance and frequency of a baby's or child's stools vary enormously. Breastfed babies will have fewer stools, which barely smell, than bottle-fed babies; older babies and toddlers may have up to four to six motions a day.

Diarrhoea can be caused by overconsumption of fruit juice as well as overfeeding; food intolerance; viral infections; bacterial infections, particularly from food poisoning (see **Gastroenteritis**); *otitis media* (see **Ear problems**); and forms of malabsorption such as the very rare cystic fibrosis and coeliac disease. Two- and three-year-olds may suffer an attack of diarrhoea when they are excited or apprehensive.

If you suspect the diarrhoea is caused by fruit juice, try diluting it with cooled boiled water. If you believe it is caused by a particular food, stop offering the food until your child has seen a doctor.

Infectious diarrhoea, whether it is caused by a virus or bacteria, may be associated with vomiting and high fever. Dehydration is one of the greatest dangers (see **Dehydration**).

If the diarrhoea is associated with vomiting, fever or dehydration, the child needs immediate medical attention. As infectious diarrhoea is highly contagious, keep other children away and be scrupulous about hygiene — your own and your child's.

Diarrhoea can cause the skin on a baby's bottom to become red and raw. You will need to change your child's nappy frequently and clean his skin thoroughly with mild soap. Applying a soothing cream will help.

Take the child to a doctor if you are concerned, or if the diarrhoea persists for more than a day or two.

Ear problems

Earache is common in children, particularly when they have a cold. It may be caused by a middle ear infection, immersion in water, or an object the child has poked in his ear.

When the middle ear is inflamed it is known as *otitis media*. It is caused when a bacterial or viral infection spreads up the narrow canal that connects the middle ear to the back of the throat (the eustachian tube). The infection produces fluid or pus that blocks the tube and results in pain. 'Glue ear' is the term used to describe thick glue-like secretions that can be a consequence of frequent middle ear infections.

However, earache is the main symptom of *otitis media*. Often a young child is unable to locate the pain. Fever and vomiting, irritability or drowsiness, loss of appetite, and occasionally diarrhoea and headache may be the symptoms that will necessitate a visit to the doctor. A baby may pull at the sore ear.

Ear infections can result in a temporary reduction in the child's ability to hear, and occasionally the eardrum may rupture with a thick and sometimes bloody discharge; however, this eases the pain and relieves the pressure.

A child who may have an ear infection needs to see a doctor, but in the short term a warm water bottle and paracetamol may help. The doctor will examine the child's ear and may prescribe antibiotics. A hearing test may also be necessary.

As a child grows, so does his eustachian tube, so middle ear infections are less common after a child is eight years old.

The outer ear can be inflamed by bacterial infections, dermatitis, eczema (see **Eczema**), by water or by a foreign body. When the outer ear is inflamed, it will be tender when touched or moved, there may be a discharge that is thick or yellow, and there may be blisters.

Treatment by a doctor is essential. He or she may have to remove a foreign body or prescribe drops.

Eczema

Eczema or atopic dermatitis is an inflammation of the skin. When it first appears it consists of itchy, red bumps or blisters. In the long term it can lead to scaly, thick skin that is dry.

Atopic eczema comes and goes. Those most susceptible have a family history of the condition. It can appear as early as two months of age, usually on the face, neck, ears and trunk. Toddlers with eczema may have patches on the backs of their knees, the fronts of their ankles and inside their wrists. Eczema concentrates in the moist creases, and if it is scratched it will weep a clear fluid and form crusts.

In a family with a history of eczema, breastfeeding your child for at least six months is the best precaution. Once he starts on family foods, certain ones may make the condition worse. Other things — such as woollen clothing, perfumed products, some detergents, chlorine and rapid changes in temperature — may aggravate the condition. Eczema is more common in urban areas and tends to worsen in cold conditions. Moisturizers, such as sorbolene cream with 10 per cent glycerine, are the usual treatment, although cortisone treatment may be necessary in severe cases.

Encephalitis

This rare condition is an inflammation of the brain that can be caused by a virus. In newborn babies herpes simplex (see **Herpes simplex**) is the most common cause. Symptoms of abnormal drowsiness, fever, irritability, vomiting, weak limbs and convulsions mean you must seek immediate medical attention. A child suffering from encephalitis will undergo a brain scan. Most children will recover completely.

Epilepsy

When a person suffers recurrent seizures, the condition is known as epilepsy. The symptoms are loss of consciousness and sometimes uncontrollable movements of the limbs or head caused by chaotic, unregulated electrical brain activity. Seizures can be caused by other conditions and one fit does not signify epilepsy (see **Convulsions**). Children suspected of having epilepsy are usually referred to a paediatrician or neurologist for further investigation. Blood tests and an electroencephalogram (EEG) will be performed. Treatment, likely to be anticonvulsant medication, will allow the child to carry on a normal life.

Eye problems

Blocked tear duct

A newborn baby can suffer from tear ducts that were blocked during the birth. The baby's eyes will water and the eye may become infected. A blocked tear duct will open naturally by the time a child is one year old; however, it may open sooner if it is treated. A doctor will explain how to gently massage the duct, and if there is an infection he or she will prescribe an antibiotic ointment. Once the block is removed the eyes will stop watering.

Conjunctivitis

Conjunctivitis, also called pink eye, is an inflammation of the conjunctiva, the membrane that covers the whites of the eyes and lines the eyelids. It can be caused by allergies, contact with irritants, or by viral or bacterial infections.

The eyes will be red, noticeably scratchy, and there may be a yellow discharge or crusts around them. If the conjunctivitis is viral, it will clear up without treatment within about seven days. If it is bacterial, antibiotics will be required.

Conjunctivitis is infectious so it is important to be scrupulously clean when treating the eye. Keep your child away from other children until the infection has cleared up. If conjunctivitis is suspected, your child will recover faster if you follow a treatment recommended by your doctor.

Eyelid problems

Styes and blepharitis are common problems with children's eyelids. When bacteria forms at the base of an eyelid, a stye will form. It will develop a pus-filled lump and will be painful. It will usually clear up of its own accord, but a fresh and clean warm cloth on the infected area will help with the discharge of pus.

Blepharitis is an inflammation of the edges of the eyelids and is a form of seborrhoeic dermatitis. Symptoms include burning redness around the eye and scales at the roots of the lashes. You will need a health professional to show you how to wipe off the scale. An antibiotic ointment may be necessary. The condition tends to be persistent, so your child may need regular treatment.

Squint (lazy eyes or cross eyes)

Lazy eyes or cross-eyes may be present when the child is born, or it may appear later. Children do not outgrow this condition. If your child develops a squint, also known as strabismus, see a doctor to assess if there is a serious eye problem. It needs immediate treatment by an ophthalmologist to prevent vision problems from developing.

It is not true that babies are unable to see clearly. Healthy newborn babies can focus on the faces of their parents within minutes of being born, and can see clearly to a distance of about 20–30 cm (8–12 in).

Fever

A fever may accompany a number of illnesses. It is a defect in the body's control of temperature and can be caused by arthritis, bronchiolitis, bronchitis, cold, ear infections, encephalitis, hand-foot-mouth disease, immunizations, meningitis, pneumonia, respiratory illnesses, *Roseola infantum* or tonsillitis. Signs of a fever include a flushed look, feeling hot to touch and unhappiness. A daily variation in temperature of 2°C (35.6°F) is quite normal in a baby, but it is important to take your child to the doctor for a check-up if you are worried about a fever. Ask the nurse or doctor to show you how to take your baby's temperature properly.

Foot problems

A baby's feet and ankles may be cramped when they are in the womb, but in the first month they will straighten out and the legs will become less bowed. The arches of your baby's feet are padded with fat to prevent heat loss and as he learns to walk his bow-leggedness and turned feet will gradually straighten.

Overlapping toes in newborn babies usually correct themselves. If they do present a problem, then a paediatrician will advise the treatment. A clubfoot (*metatarsus varus* — feet angled inwards from the instep) will be obvious from birth and a paediatrician will explain the treatment. Fusing of toes will be corrected by surgery.

Most children under three have flat feet; in 70 per cent of children these will have corrected themselves by the age of four.

Badly fitting shoes and socks can cause foot problems, so they should be fitted by a trained person. Keep your child's toenails trimmed in a straight line across the end of the toe.

Gastroenteritis

Diarrhoea, vomiting, nausea and general ill health are the common symptoms of digestive upset known as gastroenteritis. Viruses, bacteria — particularly from food poisoning — and intestinal parasites are the most common causes.

Viruses are spread by children not washing their hands properly after going to the toilet or before eating, and by adults not washing their hands properly after changing soiled nappies or before preparing food. Food that has not been prepared properly or that has been stored incorrectly can carry bacteria, which trigger gastroenteritis. Intestinal parasites can be spread to children on dirty hands, on surfaces such as toilet seats or even toys, and in contaminated water or food. The most common of these parasites is *Giardia lamblia*, the main parasitic cause of diarrhoea among children in nurseries or childcare centres.

Most children have such mild symptoms that they do not need to be taken to the doctor. However, seek medical advice if:

- there are signs of dehydration (see **Dehydration**);
- there is excessive diarrhoea;
- the vomiting is frequent;
- even drinking water is difficult;
- the child is suffering from severe abdominal pain; and
- the child is taking oral medication for another condition and cannot keep the medication down.

In most cases gastroenteritis will last about two or three days, although the diarrhoea may take longer to cease.

Gastro-oesophageal reflux (GOR)

This condition usually starts in the first month or so after birth and is quite common. Because the muscle at the entrance to the stomach is weak, the contents of the stomach pass back up the oesophagus (the tube leading to the stomach) and the baby regurgitates. This is different to possetting, where your baby does little 'sick-ups' after a feed — this is normal. Gastro-oesophageal reflux, or (GOR) as it is sometimes called, causes persistent vomiting that can be blood-stained. Baby may cough when milk is breathed into the lungs, he will usually be unhappy and may fail to gain weight. It is important to see a doctor if:

- baby is vomiting large amounts;
- the vomit contains blood or bile;
- baby has diarrhoea;
- there is blood in the stools;
- he is not gaining weight; or
- baby is still regurgitating past the age of 18 months.

Treatment may include raising baby's mattress so he sleeps on an angle, keeping baby sitting and possibly medication. Most babies outgrow the condition by the time they are one year old.

Giardiasis

See **Gastroenteritis**.

Hand-foot-mouth disease

Blisters in the mouth and on the hands and feet are the obvious symptoms of this viral illness. The other symptom is fever. Generally, the child is reluctant to eat because of the blisters in his mouth. This is another virus that can sweep through a nursery or childcare centre because it is passed on by droplets from the mouth. There is no specific treatment. The main aim is to relieve the symptoms while the virus takes its course; paracetamol is usually given for fever. Rinsing the mouth out with salty water may help, and the child will only want to drink non-acidic fluids and avoid fruit juice. Plenty of water and milk will help him get back to normal and eat food again. Keep your child away from other children until the blisters have gone.

Hay fever

Hay fever, also called allergic rhinitis, is an allergic reaction of the nasal membranes and sinuses to inhaled substances. Hay fever is triggered by many things; some of the most common include pollens, house dust and cat fur. The symptoms are nasal congestion, sneezing, an itching nose and watery eyes. Sometimes a headache follows.

Keeping the house as dust-free as possible may help. You could also try the following.

- Use covers for pillows and mattresses, and wash them regularly in hot water (that is, over 55°C/131°F) to kill dust mites.

- Remove carpets and polish the floorboards where possible — floorboards can be kept clean and free of dust more easily.

- Replace curtains with slatted blinds.

- Wash soft toys and sheepskins regularly.

- Put rugs and soft furnishings in the sun to air as frequently as possible.

- Keep cats out of the bedrooms, and preferably outside.

Head lice

Head lice like hair — clean or dirty. They are not easy to see and look like tiny flakes of dandruff stuck on the hair shaft. Usually, the first sign that someone has lice is constant scratching. Lice hardly ever cause medical complications. Their main problem is a societal one, as children are often asked to stay away from the nursery or childcare centre until the lice have been treated and are no longer visible.

Insecticide shampoos are often recommended; however, there is concern among health professionals that these shampoos have been over-used and are no longer effective. The best method of lice removal is close preening. This means combing hair conditioner through your child's hair with a fine-tooth metal comb. The conditioner 'catches' the lice, making them easier to see and comb out. Use a paper towel to catch the fallen lice. Sitting in sunlight is also the best way to see the lice and the nits (eggs). A second wash, a dry with a hair dryer and another comb with the fine metal comb may finish off the stragglers. Repeat this process every couple of days so you catch the head lice soon after they hatch.

Alternatively, apply olive oil evenly to the hair, then leave it overnight (protect the pillow with a towel). Comb out the lice and nits the next morning, then wash and condition as usual.

A few myths about head lice do exist. Head lice are often seen as a preschool problem, but they are most common in four- to 16-year-olds. Head lice do not leave a head voluntarily unless they are in contact with another head; sharing hats can cause the head lice to spread. Another myth is that head lice are damaged by combs and brushing. This is not so — the louse will simply reattach itself to the hair if it is brushed back on.

Headaches

Headaches are a common complaint in children and may be caused by sinusitis, fever or eye problems. They can also be associated with a rare condition, such as meningitis or brain tumour. A child with a headache may continue his daily activities or he may need to lie down. Keeping him quiet and giving him a massage may help. Paracetamol may also relieve the symptoms (never give a child aspirin). Take your child to see a doctor immediately if he has any of the following symptoms.

- The headache is severe and sudden.
- There is nausea or vomiting.
- He is drowsy or confused.
- Your child suffers from recurrent headaches.
- He has a stiff neck.
- There is fever associated with the headache.
- There is a rash associated with it.

Hepatitis

There are seven types of hepatitis, which is an inflammation of the liver. Hepatitis A is a virus with a number of causes; the younger the child, the less severe the infection. Hepatitis B is transmitted in children mainly via needle injuries, or via close contact with an infected person, or from birth if the mother is a carrier. It can be prevented with immunization (see 'Hepatitis B' on page 89). Hepatitis C is mainly confined to intravenous drug users. The other types are rare.

Hernias

A hernia is a part of the intestine protruding through the intestinal wall. The most common hernias found in children are umbilical, where the intestine bulges through the muscle wall at or above the navel, and inguinal, when the intestine protrudes into the inguinal canal which is in the groin.

Umbilical hernias are not usually treated, as they generally do not obstruct. They are left alone until the child is around five years old, when an operation may be necessary to correct the underlying defect. (See also page 40.)

Inguinal hernias, on the other hand, require an operation because they occur when the inguinal canal remains open, thus leaving a space through which a loop of intestine can pass into the groin or scrotum. The opening is small and a loop of bowel can get caught, swell and become obstructed, leading to a medical emergency.

Herpes simplex

Herpes simplex is a highly contagious virus. The blisters, called cold sores, appear in and around the mouth and nose. The virus is caught by direct contact with a blister. While the blisters are present, avoid hugging and kissing. Once contracted, herpes simplex stays for life and may recur at times when immunity is low.

The herpes blisters are not serious unless they occur around the eyes, but it is important to stop a child from touching them. They can be treated with antiviral ointment, which your doctor can prescribe.

Hives

Hives, also known as urticaria, can be an allergic rash caused mostly by foods or medication, but they can also be triggered by an allergen such as a plant, ointment, insect bite or extremes of temperature. Hives are often triggered by a viral infection, but often no cause is found. They appear on any part of the body as an itchy white rash on a red base. Hives are not contagious. Sometimes they are accompanied by a fever, and in this case a visit to the doctor would be wise. Antihistamines may help. Calamine lotion and cold compresses are generally recommended (see **Arthritis**).

Hives can also be part of a more severe allergic reaction, called anaphylatis, which is a medical emergency.

Impetigo

Common, highly contagious and occurring mainly in young children, impetigo is a bacterial skin infection that starts as small blisters. It mostly affects the mouth, nose and nappy area. The bacteria that cause the infection enter the skin when it is broken, often by an insect bite or eczema.

The first signs are red skin and the beginnings of blisters. These burst, leaving sores that then crust over. You need to treat these or they will last for weeks. It is necessary to see a doctor, who will prescribe antibiotics. As impetigo is so contagious, keep the child's clothing, bedding and towels separate from the rest of the family's. It is also essential to keep the child away from other children.

Good hygiene and short fingernails can help prevent impetigo.

Influenza

Commonly called flu and used to describe any of a number of mild infections and illnesses, influenza is actually a viral illness. True influenza is highly contagious and occurs in epidemics.

It is passed through droplets from the mouth and nose, and has a short incubation period of one to three days, but is contagious for around seven days.

Symptoms include fever, dry cough, muscular aches, tiredness, headache and sometimes a sore throat. Influenza can spread to the lungs and cause pneumonia, or lead to a secondary bacterial infection.

See a doctor as soon as possible if any of the following apply.

- The child is under two, is very ill or is at risk of complications.
- The child's temperature rises above 40°C (104°F), or he has a persistent fever, even if it is not this high.
- He is breathing quickly.
- He refuses to eat.

Your doctor will only prescribe antibiotics if there is a secondary bacterial infection. Bed rest, plenty of fluids and paracetamol are usually recommended. Annual vaccination against influenza is possible, but is not recommended for children unless there are other medical problems present.

Lactose intolerance

Children, particularly Asian and African children, can be intolerant to lactose, the sugars found in milk. This intolerance is caused by a deficiency of the enzyme lactase, responsible for digesting lactose in the small intestine. Your child may become temporarily lactose intolerant after an infection such as gastroenteritis or a parasite such as *giardia*. The symptoms may include diarrhoea and vomiting. If persistent lactose intolerance is diagnosed, then the child needs to eat a balanced diet designed by a dietitian. It is not always necessary to avoid cow's milk products, as these are a valuable source of calcium and other nutrients. There are certain products that can reduce the lactose content and these will be recommended by your child's doctor.

Malaria

Malaria is a serious health problem in tropical and subtropical areas. It is spread by infected anopheles mosquitoes. Young children are among those at greatest risk.

Symptoms usually appear 6–30 days after infection, and include high fever, headache, nausea and vomiting, and joint pain. A child who is infected with malaria will need to be treated in hospital.

Children who live in malarious areas, or who are travelling to these areas, need to wear protective clothing, sleep under mosquito nets and take antimalarial medicines. See your doctor for advice before travelling to a malarious area.

Measles

A potentially fatal disease now immunized against in most industrialized countries, measles is spread by droplets from the nose and mouth of the infected person (see 'Measles, mumps, rubella (MMR)' on page 89). It incubates for around 7–18 days and starts with a runny nose, dry cough and headache. A high fever is often present, then small white spots appear, first in the mouth. The child's eyes are sore and cannot tolerate bright light. Next, reddish spots appear and spread over the whole body.

A child with suspected measles needs to see a doctor. Plenty of fluids are important. Complications of measles include bronchitis, pneumonia, acute *otitis media*, encephalitis and, in the following years, possibly subacute sclerosing panencephalitis (SSPE — see 'Subacute sclerosing panencephalitis' on page 89), a degenerative disease that is rare, but fatal.

Medication

Aspirin should only be given to babies or children on doctor's orders. It is associated with a rare but fatal condition known in children as Reye's syndrome.

Antibiotics are used to kill bacteria; they are useless against viruses. They have revolutionized medicine, but health professionals are currently concerned that they are being overprescribed and that their effectiveness is diminishing. If a child is prescribed antibiotics, it is important that the full course is taken as directed — that is, before or after food. Stopping antibiotics because the condition appears to have cleared is likely to result in a recurrence. It is also important that you are made aware of any possible side effects and that you consult your doctor if you are not happy with the treatment.

Paracetamol is generally recommended as the pain relief medication for children. Always give it strictly according to the instructions, and work out the dose according to your child's weight.

There may be reasons why a doctor will prescribe medication other than paracetamol for the same purposes.

Meningitis

When the meninges, the membranes lining the brain and spinal cord, are infected, the condition is called meningitis. It may be caused by bacteria, a virus or a fungus, and can incubate for two to four days.

Symptoms of meningitis include a high fever, headache, loss of appetite and drowsiness or irritability. The child may complain that the light hurts his eyes. He may have a stiff neck. A young baby may have a bulging fontanelle. Increasing confusion and drowsiness followed by fits (convulsions) and unconsciousness will follow. A purple rash (either dots or bruises) can occur with one type of meningitis, although most children with meningitis have no rash.

It is vital that a child with meningitis receives urgent medical treatment. Any suspicions of this condition warrant investigation.

In countries where the Hib vaccine has been introduced into the immunization schedule for young children, the incidence of the most common bacterial meningitis has dropped considerably (see 'Meningococcal vaccination' on page 93).

Generally, viral meningitis is less severe than bacterial meningitis, although it can be fatal. Viral meningitis is caused by diseases such as mumps, measles and polio, all preventable with immunization. Among viruses, entroviruses are the most common causes of meningitis. These viruses reach the mouth from infected faeces via contaminated food or drink. This can be prevented by thoroughly washing your hands and making sure your child washes his hands properly — both after going to the toilet and before eating.

Motion sickness

Motion sickness particularly affects children. It is thought to be caused by changes in the movement of the head, which in turn affect the labyrinth in the inner ear. Once the child experiences the symptoms — which may include vomiting, nausea and perspiration — the best treatment is to remove the cause. If your child is prone to motion sickness, your doctor may prescribe some medication.

Preventative measures that could work include: keeping the environment free from tobacco smoke; not giving your child fatty or fried foods to eat; providing good air flow in the vehicle; and offering amusements, such as listening to music or story recordings, that do not include looking down.

Mumps

Immunization against mumps is available on most immunization schedules and is given to children under five, although the disease most commonly affects children aged from five to 15.

The virus, which is spread by droplets, takes between 14 and 21 days to incubate. Symptoms include fever, pain around the ears, and sudden swelling below and in front of one or both ears.

Your doctor may advise treatment of the fever. The contagious time for mumps is before the symptoms appear. Once considered a common childhood illness, mumps can have serious complications, including meningitis, pancreatitis, deafness and orchitis (an inflammation causing painful swelling of the testicle), which can lead to sterility.

Nappy rash

See 'Treating nappy rash' on page 72.

Pertussis

See **Whooping cough**.

Pneumonia

This illness is an infection of the lungs and may be caused by bacteria or a virus. It can be a complication of an upper respiratory infection, or a more serious infectious disease such as chickenpox (see **Chickenpox**) or whooping cough (see **Whooping cough**). A child with pneumonia has a fever and will be breathing rapidly. The chest wall may sink with every breath and he may have a dry cough and chest pain if pleurisy is also present. He may be vomiting and have diarrhoea. Pneumonia is always serious and needs urgent medical attention. The child will need plenty of fluids and, possibly, antibiotics. He may be hospitalized during the acute stage of the illness.

Roseola infantum

Roseola infantum, one of the little known but common rashes in babies, is characterized by a high fever for about three days. As the fever goes, small, possibly bumpy pink spots appear all over the baby's body. This rash only lasts about 24 hours and may be mistaken for a rubella-like rash.

Usually a doctor will recommend that the fever is treated with medication, such as paracetamol.

Rubella

Rubella, once commonly called German measles, is included in immunization schedules because of the serious effect it can have on the unborn babies of pregnant women who contract the infection (see page 90).

Rubella will incubate for between 14 and 21 days, and begins with a headache, a slight sore throat, runny nose and fever. Then small pink spots appear on the face, spreading rapidly over the rest of the body. The glands at the back of the neck and behind the ears enlarge.

When a child is suspected of having rubella, he should not be taken into public places, including a doctor's surgery. Contact the doctor by telephone. Your doctor may recommend paracetamol to reduce the fever. Report any complications such as a stiff neck to your doctor immediately, as encephalitis is a possible, although rare, complication.

Seborrhoeic dermatitis

This inflammation of the skin, which commonly affects babies and may reappear after puberty and then recur periodically, has no known cause. The symptoms generally clear up by the time a child is around two years old. A scaly rash, commonly found in the nappy area, itchiness and cradle cap are the main symptoms. Keeping the affected areas clean with an emulsifying ointment (not soap) is important. Your doctor may prescribe a corticosteroid cream (see 'Cradle cap' on page 77).

Once it is treated, seborrhoeic dermatitis usually clears up within a few weeks.

Slapped cheek disease

A mild contagious virus, also known as fifth disease and medically as *Erythema infectiosum*, slapped cheek disease is caused by parvo virus and usually occurs in children over the age of two years. The virus is passed on in the droplets of a cough. The red rash on both cheeks is the most obvious symptom; others include fever and, occasionally, joint pain. Then the rash usually develops on the trunk and the limbs. It is only a problem in children with uncommon blood disorders, such as sickle cell anaemia. There is no specific treatment. The rash usually reduces quickly. Paracetamol may be given for the fever and body aches. Parvo virus may be associated with increased miscarriage rates and problems with the foetus if the mother contracts it while she is pregnant. Once the rash appears, the child is no longer infectious, so there is no need to isolate him.

Stomach ache

Abdominal pains or tummy aches are symptoms of different conditions, including colic (see 'Colic' on page 59), constipation (see **Constipation**), diarrhoea (see **Diarrhoea**), food poisoning, gastroenteritis, *giardia* (see **Gastroenteritis**) or urinary tract infection (see **Urinary tract infections**). Seek medical advice if any of these symptoms persist or if the child is unwell.

Teething

Teething has been blamed for all sorts of ills, but in most cases these are caused by other infections or viruses and not by the budding teeth. Many children will get their teeth with no problems at all, while others will find it quite painful. Those who are unhappy will be grizzly and may eat less than normal. Their bowel motions may be loose, but if it is diarrhoea it is not caused by teething. The discomfort may be relieved by chewing on a hard or cooled (not frozen) teething ring. Occasionally, a doctor may recommend pain relief, but teething remedies should be used with caution and preferably not at all.

Tetanus

Tetanus is easily and best prevented by immunization (see 'Tetanus' on page 90). A serious illness that affects the central nervous system, it is caused by an infection of bacterial spores that enter the body via a wound. Garden soil and animal manure are the most common sources.

Tetanus is characterized by an inability to open the mouth (lockjaw), difficulty swallowing, contraction of facial muscles, muscular spasms and death. It is a medical emergency and will require treatment in hospital.

If a child suffers a deep wound and has been immunized against tetanus, he should still be taken to hospital as he may require further injections of the tetanus vaccine.

Throat infections

Usually a sore throat is caused by a minor viral infection and will clear up quickly. Over-the-counter preparations have not been found to be effective and should only be given to your child on your doctor's advice. A sore throat may also be one of the symptoms of an illness such as tonsillitis, a common cold or hay fever, so see your doctor if you are concerned.

Thrush

Babies under the age of 12 months are susceptible to oral thrush caused by the abnormal growth of the fungus *Candida albicans*. The symptoms are yellow-white spots on the tongue and inside a sore mouth. Antifungal gel or drops, prescribed by a doctor, are the usual treatment. A mother who is breastfeeding will also need to apply the gel or drops to her nipples. You will need to be meticulous when sterilizing bottle-feeding equipment.

Tonsillitis

Tonsillitis is a bacterial infection of the tonsils. The common symptoms of tonsillitis are: a sore, inflamed throat with enlarged tonsils, fever, difficulty swallowing, enlarged neck glands and earache. If tonsillitis persists, throat swabs and blood counts are used to differentiate a bacterial from a viral infection. There is no way to prevent tonsillitis, and in the under-threes a tonsillectomy (removal of the tonsils) would rarely be considered.

Antiobiotics are used to treat tonsillitis. Pharyngitis is usually a viral infection of the back of the throat.

Ulcers

Ulcers are one of the symptoms in illnesses such as herpes simplex and hand-foot-mouth disease. They may also be caused by trauma, or develop for no obvious reason and recur. The child may find it difficult to drink if there are ulcers in his mouth. Avoid giving him fruit juices.

Undescended testes

At birth, a baby boy's testes are usually descended into the scrotum, but when one or both haven't, they are known as undescended testes. These testes may descend of their own accord in the first three to six months; if they don't, an operation will be necessary some time during the child's second year. Undescended testes that are not corrected surgically can result in infertility.

Urinary tract infections (UTIs)

Urinary tract infections are common in children, with girls and newborn boys the most susceptible. UTIs are caused by an infection in the bladder and need prompt treatment to prevent scarring of the kidneys.

The most common cause is bacteria from the rectum entering the urethra. In children under the age of three, it is possible for a UTI to go undetected, as adults may not notice that the child has discomfort passing urine and is going to the toilet more frequently. A fever is another symptom of a UTI, but it may be attributed to another cause.

Once your doctor has ordered a urine test, he or she may start your child on a course of antibiotics. The child will also need to undergo tests for underlying infections of the kidney and bladder.

Vaginal infections

Newborn girls may have a slight vaginal discharge, including bleeding, but any offensive or worrying vaginal discharge or bleeding needs to be checked out by a doctor.

Vulvovaginitis is an inflammation of the vulva and vagina. Usually minor, it may be caused by irritation of the genital tissues.

Often the culprit is bubble bath. Sometimes it may be a bacterial or yeast infection, and occasionally it may be a foreign body poked into the vagina. If the infection is bacterial, your doctor may prescribe antibiotics. If it is thrush, you may be advised to apply an antifungal cream.

Vomiting

In babies under 12 months of age, vomiting may be caused by bronchiolitis, gastric oesophageal reflux (GOR), gastroenteritis, intestinal obstruction, meningitis, pyloric stenosis (a rare condition) or whooping cough. Or it may simply be possetting, usually due to wind and rarely serious. In older children it could be caused by head injury, hepatitis or a urinary tract infection. For further information on any of the conditions listed, refer to the individual entries in this section. If vomiting persists, see your doctor.

Dehydration is a possible complication of vomiting, and carers need to monitor a child who is suffering from this condition for any signs of this and other worrying symptoms (see **Dehydration**).

Warts

Warts are caused by a virus and are harmless. They can appear on hands and feet, and some people are more susceptible than others. Warts are first contracted by touch and can be very persistent, appearing and disappearing, or simply staying put for years. They come in three types.

- Common warts. These are raised growths with a hard, flat surface.
- Plantar warts or verrucas. These have a hard flat surface but grow into the foot and can be quite painful.
- Plane warts. Smooth growths that occur on the hands or face, these warts may be slightly itchy.

Warts may disappear if untreated. Plantar warts and sometimes other warts are best treated by your doctor.

Whooping cough

Bordetella pertussis is the name of the bacteria that causes whooping cough, hence its other name of pertussis. Whooping cough is a dangerous and potentially fatal disease in babies and young children. Adults and older children can have whooping cough and pass it on to unimmunized children, and even to those who have been immunized, although these people will suffer to a lesser degree (see 'Pertussis' on page 90). It is passed by droplets from coughs.

Whooping cough is characterized by a cough followed by a 'whoop', which is air being forced in while the larynx is in spasm and partly closed. Babies with whooping cough become short of oxygen very quickly and develop a blue-grey pallor. Vomiting and pneumonia, lung damage, ear trouble and convulsions from brain haemorrhage are possible complications.

Any child with suspected whooping cough needs medical treatment and may need to be admitted to hospital.

Worms

Pinworms are thin white parasites, about 1 cm (½ in) in length, which live in the digestive tract. Symptoms are an itchy anus that may keep the child awake, and scratching of the anal area. The scratching can lead to reinfestation when the child puts his hand to his mouth.

The worms can sometimes be seen wriggling around the anus, especially at night by torchlight when the female worm is laying eggs around the anal passage.

The treatment for pinworm is antiworm medicine prescribed by a doctor. The whole family may be advised to take the treatment. Everyone in the household should wash their hands very carefully to prevent reinfestation. Pinworms are not the same worms as those that infest pets.

First aid and emergency procedures

This guide to first aid and emergency procedures is not intended to replace an accredited first aid course run by an approved training organization. We highly recommend that all parents gain a first aid qualification. It could help you save your child's life.

Principles of first aid

■ Before you start applying first aid to a sick or injured child, make sure the environment, and everybody in it, is safe.

■ Do not be afraid to call for help, if necessary, or to contact the appropriate authority for assistance.

■ If possible, try to remain with the child until help arrives.

■ Do not apply a treatment if you doubt its effectiveness. Look for symptoms and signs, then use the treatment that will result in the best outcome.

■ Adhere to the ABC of resuscitation:

– **A** is for airway, which should be unobstructed and cleared;

– **B** is for breathing — you can help a person who has stopped breathing by giving expired air resuscitation (EAR); and

– **C** is for circulation — using a clean cloth, put pressure on any accessible bleeding area.

If the heart has stopped, chest compressions are applied in combination with EAR to oxygenate the blood.

Basic first aid kit

Here is a list of first aid essentials to have in your home, car and on holidays.

✱ Scissors	✱ Roller bandages
✱ Assorted safety pins	✱ Sterile eye-pad
✱ Medicine cup	✱ Triangle bandage (for sling)
✱ Splinter tweezers	✱ Roll of cotton wool
✱ Disposable gloves	✱ Cotton buds
✱ Thermometer	✱ Ice pack
✱ Antiseptic lotion	✱ Antihistamine cream for bites or stings
✱ Adhesive dressing strips in assorted sizes	✱ Sealed bottle of distilled water or large saline capsules (for an eye wash)
✱ Sterile non-adhesive absorbent dressings	

Emergency procedures

It's a good idea to familiarize yourself with resuscitation techniques so that if you're faced with an emergency, you'll know what to do and in the correct sequence. The important thing is to try to remain calm and reassure your child. Panic only frightens the child and wastes valuable time.

What do you do when a child collapses?

1 Assess the situation by ensuring that everybody at the scene, including the child, is not in any danger.

2 Shout for help or ask someone to call an ambulance.

3 Check for a response: for the younger child, tap or flick the foot; and for the older child, gently squeeze her shoulders and/or ask her to squeeze your hand or blink her eyes. Never shake a child.

4 Make sure the child is comfortable, then check her breathing and pulse every few minutes until help arrives.

What if the child does not respond and remains unconscious?

1 Gently turn the child onto her side into the recovery position. A child over 12 months should be positioned on her side with her upper leg at a right angle to her body for stability, and with her upper arm also at a right angle to her body. A baby should be resting on her side on a stable surface, with your hand supporting the top of her head.

2 Open the airway by gently clearing the mouth: scoop the mouth with your finger. Next, slightly tilt back the head of the older child, and support the jaw with the thumb and index finger in a 'pistol grip'. Do not tilt the head of a child less than 12 months old. Use two fingers to support the chin.

3 Check for breathing for up to ten seconds by looking and feeling for chest movement, and listening and feeling for breath on your cheek.

What if the child is breathing?

1 Keep the child in the recovery position.

2 Continue checking her breathing and pulse every two minutes.

3 If an ambulance still hasn't arrived, call emergency again.

4 Maintain close observation, and stay by the child's side until help arrives.

What if the child has stopped breathing?

1 Turn the child onto her back.

2 Start expired air resuscitation (EAR) (see the instructions given for 'Expired air resuscitation' below).

3 Check her pulse and breathing.

What if there is a pulse?

1 Continue with the EAR.

2 Check the child's breathing and pulse after one minute and then every two minutes.

How to check a pulse

Place your index and middle fingers on the carotid artery on the side of the child's neck, beside the windpipe and just below the jawbone, and apply gentle pressure for up to ten seconds.

What if there is no pulse?

1 Start cardiopulmonary resuscitation (CPR) (see the instructions given on page 325).

2 Check the child's breathing and pulse after one minute and then again every two minutes.

3 Continue until the ambulance arrives.

Expired air resuscitation

Expired air resuscitation (EAR) is used to give oxygen to a child who is not breathing. She may or may not have a pulse.

For a baby younger than 12 months

1 Do not tilt the child's head, but support the top of the head with one hand and the jaw with two fingers.

2 Seal your lips tightly around the mouth and nose.

3 Give five gentle puffs into the lungs until the chest rises. Remove your lips between each puff to allow the air to escape.

4 Check the child's pulse.

5 If there is a pulse, continue with EAR until help arrives.

6 If there is no pulse, begin CPR.

For a child over 12 months

1 Slightly tilt the child's head back and hold the jaw in the 'pistol grip'.

2 Place your lips around the mouth and seal the nose with your cheek.

3 Give five gentle breaths into the lungs until the chest rises. Remove your lips between each breath to allow the air to escape.

4 Check the child's pulse.

5 If there is a pulse, continue with EAR until help arrives.

6 If there is no pulse, begin CPR.

Cardiopulmonary resuscitation

Cardiopulmonary resuscitation (CPR) is used when a child is unconscious, not breathing, and has no pulse.

For a baby younger than 12 months

1 Call an ambulance.

2 With two fingers, press down firmly on the child's chest to a depth of about 1–2 cm (½–1 in). To effectively estimate where to compress, place one index finger in the middle of the lowest part of the breastbone — you can find it by running your fingers along the lowest rib on each side from the outside towards the middle. Place your other index finger at the base of the windpipe, which is the highest end of the breastbone. Extend the thumbs of both hands so they meet in the middle. Keep the thumb of the hand closest to the child's head in position and place your two fingers below it. Repeat the compressions 15 times at a rate of about 100 compressions per minute.

3 Give two puffs of EAR, then 15 chest compressions with two puffs of EAR. Continue until the child regains a pulse.

For a child over 12 months

1 Call an ambulance.

2 Using the heel of your hand, press down firmly to a depth of around 2–3 cm (1–1½ in) (see the instructions for positioning in point 2 above). Use the heel of one hand to compress the chest on the lower part of the breastbone. Repeat this 15 times at a rate of about 100 compressions per minute.

326 A commonsense guide for new parents

3 Give two breaths of EAR, then 15 chest compressions with two breaths of EAR. Continue until the child regains a pulse.

How to secure a pressure immobilization bandage

A pressure immobilization bandage is used as first aid for snake or dangerous spider bites.

1 Apply a firm compression bandage over the site of the bite, but not so tightly that it restricts the blood flow to the limb above and below the bandage.

2 Use a second bandage, such as a roller bandage, to bandage from the site of the injury (for example, from the fingers or the toes) and then up to the armpit or groin.

3 Bandage as much of the limb as possible.

4 Apply a splint to the bandage, such as a piece of wood, ensuring it covers as much of the limb as possible.

5 Do not remove the splint or bandage once it has been secured.

Treating common injuries

Below is an A–Z guide to some of the most common injuries or accidents, what you should know, how to treat them and when to call for medical assistance.

Bites

Be careful to administer the correct treatment, which varies depending on the type of bite.

Superficial bites

1 Wash the wound thoroughly with warm soapy water.

2 Pat it dry with clean gauze swabs.

3 Apply antiseptic or a sterile dressing.

4 If you are concerned about infection, seek medical advice. Check whether the child requires a tetanus or hepatitis B vaccine.

Serious animal bites

1 Apply direct pressure to the wound to control bleeding. If possible, splint the affected limb to immobilize it.

2 After immobilizing the injury, raise the affected area, if possible. Try to keep the child still, and organize transport to hospital.

Spider and snake bites

Symptoms

- Swelling and soreness around the bite
- Headache
- Blurred vision
- Nausea, sweating, vomiting
- Difficulty breathing

Treatment

1 Call an ambulance.

2 Reassure the child.

3 Do not wash the bite.

4 Do not use a tourniquet.

5 Keep the child still to prevent the spread of the venom.

6 Use a pressure immobilization bandage (see 'How to secure a pressure immobilization bandage' on page 326) to apply firm pressure over the bitten area and affected limb.

7 If it is safe to do so, identify the type of spider or snake.

Funnel web spider (Australia) bite

1 Call an ambulance.

2 Apply a pressure immobilization bandage (see 'How to secure a pressure immobilization bandage' on page 326) over the bitten area and over as much of the limb as possible.

3 If the child becomes unconscious or stops breathing, refer to 'Emergency procedures' on page 323.

Redback spider (Australia) bite

1 Call an ambulance.

2 Reassure the child.

3 Apply an ice pack wrapped in a clean cloth to the bite.

Insect bites and stings

Bees

1 To remove the sting, scrape it sideways with your fingernail to reduce the chance of more venom being released into the wound. Do not pull the sting out directly.

2 Wipe the affected area clean.

3 Apply an ice pack wrapped in a clean cloth for about ten minutes to relieve the pain and reduce the swelling.

4 Watch for signs of allergic reaction such as rash, raised lumps on the skin, swelling of the throat that causes difficulty in breathing, wheezing, nausea, vomiting and unconsciousness.

5 If there is an allergic reaction, call an ambulance.

Bull ant and centipede bites

1 Make the child comfortable and reassure her.

2 Elevate the injured area, and apply an ice pack wrapped in a clean cloth for about ten minutes to relieve the pain and reduce the swelling.

3 Closely observe the child for signs of an allergic reaction such as a rash, swollen lips and eyes, or wheezing.

4 If there is an allergic reaction, call an ambulance, and refer to 'Emergency procedures' (page 323) for instruction on resuscitation technique if the child collapses.

European wasp

This nasty creature resembles a bee, but it doesn't leave its stinger behind and can sting more than once.

1 Wash the area of the sting clean.

2 Apply an ice pack wrapped in a clean, damp cloth to the affected area.

3 If there is an allergic reaction, call an ambulance.

Ticks

Ticks tend to find their way into body creases and crevices where they bury their heads into the skin. Do not pull the tick out with tweezers as this can leave the head embedded in the skin.

1 Remove the tick by pressing tweezers or small scissor blades into the skin around the head of the tick, and gently lever the tick out with a twisting motion, trying not to squeeze it.

2 If the tick is in the ear, or the child is very young, seek medical advice.

3 If the area becomes infected, seek medical advice.

Bites and stings from marine creatures

Non-tropical jellyfish and bluebottles

1 Do not let the child rub or scratch the sting as this only causes the venom to spread.

2 Reassure the child.

3 Gently pick off any remaining tentacles with tweezers or gloved fingers.

4 Apply an ice pack wrapped in a clean, damp cloth until the pain is relieved.

Tropical jellyfish

1 Call an ambulance.

2 If vinegar is available, flood the affected area with it for at least 30 seconds to deactivate the stinging cells.

3 If there is no vinegar available, remove the tentacles with tweezers.

4 Apply ice to relieve the pain.

5 If the child becomes unconscious, refer to 'Emergency procedures' for instructions on resuscitation technique (see page 323).

Blue-ringed octopus and coneshell

1 Do not let the child rub the sting as this may cause the venom to spread.

2 Call an ambulance.

3 Apply the pressure immobilization bandage (see 'How to secure a pressure immobilization bandage' on page 326).

4 Keep the child still, do not leave her side, and reassure her until help arrives.

Stonefish and stingrays

1 Call an ambulance.

2 Do not apply any pressure.

3 Place the injured part in hot water for about 30 minutes.

Bleeding

To minimize the risk of infection to the child and to yourself, wash your hands thoroughly before and after treatment.

Bleeding from a limb

1 Raise the limb so it is higher than the heart, and place firm pressure on the affected area until the bleeding is controlled.

2 Cover with a sterile dressing.

3 Bandage, but not too tightly.

4 If the bleeding does not stop or the child goes into shock (see 'Shock' on page 344), call an ambulance.

Bleeding from the ear

1 Turn the child's head so the bleeding ear is facing downwards, allowing the blood to drain.

2 Cover the ear with a sterile dressing, and secure it with a bandage or tape.

3 Seek medical advice.

Foreign body in a wound

1 Apply dressings around it, being careful not to place any pressure on the foreign body.

2 Seek medical advice.

Nose bleed

1 Sit the child in a comfortable position with her head forward.

2 Pinch the child's nose just below the bridge for around ten minutes or until the bleeding stops. If it's a hot day and she has been active, this could be another ten minutes. An ice pack may help to stop the bleeding.

3 Do not allow her to blow her nose for several hours afterwards, as this could disturb a blood clot.

4 If the nose bleed persists for more than 30 minutes, seek medical advice.

Blisters

A blister may not require treatment.

1 If the blister bursts or is irritating the child, cover it with a dry, non-adhesive dressing.

2 Do not burst a blister, as this could lead to the area becoming infected.

3 Do not apply lotions, ointments or gels as they could irritate the affected area.

Bruises

A slight bruise may not require treatment.

1 For a more serious bruise, raise and support the affected area for ten minutes to prevent potential bleeding under the skin. Apply an ice pack.

2 If required, wrap a stretch bandage around the bruised area after each ice pack application.

Burns and scalds

1 Run cool tap water over the burn for at least 20 minutes.

2 If the child has been scalded and there is no water available, always remove the child's clothing because clothing soaked in hot liquids retains heat.

3 Closely observe the child for signs of shock (see 'Shock' on page 344).

4 Remove jewellery, a belt or clothing from the affected area (but not if it is sticking to the burn).

5 Protect the burn with a sterile dressing.

6 Seek medical treatment or, if the burns are serious, call an ambulance.

never

* Never apply butter, lotions, gels or ointments to a burn.

* Never touch the affected area.

* Never burst any blisters.

* Never attempt to remove anything sticking to the burn.

Chemical burns

1 Remove affected clothing.

2 Flush the affected area with cool tap water for at least 20 minutes.

3 Protect the burn with a sterile dressing. Do not use a fluffy cloth.

4 If the burns are severe, call an ambulance or take the child to hospital.

Choking

Do not poke your fingers randomly down a child's throat if she is choking.

Symptoms

- Difficulty breathing and coughing
- Problems talking
- Distress
- Flushed face and neck
- Strange wheezing noises or no sound
- Possibly later — grey-blue skin tone, unconsciousness

Treatment for a baby

1 If the baby is distressed but still breathing, help the baby to cough by sitting her on your lap. Remain with her and observe her closely.

2 If the baby is still unable to breathe, get someone to call an ambulance.

3 Turn baby face down across your lap, with her head off your knees and slightly lower than her body.

4 With the heel of your hand, apply four back slaps between the shoulder blades.

5 Check her breathing.

6 If she is still not breathing, turn her onto her side, facing away from you, and clear her airway by scooping inside her mouth with one finger.

7 Put the baby on her back. Place two fingers on either side of baby's ribcage, just under the armpits.

8 Apply about four chest thrusts, one every three seconds.

9 Check for signs of breathing.

10 If the baby is still not breathing, check her mouth for foreign material. If there is any, scoop it out with one finger.

11 Give five puffs of EAR.

12 Continue with cycles of back slaps, chest thrusts and EAR/CPR (see 'Emergency procedures' on pages 323–5) until help arrives.

Treatment for a young child

1 Encourage the child to cough to clear her airway.

2 Remain with the child and reassure her so she does not panic.

3 If the child is unable to breathe or becomes unconscious, call an ambulance.

4 Position the child on her side in the recovery position.

5 With the heel of your hand, apply up to four back slaps between the child's shoulder blades.

6 Check her breathing.

7 If she is still not breathing, place your hands on either side of her ribcage just below the armpits and squeeze together firmly.

8 Repeat this up to four times.

9 Check her breathing.

10 If she is not breathing, check her mouth for any foreign material and remove it with one finger.

11 If the child is still not breathing, give five breaths of EAR.

12 Continue with back slaps, chest thrusts and EAR/CPR until help arrives (see 'Emergency procedures' on pages 323–5).

Convulsions

See 'Convulsions' on page 298.

Dehydration

See also 'Dehydration' on page 299, as dehydration can be a complication of an illness.

Early signs

- Dry mouth and tongue
- Passing urine less frequently than normal
- Thirst
- Lethargy

Late signs

- Sunken eyes
- Drawn and pale complexion

- Headaches
- Weight loss
- When the back of the hand is gently pinched, the skin remains pinched and fails to 'bounce' back.

Treatment

1 Move the child to a cool shaded area and give her diluted water-based fluids, such as rehydration drinks or diluted cordial.

2 Make sure you give the child sips of fluids at regular intervals. Avoid giving large quantities of fluids at once.

3 If the child is conscious but continues to vomit, or if diarrhoea persists, seek medical advice.

4 If the child becomes unconscious, call an ambulance and refer to 'Emergency procedures' on page 323 for instructions on resuscitation.

Dislocation, fractures and sprains

Dislocation

Dislocation is the partial or full displacement of bones at the joint. Never try to manipulate a dislocation back into place. Seek medical advice.

Elbow injuries

Children often fracture the upper arm bone (humerus) just above the elbow.

Symptoms

- Pain
- Tenderness in injured area
- Swelling and, later, bruising
- Limited or no movement

Treatment

1 If the child can bend the arm, place the injured arm across her chest so she is comfortable.

2 Hold the arm in place with a sling that is buffered by soft padding.

3 To limit movement further, tie a bandage over the sling and around the child's chest.

4 Take the child to hospital.

5 If the child cannot bend the elbow, lay her down and place padding such as towels around the elbow.

6 Call an ambulance.

Fractures

A fracture is a break, partial or complete, of the bone itself.

Symptoms

- Severe pain
- Impossible to move affected limb, or it is painful when moved
- Signs of shock (see 'Shock' on page 344), although often the child is not in shock
- Shortening, bending, twisting of affected limb

Treatment

1 Prevent the child from moving, and support above and below the injured part with your hands.

2 For greater support, secure the injured part to an uninjured part of the body. For instance, secure the arm to the torso using a sling; for a leg injury, secure the injured leg to the other leg with bandages.

3 Do not let the child eat or drink in case an anaesthetic needs to be administered.

4 Take the child to the nearest doctor. Only call an ambulance if the pain is severe or if there is no other transport available.

Sprains

A sprain is where a joint has been forced beyond its normal range of movement, and the ligaments that hold it together are stretched.

Symptoms

- Pain
- Swelling
- Tenderness

Treatment

1 Support the injured part in the most comfortable position for the child.

2 Compression and elevation help reduce swelling, so wrap the injured part firmly, but not too tight, in a crepe or elastic bandage.

3 Elevate the injured part on pillows (if necessary, resting on top of telephone books) for around 15 minutes.

4 Remove the layers and cool the still elevated limb with an ice pack (you could use frozen peas wrapped in a tea towel) for 20 minutes every two hours.

5 Repeat compression and elevation.

6 If the swelling and bruising look severe, and the child appears to be in a lot of pain, seek medical advice.

Drowning

When carrying a child from the water, keep her head lower than the rest of her body to reduce the risk of inhaling water.

1 If the child is unconscious, lay her in the recovery position (lay a baby on her side), and check for breathing and a pulse. Be prepared to follow 'Emergency procedures' (see page 323) with the child positioned on her back. If there is water in the lungs increasing resistance, breathe at a slower rate when giving EAR.

2 If the child vomits during resuscitation, roll her back onto her side and clear the airway. Continue resuscitation. Call an ambulance.

3 Place dry blankets or other warm garments on top of the child to help prevent hypothermia.

4 Even if the child appears to have recovered, call an ambulance or take the child to hospital, as there could be water damage to the lungs.

Ear injuries

Do not probe the ear or attempt to remove a foreign object. Seek medical advice.

Bleeding from the ear

1 Lay the child on her side to allow the blood to drain from the bleeding ear.

2 To protect the ear from dirt, cover it with a sterile cotton pad and secure it with tape.

3 Seek medical advice.

Insect in the ear

1 Wash the ear gently with tepid water to flush out the insect.

2 If the insect remains lodged in the ear, seek medical advice.

Object in the ear

Seek medical advice. Do not attempt to remove the object yourself.

Electric shock

1 Switch off the electricity at the mains or the power point.

2 If this is not possible, drag the child away from danger, with a dry non-conducting item, such as a wooden mop handle or chair. You could also grab onto the child's clothing, being careful not to make skin-on-skin contact. Dry clothing can provide insulation against electric shock. Avoid metal surfaces and beware of metal studs, buttons or belt buckles. Stand on a thick wad of newspaper to avoid electric shock.

3 If the child's clothes are burning, smother the flames. Don't use water if the electricity is still on.

4 If the child is unconscious, place her in the recovery position (place baby on her side), and clear and open the airway.

5 Check her breathing and pulse, and refer to 'Emergency procedures' on page 323.

6 Call an ambulance or seek medical advice.

7 Cool burns with cold water.

Eye injuries

Do not let the child rub the sore eye. Wash your hands thoroughly before commencing treatment.

Chemical in the eye

1 Wash the affected eye thoroughly in cool water for 15 minutes, taking care to clean under the eyelids.

2 Contact the poisons information centre in your area, or take the child to hospital.

Object stuck in the eye

It is very important that you do not remove the object from the eye.

1 The child should sit up, and avoid coughing or vomiting, if possible.

2 Cover the injured eye with a sterile dressing or clean pad.

3 Tell the child to close the other eye, to avoid the injured eye moving.

4 Call an ambulance.

Small, loose objects in the eye

1 Thoroughly wash your hands before touching the child's eye.

2 Ask the child to look up. Gently pull out the lower lid. If you can see the object, gently flush it out with drops of tepid water, or gently remove it using the corner of a moist, clean cloth.

3 If the object is not visible, get the child to look down. Gently pull the lashes of the upper lid down and over the lower lid.

4 If this fails to dislodge the object, flush the eye with a stream of tepid water. Lay the child down with her affected eye closest to the ground and pour the water across the eye, so it doesn't pour directly onto the child's clothing.

5 If you are unsuccessful, seek medical advice.

Fainting

1 Lay the child down, and lift and support the legs so they are higher than the body.

2 Make sure the room is well ventilated and that the child is not too hot.

3 Help the child sit up slowly after she recovers.

4 Check if the child sustained any injury when falling.

5 If the child is not regaining consciousness quickly, place her in the recovery position and check her airway and breathing.

6 Be prepared to refer to the 'Emergency procedures' section on page 323.

7 Call an ambulance if the child does not recover as you would expect if she had fainted.

Finger injuries

Amputation

1 Raise the injured hand to control blood loss.

2 Apply a sterile dressing or clean pad (a non-fluffy one).

3 Treat the child for shock (see 'Shock' on page 344).

4 Wrap the severed finger in plastic film and then again in a soft cloth.

5 Place the wrapped finger in a container of crushed ice.

6 Write the child's name and the time of injury on the container, so it is ready to hand over to hospital emergency staff.

7 Call an ambulance and make sure that the amputated piece accompanies the child to hospital.

Nail injuries

A typical injury is bruising to fingernails, as little children tend to get their fingers caught in doors and drawers. However, if the nail bed is affected, seek medical advice.

Foreign bodies

Foreign body in the nose

1 Do not attempt to remove the foreign body, as you could move it further up the nose.

2 Keep the child calm and encourage her to breathe through her mouth.

3 Seek medical advice.

Swallowed or inhaled objects

1 If necessary, treat the child for choking (see 'Choking' on page 332).

2 If the child is unconscious, call an ambulance; otherwise seek medical advice.

3 Reassure the child.

4 Try to find out what the child has swallowed or inhaled.

5 Do not give the child anything to eat or drink.

Frostbite

Frostbite usually occurs on the extremities of the body — such as the fingers, toes and nose. These parts freeze, which causes tissue destruction.

Symptoms

- Numbness and tingling in affected areas
- Unnaturally pale, wax-like complexion which feels odd to the touch
- Skin then turns mottled and blue before going black
- Skin lastly turns red, and there might be blistering

Treatment

1 Move the child to a warm, dry place.

2 Do not attempt to reheat the child quickly.

3 Gently remove gloves and boots, and warm the affected areas with your hands in your lap or place the child's hands under her armpits.

4 Try not to rub as this could harm the skin.

5 Place the frostbitten part in warm water.

6 Dry gently and apply a dry sterile dressing covered in soft padding.

7 Raise and support the limb.

8 Take the child to hospital.

Grazes

1 Wash your own hands before washing the affected area with clean water to remove any dirt or gravel particles.

2 Apply an antiseptic to the wound.

3 If necessary, cover the wound with a sterile dressing or adhesive strip dressing.

Hand injuries

Palm

1 Place a sterile dressing firmly onto the part of the palm that is bleeding, and have the child firmly clench her fist over it, or ask her to apply pressure with the uninjured hand.

2 Bandage over the clenched fingers. Tie the knot over the fingers.

3 Keep the arm elevated in a sling, or hold the arm upright by cupping the child's elbow.

4 Seek medical treatment.

Fracture

1 Keep the hand raised to reduce swelling.

2 Wrap the injured hand in soft padding, such as cotton wool.

3 Gently support the hand by raising it up and across the chest in a sling, which is elevated.

4 Take the child to the hospital.

Head injuries

All head injuries caused by a fall or a blow should be treated as potentially serious. However, a minor bump on the head can be treated with an ice pack wrapped in a clean tea towel.

Symptoms

- Unconsciousness (or was unconscious after the accident)
- Headache
- Memory loss
- Blurred vision
- Nausea and vomiting
- Drowsiness
- Responds oddly or twitches when touched or spoken to
- Bleeding, or losing clear fluid, from nose, ears or eyes
- Wounds to the scalp or face

Treatment

1 Call an ambulance. If the symptoms are less severe, it is still imperative that you seek medical treatment.

2 Lay the child on her side in the recovery position (lay baby on her side).

3 Check the airway is clear and that the child is breathing, and refer to 'Emergency procedures' on page 323.

4 Support the head and neck in line with the spine in case there is a spinal injury.

5 Control the bleeding, but only apply gentle direct pressure to the skull if you suspect a fracture.

6 If blood or fluid is leaking from the ear, cover it gently with a sterile dressing and, if possible, turn the child so the affected ear is facing downwards.

Heat exhaustion and heat stroke

Heat exhaustion

Heat exhaustion is a mild version of heat stroke.

Symptoms

- Headache, dizziness, confusion
- Nausea or vomiting
- Loss of appetite
- Sweating
- Cramps — legs, arms, abdomen
- Rapid, weakening pulse and breathing

Treatment

1 Find a cool place. Get the child to lay down with her legs elevated.

2 Give the child plenty of water to drink.

3 Even if the child recovers, seek medical advice.

Heat stroke

Heat stroke is where the body becomes dangerously overheated due to a high fever or prolonged exposure to heat.

Symptoms

- Headache, dizziness, vomiting
- Confusion
- Hot and dry skin
- Fast pulse rate
- Body temperature of about 40°C (104°F)

Treatment

1 Move the child to a cool place.

2 Remove any hot clothes.

3 Call an ambulance.

4 Apply ice packs to the armpits, groin and sides of the neck to get the child's temperature down quickly, until her temperature falls to 38°C (100.4°F) under the tongue and 37.5°C (99.5°F) under the armpit.

5 Remove as many clothes as possible.

6 If the child becomes unconscious, gently turn her onto her side into the recovery position.

7 Check her breathing and pulse, and refer to 'Emergency procedures' on page 323 for resuscitation information.

Hypothermia

Hypothermia occurs when a person has been overexposed to the cold.

Symptoms

- Slow pulse
- Shallow breathing
- Blurred vision
- Shivering (although this may be absent if hypothermia is severe)
- Cramps
- Unusually quiet

- Drowsy
- Loss of appetite
- Unconsciousness

Treatment

1 Do not place a hot water bottle or heater next to the child.

2 If she has been brought in from outside, make sure the child is wearing warm, dry clothes.

3 A young child, if she is responsive, could get into a warm bath. Heat the water to a temperature of 37°C (98.6°F).

4 Put the child to bed and cover her with warm blankets. Remain with her until the colour returns to her cheeks.

5 Give the young child warm drinks and soups to slowly warm her up.

6 Gradually warm a baby by wrapping her in blankets. While she is awake, keep her head covered with a woollen beanie. Hold her close to you.

7 Seek medical advice.

Poisoning

Chemicals or detergents

1 Do not make the child vomit.

2 Clear the child's mouth to retrieve anything she hasn't yet swallowed.

3 If the poison is corrosive, wipe her mouth and face, and rinse her mouth with cold running water, or give frequent sips of cold milk.

4 Get a sample of the poisonous substance to take to the hospital for identification.

5 Call the poisons information centre in your area, or call an ambulance.

6 If the child becomes unconscious, refer to 'Emergency procedures' for resuscitation information (see page 323).

Poisonous plants

Symptoms

- Skin reactions such as a rash, flushed dry skin
- Swelling around lips and eyes
- Severe stomach pains

- Palpitations
- Dizziness
- Vomiting
- Diarrhoea
- Possibly later — unconsciousness

Treatment

1 Do not make the child vomit.

2 If the child is conscious, contact the poisons information centre in your area, or call an ambulance.

3 Keep a piece of the plant you suspect the child has eaten, or any part that has been vomited, for identification purposes.

4 If the child is unconscious, place her in the recovery position (baby on her side) and refer to 'Emergency procedures' for resuscitation information (see page 323).

Shock

Shock may occur as a result of serious injury or illness, particularly when there is severe bleeding or fluid loss from burns, or severe dehydration.

Symptoms of shock

- Pale face, fingernails and lips
- Toes, fingers and lips turn a bluish colour
- Cold, clammy and sweaty skin
- Weak but rapid pulse accompanied by rapid breathing
- Dizziness
- Nausea

Symptoms of severe shock

- Extreme thirst and restlessness
- Gasping for air
- Drowsiness and confusion
- Unconsciousness

Treatment

1 Call an ambulance.

2 Do not let the child move.

3 Do not leave the child alone; stay with her, giving constant reassurance.

4 Do not allow the child to drink or eat in case an anaesthetic needs to be administered.

5 Do not overheat the child, but strive to maintain her body warmth.

6 Lay the child down and raise her legs (unless they are seriously injured and require immobilization) above the level of her heart.

7 Loosen any tight clothing.

8 Give first aid for the external injuries — check that you have immobilized all fractures (see 'How to secure a pressure immobilization bandage' on page 326), and dress wounds and burns.

9 Attempt to control any bleeding.

10 Closely monitor the child's airway, breathing and pulse, and place her in a stable position on her side if there is any breathing difficulty, if she is going to vomit or if she loses consciousness.

11 If the child is unconscious, refer to 'Emergency procedures' for resuscitation information (see page 323).

Spinal injuries

Always suspect spinal injury in a major fall or injury.

Symptoms

- Pain in the neck or back
- Any loss of feeling or unusual sensations such as a tingling or burning in the hands or feet
- Loss or reduction of the ability to move the limbs below the injured part
- A bulge, twist or any other irregularity in the normal curve of the spine
- Unconsciousness following a head injury

Treatment

1 Call an ambulance.

2 Leave the child on her back and protect her neck from movement. If she vomits, roll her onto her side.

3 If the child is breathing, continue to support her in a secure position until help arrives.

4 If the child has stopped breathing, see 'Emergency procedures' for resuscitation information (see page 323).

Splinters

1 Clean the area around the splinter with warm, soapy water.

2 Using clean tweezers, grasp the splinter and pull it out on the same angle it went in.

3 Wash the area again, apply antiseptic, and cover it with an adhesive dressing.

4 Check that the child's tetanus immunization is current.

5 If the splinter is in deep and difficult to remove, seek medical advice.

Strangulation and suffocation

1 Remove any constricting item around the child's neck or any obstruction to her breathing. Take care to keep movement to a minimum in case the neck is injured.

2 In the case of suffocation (in particular, from fumes or smoke inhalation) it may be necessary to move the child outside.

3 If the child is unconscious, place her in the recovery position (lay a baby on her side), and clear and open the airway.

4 Check her breathing and pulse.

5 If the child becomes unconscious, refer to 'Emergency procedures' for resuscitation information (see page 323).

6 Call an ambulance.

Teeth injuries

1 Do not place a child's milk/baby tooth back in the socket (this is only done with adult teeth).

2 If possible, find the tooth and place it in milk or saliva.

3 Visit the dentist immediately.

Traffic accidents

Refer to 'Principles of first aid' and 'Emergency procedures' on pages 322–3.

Unconsciousness

Refer to 'Principles of first aid' and 'Emergency procedures' on pages 322–3.

Notes

Birth to six months

1 Erik Lykke Mortensen et al, 'The association between duration of breastfeeding and adult intelligence', *Journal of the American Medical Association*, 2002, 287, pp. 2365–71.

2 Collaborative Group on Hormonal Factors in Breast Cancer, 'Breast cancer and breastfeeding: Collaborative reanalysis of individual data from 47 epidemiological studies in 30 countries, including 50302 women with breast cancer and 96973 women without the disease', *Lancet*, 20 July 2002, 360 (9328), pp. 203–10; and M H Labbock, 'Health sequelae of breastfeeding for the mother', *Clinical Perinatology*, June 1999, 26(2), pp. viii–ix, 491–503.

3 Results from research (much of it funded by the National Institute of Health in the United States) conducted by Dr Tiffany Field, director of the Touch Research Institute at the University of Florida's medical school (from a 1999 article written by Julie Robotham, medical reporter for *The Sydney Morning Herald*, which appeared on the Families Worldwide website).

4 Lyn Quine, *Solving Children's Sleep Problems: A Step by Step Guide for Parents*, Becket Karlson, Cambs, 1997.

5 Penelope Leach, *Your Baby & Child: New Version for a New Generation*, Penguin Books, London, 1997, pp. 17–18.

Six months to one year

1 Child Accident Prevention Foundation Australia.

2 Child Accident Prevention Foundation Australia.

3 Penelope Leach, *Your Baby & Child: New Version for a New Generation*, Penguin Books, London, 1997.

4 E R Mondschein, K E Adolph & C S Tamis-LeMonda, 'Gender bias in mothers' expectations about infant crawling', *Journal of Experimental Child Psychology*, 2000, Dec 77 (4), pp. 304–16.

5 Leach, *op. cit.*, pp. 310–12.

One to two years

1 Penelope Leach, *Your Baby & Child: New Version for a New Generation*, Penguin Books, London, 1997, p. 386.

Two to three years

1 Penelope Leach, *Your Baby & Child: New Version for a New Generation*, Penguin Books, London, 1997, p. 377.

Resources

These are some of the many parent support organizations that may help you. You can find them in your telephone directory.

Australia

Breastfeeding

Australian Breastfeeding Association: www.breastfeeding.asn.au

Childcare

National Childcare Accreditation Council Inc.: www.ncac.gov.au/

Children with special needs

For a list of organizations, see: ww.geocities.com/australianparentsonline/specialneeds.htm

These are just a few of the organizations listed:

Association for Children with a Disability: www.acd.org.au/

Royal Institute for Deaf and Blind Children: www.ridbc.org.au/

Early Childhood Intervention Australia: www.ecia.org.au/

Health

Better Health Victoria, established by the Victorian Government: www.betterhealth.vic.gov.au/

Health Insite — Australian Government health site: www.healthinsite.gov.au/

The Cochrane Consumer Network: www.informedhealthonline.org/item.aspx

Immunization

Immunise Australia program: immunise.health.gov.au/

Australian Childhood Immunisation Register 1800 653 809

Parenting

To find resources and information:

www.australianbaby.info

www.geocities.com/australianparentsonline/homepage.htm

www.rch.unimelb.edu.au/ecconnections/

Parentline 13 22 89

Postnatal depression

Dona Maria Pre and Post Natal Support Network

National Helpline 1300 555 578

The National Postnatal Depression Support Program: www.beyondblue.org.au

Safety

Kidsafe (Child Accident Prevention Foundation of Australia): www.kidsafe.com.au

Twins and triplets

Australian Multiple Birth Association: www.amba.org.au

Playgroup Associations including Baby Playgroup: www.playgroupaustralia.com.au

Single parents

National Council for Single Mothers: www.ncsmc.org.au

Parents Without Partners: pwp.freeyellow.com/

United Kingdom

Breastfeeding

Association of Breastfeeding Mothers: www.abm.me.uk/

La Leche League: www.laleche.org.uk

Childcare & Playgroups

ChildcareLink freephone 08000 96 02 96: www.childcarelink.gov.uk/index.asp

Disability

Department for Work and Pensions, Disability Unit: www.disability.gov.uk/)

Health

National Health Service Direct: www.nhsdirect.nhs.uk/

The Cochrane Consumer Network: www.informedhealthonline.org/item.aspx

Immunisation

National Health Service: www.immunisation.nhs.uk/

Parenting

The National Childbirth Trust: www.nctpregnancyandbabycare.com/

Single Parents

Gingerbread: www.gingerbread.org.uk/

Single Parent Action Network: www.singleparents.org.uk/

Twins and triplets

Twins and Multiple Births Association (TAMBA): www.tamba.org.uk

Bibliography

Australian Consumers' Association, *The Choice Guide to Baby Products*, 8th edn, Choice, Australia, 2003.

Biddulph, Steve, *The Secret of Happy Children*, HarperCollins, Sydney, 1998.

Biddulph, Steve & Shaaron, *Love, Laughter and Parenting in the Precious Years from Birth to Six*, Dorling Kindersley, Sydney, 2000.

Brazelton, T. Berry, *Touchpoints: The Essential Reference Guide to Your Child's Emotional and Behavioural Development*, Doubleday, Sydney, 1993.

Cafarella, Jane (ed.), *Breastfeeding... Naturally*, Nursing Mothers Association of Australia, Merrily Merrily Ent., Mitchan, Victoria, 1996.

Campbell, Don, *The Mozart Effect for Children*, Hodder Headline, Sydney, 2000.

Child and Youth Health website. www.cyh.com/cyh/index.html

Fallows, Carol, *Baby Basics, Baby Food, Baby Health, Baby Sleep*, 2001; *Toddler Food, The Toddler Years, Raising Happy Children*, 2003 (seven booklets), The Australian Women's Weekly Parenting Guides, ACP, Sydney.

Fallows, Carol, *Parents When-Not-To-Worry Book*, Transworld, Sydney, 2001.

Fallows, Carol, *The Australian Baby & Child Care Handbook*, Penguin, Melbourne, 1997.

Heath, Dr Alan & Nicki Bainbridge, *Baby Massage: The Calming Power of Touch*, Dorling Kindersley, 2000.

Karmel, Annabel, *Annabel Karmel's New Complete Baby and Toddler Meal Planner: Over 200 Quick and Easy Recipes*, Viking, 2001.

Kitzinger, Sheila, *Breastfeeding Your Baby*, Dorling Kindersley, London, 1998.

Leach, Penelope, *Your Baby and Child. New Version for a New Generation*, Dorling Kindersley, 2003.

Martin, Elaine, *Baby Games: The Joyful Guide to Child's Play from Birth to Three Years*, 2nd edn, Choice, Sydney, 1999.

McKay, Pinky, *100 Ways to Stop the Crying*, Lothian Books, Melbourne, 2002.

McKay, Pinky, *Parenting by Heart*, Lothian Books, Melbourne, 2001.

Murray, Lynne & Liz Andrews, *Your Social Baby: Understanding Babies' Communication Since Birth*, ACER Press, 2001.

Opray, Annie, *Solid Start*, Penguin Books, Melbourne, 2003.

Ronnebeck, Reinhard, *7000 Days: Creating a Happy Family from Day One*, ABC, Sydney, 2002.

Sears, William & Martha Sears, *The Baby Book: Everything You Need to Know About Your Baby — From Birth to Age Two*, Little, Brown and Company, London, 1993.

St John Ambulance Australia, *First Aid for Children Fast: Emergency Procedures for All Parents and Carers*, Dorling Kindersley, Sydney, 1999.

Tyler, Ella (consultant), *Australian First Aid Manual. The Authorized Manual of the National Safety Council of Australia*, Dorling Kindersley, 2001.

Valman, Bernard, *When Your Child is Ill. A Home Guide for Parents*, Dorling Kindersley, London, 2002.

Warren, Jean & Theodosia Sideropoulos Spewock, *A Year of Fun Just for One's*, Totline Books, Frank Schaffer Publications, Inc., d.b.a. Warren Publishing House, 1995.

Whitby, Joanna, *Practical Cooking for Babies and Toddlers*, Choice, Sydney, 1999.

Index

Index

a

absorbent fold (nappy), 69
accidents
    baby walkers, 183
    change tables, 65
    dental, 209, 346
    drowning, 162, 235, 237
    plastic bags, 161, 253
    prevention, 252–4
ADHD *see* attention deficit
    hyperactivity disorder (ADHD)
aggression, 265–6
alcohol, 101, 158
all-in-one suits, 12, 15, 203
allergies, 44
    food, 138, 139, 141, 143–4
anaemia, 294
antibiotics, 311–12
antibodies, 88, 89
apnoea, 35, 80
appendicitis, 294–5
areolae, 41, 45, 46
arthritis, 295
aspirin, 311
Association of Breastfeeding
    Mothers (UK), 349
Association for Children with a
    Disability (Australia), 348
asthma, 295–6
attention deficit hyperactivity
    disorder (ADHD), 262
attention seeking, 263–4
Australian Breastfeeding
    Association, 348
Australian Childhood
    Immunisation Register, 348
Australian Multiple Birth
    Association, 348
autism, 95

b

babies
    micro-prems, 34–5
    premature, 34–7
    small-for-dates, 34
Babinski reflex, 41
baby blues, 127
baby bouncers, 29
baby capsules, 22
baby carriers, 19–21
baby food, commercial, 140
baby jumpers, 182
baby massage, 80–6

baby pants, 63–4
Baby Playgroup (Australia), 349
baby talk, 220, 224
baby walkers, 183
baby's room
    decorating, 28–9
    lighting, 28
    safety, 160
    set-up, 24–9
    sharing with parents, 24,
        100–1
    storage, 29
back problems (mother), 62, 64–5
backpacks, 19, 21, 124
balance, 156, 182, 216, 217, 253
balloons, 241
banana muffins, 200
banana smoothie, 198–9
bassinet, 24, 26, 28
bathing, 74–7, 114, 159
    sponge bath, 78–9
bathroom
    cleaning, 168
    safety, 158–9, 228
bedclothes, newborn, 28
bedroom, safety, 159–60
bedtime routine, 102–3, 137,
    174, 177, 210
bee stings, 328
Better Health Victoria (Australia),
    348
bibs, 13
bicarbonate of soda, 169
bilirubin, 36, 38
birds, 255
birthday parties
    first, 240–1
    toddlers, 287–91
birthmarks, 39
births, multiple, 120–2, 225
bites, 327–30
biting, nipple, 173
bleach, 169
bleeding, 330–1
blepharitis, 303
blisters, 331
blocks, stacking, 230
blood stains, 170
body parts, naming, 256
boils, 296
bonding, 44, 81
books, 112, 234–5
    see also reading

booster seats, 23
booties, 13
bottle
    at bedtime, 214
    as comforter, 273–4
bottle-feeding, 51, 53–7
    equipment, 53–4
    going out, 124
    myths, 57–8
    problems, 56–7
    sterilizing equipment, 54–6
bottle-feeding caries, 214, 274
bottoms
    airing, 108
    cleaning, 79
bowel movements, newborns,
    38–9, 62
brain development, 44
Brazelton, Dr T Berry, 283
breast pump, 52
breastfeeding, 41, 43–53, 87
    on demand, 101
    latching on, 41, 46, 47, 48,
        58
    myths, 57–8
    position, 46–7
    problems, 46, 48–51
    stress, 53
    in tandem, 121
    to soothe, 116, 137
    and working, 51, 52–3,
        130
breastmilk, 36–7, 43, 44, 46,
    50–1
    expressing, 49, 50, 52
breasts, 45
    lumpy, 49, 50
bronchiolitis, 296–7
bronchitis, 296–7
bruises, 331
bunny rugs, 13
burns/scalds, 331
burping, 58
butterfly stroke (massage), 82

c

caesarean delivery, 47
cancer, 45
car restraint *see* child car
    restraint
cardigans, 12
cardiopulmonary resuscitation
    (CPR), 325–6
carriage prams, 16